MORE PRAISE FOR *PROFIT FIRST*

"Entrepreneurs commonly confuse cash flow with profitability. *Profit First* makes the process so radically simple that you no longer have an excuse not to be profitable AND have cash flow!"

—**GREG CRABTREE**, author of *Simple Numbers, Straight Talk, Big Profits*

"Not only is Mike one of the most innovative small business authors of our time, his Profit First system—simple to apply and impactful in its results—can be the difference between constantly walking the financial tightrope or being predictably profitable. And a predictably profitable business is not only less stressful and more gratifying, it allows you to focus on what really matters . . . serving your customers!"

—**BOB BURG**, coauthor of *The Go-Giver* and *The Go-Giver Leader*

"Why are so few businesses actually profitable for their owners? *Profit First* turns accepted wisdom on its head and shows the real reason business owners struggle with the bottom line. This book shows you how to take home more money almost immediately."

—**DORIE CLARK**, author of *Stand Out*

"*Profit First* is a revelation. I only wish I knew about this system when I started my first business."

—**JOHN JANTSCH**, author of *Duct Tape Marketing* and *SEO for Growth*

"Finance is the top headache of an entrepreneur. *Profit First* is a must-read to avoid bankruptcy for great business ideas. Clever, easy to implement, and absolutely effective (plus you will enjoy reading it)."

—**SOFÍA MACIAS**, author of *Pequeño Cerdo Capitalista*

"Entrepreneurs and small business advisors finally have a practical toolkit for increasing profitability! Everyone who touches the small business world should read and apply these game-changing principles."

—**JOE WOODARD**, CEO of Woodard Events and Woodard Consulting

"I took the pledge and started implementing the Profit First system after reading Chapter One. By the time I was halfway through the book my business had already turned a profit."

—**BARRY MOLTZ**, author of *How to Get Unstuck*

PROFIT FIRST

ALSO BY MIKE MICHALOWICZ

The Toilet Paper Entrepreneur

The Pumpkin Plan

Surge

PROFIT FIRST

TRANSFORM YOUR BUSINESS
FROM A CASH-EATING MONSTER
TO A MONEY-MAKING MACHINE

MIKE MICHALOWICZ

PORTFOLIO / PENGUIN

Portfolio Penguin
An imprint of Penguin Random House LLC
375 Hudson Street
New York, New York 10014

The original edition of this work was published by the author in 2014.

Library of Congress Cataloging-in-Publication Data

Names: Michalowicz, Mike, author.
Title: Profit first : transform your business from a cash-eating monster
to a money-making machine / Mike Michalowicz.
Description: New York : Portfolio, 2017.
Identifiers: LCCN 2016040957 (print) | LCCN 2016055861 (ebook)
| ISBN 9780735214149 (hardcover) | ISBN 9780735214163 (epub)
Subjects: LCSH: Small business—Finance. | Small business—Growth.
| Profit. | Success in business.
Classification: LCC HG4027.7 .M53 2017 (print) | LCC HG4027.7 (ebook)
| DDC 658.15—dc23
LC record available at https://lccn.loc.gov/2016040957

Printed in the United States of America
7 9 10 8 6

Book design by Daniel Lagin

For my daughter, Adayla, and her piggy bank

TESTIMONIALS FOR
PROFIT FIRST

Darnyelle Jervey: *"It feels good to be building a business that serves me. Profit First is helping me to live out my mission in my own business."*

Darnyelle Jervey owns Incredible One Enterprises, a business optimization consulting firm that offers coaching and consulting to advancing entrepreneurs and small business owners with million-dollar businesses. She started applying Profit First to her business in January of 2015. She had been saving 10 percent of what she brought in and had a consistent cash flow, but she hadn't been tracking profit. Any profit she earned stayed in the business for "reinvestment" purposes.

Before she implemented Profit First, Darnyelle's 10 percent profit savings was about $65,000. In the last year and a quarter, Darnyelle added another $231,763.20 to her profit account. In the last year, Incredible One Enterprises has grown 258 percent.

Bottom Line: $296,763.20 in profit, 258 percent revenue growth, and more than a million dollars in sales.

Carrie Cunnington: *"My business finances are organized and clean. I'm profitable (yeah!), disciplined, in control and motivated."*

Carrie Cunnington is the founder of Cunnington Shift, a coaching practice that empowers high-achieving professionals to create positive shifts and find greater fulfillment in their lives. When she started applying Profit First to her business in 2014, she's had a consistent cash flow, and yet she still lived month to month. No matter how hard she tried, she couldn't seem to get control of her business finances.

With the direction of Shannon Simmons, a Profit First Professional, Carrie implemented Profit First in her business, and later, inspired by what the model did for her business, she and her husband started implementing it in their personal finances as well. They eradicated all their debt by the end of 2016 and have taught their young daughters how to use the model.

Bottom Line: Debt free and posting quarterly profits.

Christian Maxin: *"I now need just 60 minutes a week to manage my financial planning."*

Christian Maxin is the owner of dP elektronik GmbH, a company based in Isernhagen, Germany, that is the market leader in electronic security solutions for doors, gates, elevators, and barriers. Before Profit First, Christian felt pressure all the time and "permanently insecure" about his company's finances. He spent hours every week updating spreadsheets and planning.

Since implementing Profit First in 2014, Christian now spends only an hour a week on financial planning, feels relaxed about his company's finances, and gets plenty of sleep! He has accumulated a significant "cushion," which allows his business to compensate for short-term losses in sales, and the monthly tax payments are taken care of without hassle. In less than two years, Christian increased profit by 50 percent, which translates to more than $250,000, and grew his business by 20 percent.

Bottom line: Christian can see the financial health of his business at a glance: $250,000 in new profit and business growth of 20 percent.

Paul Finney: *"Once you have cash, opportunities start to appear like never before."*

Paul Finney is the owner of October Kitchen LLC, a chef service offering fresh and frozen prepared meals delivered in Hartford, Connecticut, and in retail takeaway stores. Paul and his wife, Alison, were frustrated because they could not capture more of their cash flow for all of their hard work. They were not taking a paycheck, and it was affecting their motivation. In 2015, Paul found *Profit First* on Amazon and soon after began working with a Profit First Professional.

Since implementing Profit First, Paul feels "reborn." October Kitchen's sales have grown from $3,000 to $15,000 per week. Paul was able to reduce his food costs by 20 percent, and the company has a steady annual growth rate of 10 to 15 percent. Having cash available allowed Paul and Alison to identify and take advantage of growth opportunities. October Kitchen is on track for a $1 million annual revenue in 2017.

Bottom Line: 500 percent growth in weekly sales; costs cut by 20 percent.

Helen and Rob Faulkner: *"After 18 years of being in business, we finally feel we're a success."*

Helen and Rob Faulkner own and operate the Saddle Camp, a horse-riding adventure camp and riding school for girls outside Sydney, Australia. Fulfilling a childhood dream, Helen started her business at the age of twenty-one. After twenty years of ups and downs, Helen was ready to give up. Business was down, they would have to replace ponies soon, and they had no cash reserves. Helen reached a point of desperation, asking Siri on her iPhone, "Is it time to let the dream go?" Then she asked, "How do I make my business more profitable?" and *Profit First* popped up.

In the first four weeks of implementing Profit First, Helen and Rob paid off their accounts, have a system for allocating funds for big expenses and purchases, and took their very first profit distribution. They view Profit First as the "missing ingredient" in their business that enables them to sustain it.

Bottom Line: Helen and Rob turned around their business and posted a first-ever profit distribution within four weeks of starting Profit First.

CONTENTS

INTRODUCTION

1

Chapter 1
YOUR BUSINESS IS AN OUT-OF-CONTROL
CASH-EATING MONSTER

11

Chapter 2
THE CORE PRINCIPLES OF PROFIT FIRST

34

Chapter 3
SETTING UP PROFIT FIRST FOR YOUR BUSINESS

49

Chapter 4
ASSESSING THE HEALTH OF YOUR BUSINESS

59

Chapter 5
ALLOCATION PERCENTAGES

75

Chapter 6
PUTTING PROFIT FIRST INTO MOTION

89

Chapter 7
DESTROY YOUR DEBT
114

Chapter 8
FIND MONEY WITHIN YOUR BUSINESS
133

Chapter 9
PROFIT FIRST—ADVANCED TECHNIQUES
148

Chapter 10
THE PROFIT FIRST LIFE
163

Chapter 11
HOW TO KEEP IT FROM FALLING APART
177

EPILOGUE
189

ACKNOWLEDGMENTS
193

Appendix 1
THE PROFIT FIRST QUICK SETUP GUIDE
195

Appendix 2
THE INSTANT ASSESSMENT FORM
197

Appendix 3
GLOSSARY OF KEY TERMS
199

INDEX
201

INTRODUCTION

I am a fool."

I'll never forget the day Debbie Horovitch stood before me and cried. Through her tears, she kept babbling "I'm a fool" over and over again.

Debbie, the entrepreneur behind the Social Sparkle & Shine Agency—a Toronto, Canada, firm that specializes in social media services—had approached me at a CreativeLive event in San Francisco. I was there to teach business growth strategies from my second book, *The Pumpkin Plan*. During one of the event sessions, I explained the basic concept of the Profit First system. One of the tools of Profit First is the Instant Assessment, a way to quickly gauge the real financial health of your business. When I ran the assessment on a volunteer attendee, the Profit First system clicked for everyone in the room.

All CreativeLive presentations are simultaneously broadcast live online, and eight thousand viewers had tuned in for my event. Tweets and comments started flying in from all over the world. Because the Instant Assessment is so fast and easy, I wasn't totally surprised to see the many comments from online viewers saying that they had assessed their business right then and there. Entrepreneurs, CEOs, freelancers, business owners—everyone shared how relieved they were to learn this simple method. It was as though they had each experienced a sudden total clarity, an instant jolt of confidence about the money side of their businesses.

Then Debbie found me during the break and said, "Could we put my business through the Instant Assessment?"

"Sure," I said. "It only takes a minute or two."

Pen in my mouth, people bustling all around us, I ran through it right then and there, as if Debbie and I were in a world of our own. I scrawled her annual revenue number on the board. We ran the percentages. Debbie looked at the results and started to shake with sobs. She couldn't bear to look at where she was, or where the Instant Assessment said she should be.

"I've been a fool," she said, tears streaming down her face. "Everything I have done over the last ten years is wrong. I am such a fool. I am a fool. I am a fool."

Let me admit it right now: I'm a co-crier—when people cry, I go there with them. As soon as Debbie started, my eyes welled up with tears and the pen in my mouth dropped to the floor. I put my arm around her to try to comfort her.

For ten years, Debbie had put her soul into her business, giving it everything she had, sacrificing her personal life in order to give her business life, and yet she didn't have a dime (or a successful business) to show for it. Of course she knew the truth of her struggles all along, but she had chosen to dance around that truth and continued to live in denial.

Putting your nose to the grindstone is a really easy way to cover up an unhealthy business. We think that if we can just work harder, longer, better—if we can just hold out—something good will happen one day. Something big is just around the corner, right? Something just like magic will wipe away all of the debt, financial stress, and worry. After all, don't we deserve that? Isn't that how the story is supposed to end?

No, my friend, that's only in the movies—nothing like what we experience in real life.

After Debbie ran the Instant Assessment, she had to face reality: her business was sinking—for the prior ten years it had been a struggle to stay afloat—and it was taking her down with it. She kept saying, "I am a fool; I am a fool."

Those words tore into me because I'd been there. I understood exactly how it felt to face the naked truth about my business, my bank account, my strategies, and my hard-fought success.

I first designed Profit First to fix my own financial problems. It worked. Actually it more than worked: it was a miracle. Years of struggle and financial troubles were fixed, not overnight but in hours. I wondered whether

Profit First would work just for me and my flawed brain or whether it would serve others.

So I tried it with another business I co-own, a small leather manufacturer in St. Louis. It worked. I tried it with others businesses, large and small. It worked. I wrote about it in my first book, in a small, easily overlooked paragraph in *The Toilet Paper Entrepreneur*. And then something happened: I started getting email from other entrepreneurs who said they'd tried it and seen results. I wrote about it in the *Wall Street Journal*, and more success stories rolled in.

After I wrote my second book, *The Pumpkin Plan*, I included the Profit First system in my speeches. It was after I met Debbie at the CreativeLive event when I realized entrepreneurs needed more than just a paragraph or a chapter on the subject. Too many business leaders lived and worked in tormented servitude to their businesses. If I wanted to make a real difference for the Debbies (and Mikes) of the world, I knew I had to write a book about Profit First.

Profit First was first published in 2014, and since then tens of thousands of entrepreneurs have implemented the system and transformed their businesses. They are not only generating a serious profit; they are *growing* their businesses big-time. Two birds, one stone.

As I write this updated version of the book, I am thirty-five thousand feet up in the air flying somewhere over Pennsylvania or Texas, or maybe it's Russia. I travel so much these days that I rely on the pilot to tell me where I am. My fellow passengers are watching a movie they've already seen four times, catching up on work, or "resting their eyes" with a gaping mouth and occasional snort. A few are looking out the window at the clouds below. Me? I'm thinking about all of the businesses we are flying over. There must be thousands of businesses below us at any given second.

The Small Business Administration (SBA) states that there are 28 million small businesses in the United States alone. The SBA defines a small business as a company that generates $25 million or less in annual revenue. That includes my business, and I suspect it includes yours. Shoot, that even includes Justin Bieber's (his "small business" music sales pulled in only $18 million last year). So that's 28 million of us entrepreneurial "weirdos" in the United States alone. When you look at the full size of our global entrepreneurial family, you'll see that the number of small businesses soars past 125 million.* That's a lot of entrepreneurs, a lot of people with guts, smarts, and determination who decided they had something of value to offer the world and took a shot at building something out of it.

That's you, buddy, an entrepreneur. You might be in the early start-up phase, your plans and dreams written on a cocktail napkin (or toilet paper—you know who you are my TPE peeps!). If you're just getting started, props to you. You'll be focusing on profit from Day One, which will save your sanity, your bank account, and your ass.

Maybe you've built a business or are managing one. Maybe you read the first incarnation of my book, and you want to kick your Profit First system up a notch. Regardless of your entrepreneurial status, you are a miracle worker, so to speak. You convert ideas into reality. You find customers; you make stuff for them; you deliver a service to them; and they pay you for it. You keep selling; you keep delivering; you keep managing the money. All of us are smart, driven people. Really smart. Really driven. But there is one really friggin' nagging problem: eight out of ten businesses fail, and the number one reason they fail is lack of profitability. According to a Babson College report, "A lack of profitability is consistently the major reason cited for business discontinuation."† Are you surprised? Probably not. I wasn't. It's true, and it makes me want to drown my sorrows in Margaritaville. The majority of small businesses, and medium businesses and even some big ones, are barely surviving. That guy driving the new Tesla whose children go to private school via chauffeur and who lives in a massive house and runs a $3 million company, is one bad month from declaring bankruptcy. I should know; he's my neighbor.

The entrepreneur who says "Business is great" at the networking event is the same woman who, because of her tears, later tries to ask me an indecipherable question in the parking lot—she's crying because she hasn't been able to pay herself a salary for almost a year and will soon be evicted from her home. It's just one of many similar conversations I've had with entrepreneurs who are afraid to tell the truth about their financials.

---

* http://www.ifc.org/wps/wcm/connect/9ae1dd80495860d6a482b519583b6d16/MSME-CI-AnalysisNote.pdf?MOD=AJPERES.

† Global Entrepreneurship Monitor 2015–16 Global Report.

The SBA Young Entrepreneur of the Year award recipient who is changing the world, who is lauded as a member of the next generation of genius, who is destined to be on the cover of *Fortune* magazine because of his business acumen, is taking out bank loan after bank loan and racking up credit card debt to cover payroll behind the scenes. I should know; that was me.

How can that be? What's wrong with us? I mean, we get basically everything else right, or damn close. We made something out of nothing. And yet why aren't most businesses profitable?

I used to brag about the size of my business. I patted myself on the back for hiring more employees, for moving into a fancy-schmancy office space, for making big sales. The truth is, I used all that as an excuse to cover up one ugly fact: my business had never once posted a profit. The reality was, my business (and I, as a result) was drowning, and I kept trying to make it grow bigger to keep my head above water. I would say, "I don't want to post a profit, of course. I just want to break even. That way I'll save on taxes." In other words, I'd rather lose $10 than have to pay the government $3. I continued to sink month in month out. Year after year. Constant stress.

In fact, I survived check to check from the day I started my business until the day I sold it and cashed in. Man, I was relieved! My business had been dragging me down, and I'd finally gotten rid of it. But that relief came with a bitter aftertaste. When I started the business, my goal wasn't mere survival. I mean, survival is the goal for POWs and refugees, certainly not what a businessperson would aim for. I was convinced I was the problem. For the longest time, I thought I was flawed, that my brain was messed up. It took me a long time to ask, what if I'm not the problem? What if the system I have been told to follow is flawed?

Profit First works because it doesn't try to fix you. You work hard, you have good ideas, you already give 100 percent to your business. Profit First is a system designed to work with who you are already. You don't need to be fixed. The system does.

Imagine that you were told you could fly if you simply flapped your arms, and then you were encouraged to jump off the nearest cliff. That's right. Just flap your arms, and you'll not only survive the bajillion-foot drop, you'll soar. What's that? You're plunging to your death? Quick! Flap harder.

Flapping your arms in order to fly is crazy because *humans can't fly*.

Following a financial formula that isn't designed for how humans are naturally wired is like asking you to flap your arms harder and harder until you take off. Sorry, pal, it ain't gonna work no matter how hard you try.

The system for profitability we have been using since the beginning of time is totally stupid. Actually, it is horrible. Yeah, sure, it makes mathematical sense, but it surely doesn't make human sense. While some businesses succeed by following the old system, they are the exception, not the rule. Relying on traditional accounting methods to grow profitability is the equivalent of telling you to jump off a cliff and flap the living crap out of your arms. Maybe two or three of the millions of people who try it, by some miracle, live. But pointing to the miraculous survivors and saying, "See? This works!" is ludicrous. Millions die and a few survive, yet we blindly say the arm-flapping, cliff-jumping system is the best way to fly. Absurd.

If you aren't profitable, the natural assumption is that you haven't grown fast enough. I have news for you, people. You're completely fine. You don't need to change. The old formula to profit is what's wrong. It needs to change.

You know the formula I'm talking about: Sales – Expenses = Profit. That crusty, bifocal-wearing, old-person-smelling formula at first blush makes total sense. Sell as much as you can, then pay the bills, and what is left over is profit. Here's the problem: there are never any leftovers. Flap. Flap. Flap. Splat.

The old profit formula creates monsters of businesses. Cash-eating monsters. But we stay loyal to the formula, and things get worse.

The solution is profoundly simple: Take your profit first.

Yeah, it is that simple.

What you are about to learn is so simple, so obviously effective that you may hit your head and say, "Why the hell didn't I do this earlier?" But it may seem hard at times because you haven't done it before. It will challenge you because you will be required to stop flapping your arms. You will be required to stop doing what wasn't working. (It is very hard to stop doing something even though it isn't working out for you. Remember that last nasty hangover, when you said, "I'm never drinking again"? How long did that last?)

Profit First will challenge you because you will have to totally change the way you think about business. And change is scary. Most people suck at trying new stuff, let alone sticking with new systems. Chances are you'll consider trying Profit First, but you'll tell yourself it's so much easier to keep doing things the old way, even if the old way is slowly but surely sinking you and your business. So before we get started, let me tell you about the courageous people who went before you and jumped on the inaugural flight of Profit First.

As of this very second, there are 128 accountants, bookkeepers, and coaches working hand in hand with me to guide entrepreneurs on an implementation of Profit First. (No worries. You can absolutely do this on your own, but for some people, having an accountability partner who knows the ins and outs of their industry who can guide them step by step is a better approach.) Of these 128 Profit First Professionals (PFPs), on average, we have directed the Profit First implementation of ten companies per PFP. That means we have guided 1,280 businesses to success using Profit First.

But the majority of people who have read *Profit First* so far, I can only assume, have followed the process on their own. I get roughly five emails a day, every day, from entrepreneurs who tell me they have started the Profit First process or have used it to transform their businesses. Over a two-year period, that is 3,650 emails of new implementations. But I know that even more people read the book and just do it, without ever saying a thing. So my best estimate on the high end is that more than thirty thousand companies are now doing Profit First. Even if that estimate is spot on, we have barely scratched the surface. Thirty thousand is a nice number, but when compared to 125 million businesses, we are not even at the starting line. So let's move this puppy forward, and let's start with you.

But first, I'd like to introduce you to Keith Fear.

Keith is a longtime fan of my books. I know because he emailed me when I first launched *The Pumpkin Plan*. He fell in love with the book, he tells me, and his hot-air balloon business skyrocketed as a result. His business grew, but his profits didn't. He actually surpassed a million in revenue and still had to have a separate full-time job just to make ends meet. Then he read *Profit First*. And did nothing.

Nothing at all! Why? Because Keith couldn't imagine Profit First would work. He had been trying to flap his arms all his life, which seems particularly strange when you fly balloons for a living and the feedback has been the same: flap harder. The concept of taking his profit first, before anything else, was so unfamiliar that it didn't seem possible. But after two more years of check-to-check, panic-to-panic survival, he gave in and gave up the familiar and decided to give it a shot. The results were . . . well, I will let Keith explain, as he wrote in his letter:

Mike and Team,

I thought I would take a moment and share something with you. I just finished reading *Profit First* for the umpteenth time, and actually had to buy a new copy. I kind of wore out parts of the first copy I had and then gave it to a friend to help them out. I own and operate a hot air balloon ride business. We have operations in St. Louis, Missouri, Albuquerque and Taos, New Mexico, and now also in Cottonwood, Arizona, near Sedona.

When I read your book for the first time, I thought you had lost your mind. No way could this work. So for the last few months of 2014 I did nothing. I kept doing things the way I was. After all, I was making a small profit, but my cash flow wasn't the best. It was all I could do to deal with the cash issues, honestly. Finally, about the beginning of this year, I read the book again and, this time, started trying it.

To give you an idea of what this has done for us, at one point early in 2015 our net profit year over year from year to date 2014 versus 2015 was up 1,721 percent. Nope. No typo. I truly am not kidding. We ended 2015 with net profit up 335.3 percent overall. On top of that, we ran about a 22 percent net Profit percentage!

Keith

Keith's business was saved by Profit First. Today his business is thriving. And so is mine.

Profit First saved my business and ensured that every new business I started would be profitable from day one. Yes, *day one*. The day I opened my newest venture, Profit First Professionals, I did two things: I signed the incorporation documents and then went straight to the bank to open my five foundational Profit First accounts. To date, Profit First Professionals is the most profitable business I have ever owned—by a long shot. It is not the biggest I have owned, at least not yet, but it is posting profits that are 1,000 percent bigger than the best year of any of my prior companies, which sold for millions. That is not a typo—1,000 percent more profitable. This company is not even two years old and is growing so strongly that it will likely be the biggest company (on a revenue basis) that I've ever owned.

Profit First, I promise, will do the same for you. If you need to make your first profit or just need to amplify the profits you already have, this is the path.

Helping you and all of our fellow entrepreneurs become more profitable is my life's purpose. I am flying all over America and beyond to speak about Profit First. Tomorrow I will speak to more than 1,100 pharmacy owners at an event in Houston, then to 25 people (if I am lucky) in Casper, Wyoming, then over to New Orleans to talk with 200 folks in the morning and then a panic dash (via plane, train, and Uber) to Washington, D.C., for an evening keynote. Then I'll travel abroad for more events. In between, I will do interviews for about four podcasts a day, recording my own podcast (ahem—The Profit First Podcast, of course) and updating this book at night. I do *all* of these with joy. I will teach this to anyone and everyone. I will not stop. I am here to eradicate entrepreneurial poverty.

At CreativeLive, after Debbie calmed down a bit, I said, "The last ten years were not wasted. I understand you feel that way right now, but it's not true. You needed to experience those years to get you where you are today, here with me, doing this. You needed to reach a point where enough is enough." To finally change, she needed her enough-is-enough moment. We all do.

The truth is, Debbie is far from a fool. Fools never seek out answers. Fools never realize there is a different way, even when it's staring them in the face. Fools don't admit they need to change. Debbie faced the music, realized what she was doing wasn't working, and decided she would not stand for it anymore. Debbie is smart and courageous, and a hero, too. She implored me to put her story in this book and not cloak her name. Debbie wanted you to know you're not alone.

You started your business, I suspect, for two reasons. First, to do something you love. And second, for financial freedom. You did it for some degree of wealth. You did it to put profit in your pocket.

That's why this book exists. We are going to put profit in your pocket. Starting today. Literally, today. Your profit will start today and will occur permanently.

All you need to do is commit to study this and then *do it*. Don't skip the doing. Pleeease do not skip the doing. You can't read this book, think "awesome concept," and go back to business as usual. You need to get off your butt. As Debbie did, you need to push past your feelings about the choices you made in the past. And like Keith, you need to put this into action as you read the book and follow the action steps at the end of every chapter. Your (profitable) life depends on it.

I want your profitability more than anything. I know it will bring you stability in your business and in your life. And I know you are the seed for other entrepreneurs, your employees and contacts, and perhaps even family and friends to do the same. Join me. Let's eradicate entrepreneurial poverty together.

Since I published the first edition of *Profit First* two years ago, I've received tons of feedback and questions that have given me ideas for improvement. I've also learned of dozens of shortcuts, tweaks, and solutions that individuals had discovered in their own implementation of Profit First and were kind enough to share with me. All these streamlined improvements, new advanced concepts, and clarified solutions are in this revised and expanded edition of *Profit First*. If you read the first edition of *Profit First*, you will find the core system hasn't changed a bit. It is foundationally identical. But this revised and expanded *Profit First* is packed with new knowledge, new stories, and new, easier techniques.

If you are new to *Profit First*, you have the best of the best in your hands. The implementation of Profit First in your business will be easier, faster, and better than ever before.

Get ready. We are going to make your business permanently profitable, starting with your very next deposit.

Chapter 1

YOUR BUSINESS IS AN OUT-OF-CONTROL CASH-EATING MONSTER

N o matter how many years you've been at the grind, you are probably well aware of the statistic that roughly 50 percent of businesses fail within the first five years. What they don't tell you is that those failed entrepreneurs are, in fact, the lucky ones! The majority of the businesses that survive are racking up debt, and their leaders are perpetually stressed. Most entrepreneurs are living a financial nightmare, one that's populated by Freddy Krueger or Frankenstein's monster in its raw, unadulterated scariness. In fact, I am convinced that I am Dr. Frankenstein.

If you read Mary Shelley's classic, *Frankenstein*, you know exactly what I'm talking about. The good doctor reanimated life. From mismatched body parts, he stitched together a living being more monster than man. Of course his creation wasn't a monster at first. No, at first it was a miracle. Dr. Frankenstein brought to life something that, without his extraordinary idea and exhaustive hard work, could not exist.

That's what I did. That's what you did. We brought something to life that didn't exist before we dreamed it up; we created a business out of thin air. Impressive! Miraculous! Beautiful! Or at least it was until we realized our creation was actually a monster.

Stitching together a business with nothing but a great idea, your unique talents, and whatever few resources you have at hand is most certainly a miracle. And it feels like one, too, until the day you realize your business has become a giant, scary, soul-sucking, cash-eating monster. That's the day you discover that you, too, are an esteemed member of the Frankenstein family.

And just as happened in Shelley's book, mental and physical torment ensues. You try to tame the monster, but you can't. The monster wreaks destruction at every turn: empty bank accounts, credit card debt, loans, and an ever-increasing list of "must-pay" expenses. He eats up your time, too. You wake up before sunrise to work, and you're still at it long after the sun goes down. You work and work, yet the monster continues to loom. Your relentless work doesn't free you; it further drains you. Trying to keep the monster at bay before it destroys your entire world is exhausting. You suffer sleepless nights, worries about collection calls—sometimes from your own employees—and a near-constant panic about how to cover next week's bills with a few dollars and the lint in your pocket. Didn't you start a business so you could be your own boss? Now it looks as though this monster is the boss of you.

If you think operating your business is closer to a horror story than to a fairy tale, you're not alone. Since I wrote my first book, *The Toilet Paper Entrepreneur*, I've met tens of thousands of entrepreneurs; and let me tell you, most are struggling to tame the beast that is their business. Many companies—even those that appear to have it all together, even the big guys who seem to dominate their industries—are one bad month away from total collapse.

My own wake-up call came in the form of my daughter's piggy bank.

THE PIGGY BANK THAT CHANGED MY LIFE

I lost my way the day I received a check for $388,000. It was the first of several checks I would receive for the sale of my second company—a multimillion-dollar computer forensic investigations business I had cofounded—to a Fortune 500 firm. I had now built and sold two companies, and that check was all the proof I needed that my friends and family were right about me: When it came to growing businesses, I had the Midas touch.

The day I received the check, I bought three cars: a Dodge Viper (my college-fantasy dream car, and what I have subsequently found many people identify as the "that-guy-must-have-a-tiny-penis" car), something I'd promised I would get for myself "one day" when I'd "made it," a Land Rover for my wife, and a spare—a tricked-out BMW.

I had always believed in frugality, but now I was rich (with an ego to match). I joined the private club: the one where, the more money you give, the higher they place your name on the members' wall. And I rented a house on a remote Hawaiian island so my wife, my children, and I could spend the next three or so weeks experiencing what our new lifestyle would be like. You know, "how the other half lives."

I thought it was time to revel in the money I had created. What I didn't know was that I was about to learn the difference between making money (income) and taking money (profit). These are two very, very different things.

I launched my first business on ambition and air, sleeping in my car or under conference room tables in order to avoid the cost of hotels when visiting clients. So imagine the surprised look from my wife, Krista, when I asked the sales guy at the dealership for "the most expensive Land Rover you have." Not the best Land Rover. Not the safest Land Rover. The most expensive Land Rover. He skipped his way to the manager, doing a giddy hand clap.

Krista looked at me and said, "Have you lost your mind? Can we really afford this?"

Full of snark, I said, "Can we afford it? We have more money than God." I will never forget the stupidity coming out of my mouth that day; such disgusting words, such a disgusting ego. Krista was right. I had lost my mind—and, at least for the moment, my soul.

That day was the beginning of the end. I was well on my way to discovering that while I knew how to make millions, what I was really, really proficient at was losing millions.

It wasn't just the lifestyle I bought into that caused my financial downfall—the trappings of success were a symptom of my arrogance—I believed in my own mythology. I was King Midas reinvented. I could do no wrong. And because I had the golden touch and knew how to build successful businesses, I decided that investing in a dozen brand-new start-ups was the best way to use my windfall. After all, it was only a matter of time before my entrepreneurial genius rubbed off on these promising companies.

Did I care whether the founders of these companies knew what they were doing? No—I had all the answers (read that with a massive douche emphasis). I assumed that my golden touch would more than compensate for their lack of business expertise. I hired a team to manage the infrastructure of all these start-ups—accounting, marketing, social media, Web design. I was sure I had the formula for success: a promising start-up; the infrastructure; and my incredible, superior magic touch (more douche emphasis).

Then, I started writing checks—$5,000 to one person, $10,000 to another, every month more checks, and still more. One time, I cut a check for $50,000 to cover expenses for one of these companies. I was focused on one thing and one thing only: growth. Mindlessly throwing money at start-up companies wasn't even in alignment with my values about money; I was a bootstrapper and proud of it. Still, I was blind to my mistakes. I was all pump and dump. Grow the businesses, then sell them. In retrospect, it was clear that I would not be able to grow all of these companies to the point where they would eventually become niche authorities, as I had with my two previous companies. There was never enough revenue to cover the ever-increasing mountain of bills.

Because of my massive ego, I didn't allow the good people who started these businesses to become true entrepreneurs. They were just my pawns. I ignored the signs and kept funneling money into my investments, sure that King Midas would be able to turn it all around.

Within twelve months, all of the companies I'd invested in, except one, had gone belly up. When I started writing checks to pay bills for companies that had already folded, I realized that I was not an angel investor; I was the Angel of Death.

It was a monumental disaster. Scratch that; *I* was a monumental disaster. Within a couple of years, I lost nearly every penny of my hard-earned fortune. Over half a million in savings gone. A much larger (embarrassingly larger) amount of investment money gone. Worse, I had no incoming revenue. By February fourteenth of 2008, I was down to my last $10,000.

I will never forget that Valentine's Day. Not because it was so full of love (even though it was), but because it was the day I realized that the old adage "When you hit rock bottom, the only way to go is up" is total bullshit. I discovered that day that when you hit rock bottom, sometimes you get dragged along the bottom, scraping your face on every one of those rocks until you're battered, bruised, and bloodied.

That morning I got a call at my office from Keith, my accountant (not to be confused with Keith, the hot-air balloon guy). He said, "Good news,

Mike. I got a jump start on your taxes this year and just finished your return for 2007. You owe only twenty-eight thousand dollars."

I felt a sharp pain in my chest, like a knife stabbing me. I remember thinking, "Is this what it feels like to have a heart attack?"

I would have to scramble to get the $18,000 I didn't have, and then figure out how to cover my mortgage the next month plus all of the small recurring and unexpected expenses that added up to a whole lot of cash.

As Keith wrapped up the call, he said that the bill for his services would arrive on Monday.

"How much?" I asked.

"Two thousand."

I felt the knife twist. I had $10,000 to my name and bills totaling three times that amount. After I ended the call, I put my head on my desk and cried. I had gone so far astray from my values, from who I was at my core, that I had destroyed everything. Now, not only could I not pay my taxes; I had no idea how I would provide for my family.

At the Michalowicz household, Valentine's Day is a legit holiday—on a level with Thanksgiving. We have a special dinner together, exchange cards, and go around the table sharing stories about what we love about each other. This is why Valentine's Day is my favorite day of the year. Typically, I would come home with flowers, or balloons, or both. That Valentine's Day I came home with nothing.

Though I tried to hide it, my family knew something was wrong. At the dinner table, Krista asked me if I was OK. That was all it took for the dam to break. The shame was too great. I went from offering up forced smiles to sobbing in a matter of seconds. My children stared at me, shocked and horrified. When I finally stopped crying enough to speak, I said, "I lost everything. Every single penny."

Total silence. I slumped over in my chair; the shame was too great for me to face my family, not when all the money I had earned to support them was gone. Not only had I failed to provide for my family; my ego had stolen it all away. I felt pure, unadulterated shame about what I had done.

My daughter, Adayla, who was nine years old at the time, got up from the table and ran to her bedroom. I couldn't really blame her—I wanted to run away, too.

The silence continued for two painfully awkward minutes until Adayla walked back into the room carrying her piggy bank, the one she had received as a gift when she was born. It had clearly been cared for; even with all those years of use, there wasn't a single chip or crack on the bank. She had secured the rubber stopper in place with a combination of masking tape, duct tape, and rubber bands.

Adayla set her piggy bank down on the dining room table and slid it toward me. Then she said the words that will stay with me until the day I die:

"Daddy, we're going to make it."

That Valentine's Day I woke up feeling like Debbie Horovitch felt after her Instant Assessment: like a fool. But by the end of the day I'd learned what net worth really is, thanks to my nine-year-old daughter. That day I also learned that no amount of talent, ingenuity, passion, or skill would change the fact that cash is still king. I learned that a nine-year-old girl had mastered the essence of financial security: save your money and block access to it so it doesn't get stolen—by you. And I learned that I could tell myself that my natural aptitude for business, my relentless drive, and my solid work ethic could overcome any cash crisis, but it would be a lie.

Running the Instant Assessment can be like having a bucket of ice water dropped on your head (if you did the "ice bucket challenge" a couple of years ago, you know the spine-shuddering chill I am talking about). Or it can seem like the most humbling moment of your life, like when your daughter volunteers her life savings to save you from the mess you made. But no matter how sharp the pain is, it's better to face it than continue to live and operate your business in denial.

MONEY PROBLEMS

You have probably put a lot of work into growing your business. You are probably good or great at that part. That's awesome. And that's surely half of the equation. But colossal growth without financial health will still kill your company. With this book, you have an opportunity to master money.

Money is the foundation. Without enough money, we cannot take our message, our products, or our services to the world. Without enough money, we are slaves to the businesses we launched. I find this hilarious because, in large part, we started our businesses because we wanted to be free.

Without enough money, we cannot fully realize our authentic selves. Money amplifies who we are. There isn't a single ounce of doubt in my mind that there is something big you are intended to do on this planet. You wear the cape of what I believe is the greatest of all superheroes: the Entrepreneur. But your superhero powers can only yield as much power as your energy source provides. Money. You need money, superhero.

When I sat down to evaluate where I went wrong, I realized that while my own spending and arrogance definitely played a part, I also lacked knowledge. I had mastered how to grow businesses quickly, yet I never really graduated to understanding profitability. I had learned how to collect money, for sure, but I had never learned how to keep it, how to control it or how to grow it.

I knew how to grow a business from nothing, working with whatever resources I had; but as revenue increased, so did my spending. I discovered that this was the way I ran both my personal life and my business. I took pride in making magic happen with pennies in my pocket, but as soon as I got some real cash, I made sure that I had a very good reason to spend it. It was a check-to-check lifestyle, but sustainable—as long as sales were sustained and did not dip.

While my companies grew explosively, I still operated them on a check-to-check basis—and I had no idea that this was a problem. The point was to grow, right? Increase sales and the profit will take care of itself, right?

Wrong. Money problems occur when one of two things happen:

Sales slow down. The problem here is obvious when you operate check-to-check and sales slow down: when your one big client goes out of business, or that big deal you were banking on falls through, you won't have enough to cover expenses.

Sales speed up. This problem here is not obvious, but it is insidious. As your income climbs, expenses quickly follow. Big deposits feel great, but they are irregular. Consistent incoming cash flow is hard to sustain. A great quarter can trick you into believing your business is on a permanent upswing, and you start spending like this is the new normal. But drought periods come quickly and unexpectedly, causing a major gap in cash flow.

And cutting back on expenses is nearly impossible because our business (and personal) lifestyle is locked in at our new level. Exchanging the newly leased car for a rust bucket, laying off employees because we're overstaffed, saying no to our partners—all of this is very hard to do because of the agreements and promises we made. We don't want to admit we've been wrong in how we've been growing our business. So rather than reduce our costs in any meaningful way, we scramble to cover ridiculously high expenses. We steal from Peter to pay Paul, hoping for another big payout.

Sound familiar? I thought it might. Over the last eight years I've connected with entrepreneurs at every level of growth, and this "top line" (revenue-focused), check-to-check methodology is more common than you may realize. We assume that multimillion-dollar companies are turning big profits, but it's rare to find a truly profitable business. Most entrepreneurs are just covering their monthly nut (or worse) and accumulating massive debt.

Without an understanding of profitability, every business, no matter how big, no matter how "successful," is a house of cards. I made a lot of money with my first two businesses, but not because I ran a tight fiscal ship. I was just lucky enough to keep the plates spinning fast enough and the company growing big enough that someone else was willing to buy it and fix the financial problems.

BIGGER IS NOT BETTER

Why the hell is success constantly defined by applying the *Super Size Me* principle to your business? Does more revenue mean you are more successful? No. I know far too many big businesses with owners who are in pure panic and use lawn furniture to decorate the inside of their houses because they have to funnel every spare penny into their businesses to keep them from sinking. Is that success? Hardly.

Growth is the battle cry of nearly every entrepreneur and business leader. Grow! Grow! Grow! Bigger sales. Bigger customers. Bigger investors. But to what end? Bigger business means bigger problems for sure. Yet it surely does not guarantee bigger profits, especially when profit is a hopeful residual.

Growth is only half the equation. It is an important half, but still only half. Have you ever seen the guys at the gym with the massive arms and heaving chests, the ones as big as oxen who also have toothpick legs? They're only working half the equation and have become unhealthy freaks as a result. Sure, that guy can throw a monster punch, but God forbid he needs to step into it, or move a little. His puny legs will give out instantly; he'll curl up on the floor and cry like a baby. A little mutant baby.

Most business owners try to grow their way out of their problems, hinging salvation on the next big sale or customer or investor, but the result is simply a bigger monster. (And the bigger your company gets, the more anxiety you deal with. A $300,000 cash-eating monster is much easier to manage than a $3,000,000 one. I know; I have survived operating both.) This is constant growth without concern for health. And the day that big sale or customer or investor doesn't show, you will fall to the ground and curl up crying like a baby.

Jason Fried, cofounder of Basecamp, wrote an article for *Inc.** in which he talked about the demise of his favorite Chicago pizza joint. The owners did everything right—except that they grew too fast. After building their business slowly, they suddenly scaled from twenty to forty locations. Sales could not outpace their debt, and Fried's beloved pizza chain was forced to close. The perfect size for your business? It will happen naturally, when you take your profit first. You will reverse engineer all the elements of your business, and as Fried says, "the right size will find you."

So why are entrepreneurs programmed to pursue bigger and bigger and bigger? Because of an assumption that at a certain point all that revenue will yield a profit. You think you just need one more big project or one more new client or just a little bit more time, and finally that profit will pour in. But it never does. Profit is always within sight, but never attainable. It's like the donkey with a carrot dangling over its head. The jackass keeps working harder and harder, but never gets to the carrot. It's always just one more step away. The problem is, that jackass . . . is you. (Sorry about the brutal honesty. I hurt you because I love you.)

Here's the deal, my friend: Profit is *not* an event. Profit is not something that happens at year-end or at the end of your five-year plan or someday. Profit isn't even something that waits until tomorrow. Profit must happen

---

* "Why Growing Fast Will Make Your Company More Mediocre," May 2016.

now and always. Profit must be baked into your business. Every day, every transaction, every moment. Profit is not an event. Profit is a habit.

Do you know the saying "Revenue is vanity, profit is sanity, and cash is king"? It is a succinct reminder that your job is to maximize profit, regardless of the current size of your business. As you focus on profit, you'll discover new ways to both streamline and grow your business. It doesn't work the other way around. The lemming mentality of growing first with the hope of finding profit in the process, is so bass ackward it drives me nuts.

Recently I delivered a speech in tiny Georgetown, Colorado, at an event hosted by my dear friend Michelle Villalobos. As often happens in my Profit First presentations, one of the entrepreneurs said, "This sounds great and all, but I need to grow. I need to put all of my money back into my business to do that."

Perhaps you're thinking the same thing right now. If you are, it's because you're stuck in the mode of "grow now, profit someday."

I asked her, "Why do you want to grow?"

"I want to grow so that my company can manage more clients and generate more sales," she said.

"Why do you want that?"

She looked at me as if I were an alien. "So that my company is bigger, Mike."

"Why do you want a bigger company?" I asked.

"So I can make more money," she responded. I could tell from her tone that she was getting exasperated.

"Aha!" I said. Now we have peeled back that good ol' Georgetown, Colorado, onion (which, let me be clear, is not known for its onions.) "Why not just make more money now?"

She wants to grow, grow, grow so that she can make a profit one day. Alternatively, if you want to grow for ego, and to boast, that is just dumb (cough—that's exactly what I did in the past—cough—so embarrassing— cough). If you want to grow to make money for yourself one day, you are playing a game of kick the profit can down the road.

Here's the reality if you want healthy, sustainable growth—which, not so surprisingly, will spawn more healthy growth—you need to reverse engineer the profit. Take profit first. You can't grow out of your profit problem. You need to fix profit first, then grow. You must figure out the things that make profit and dump the things that don't. When you focus on growth, it is inevitably a scramble to grow at all costs. Yes, at all costs (including the quality of your life). When you focus on profit first, you inevitably figure out how to make a profit consistently. Profitability. Stability. Sanity. Forevermore.

CHECK-TO-CHECK AND PANIC-TO-PANIC

Have you ever had the thought that the universe knows exactly how much extra money you have? A customer pays up on a $4,000 past-due invoice you wrote off months ago and later that week your delivery truck breaks down—for good. Bye-bye, $4,000. You land a new client and a wad of cash drops into your lap; only minutes later you remember that this is a three-payroll month. Oh well, at least now you'll almost be able to cover it. Or you get a credit on your credit card account for an accidental billing (woo-hoo, found money!), only to discover another charge on your credit card for something you forgot all about.

It's not the universe that knows how much we have in our bank accounts. It's us. We default to managing the cash of our business by doing what I call "bank balance accounting."

If you're like most entrepreneurs, and me, this is how it works:

You look at your bank balance and see a chunk of change. Yippee! You feel great for about ten minutes, and then decide to pay all the bills that have been piling up. The balance goes to zero and very quickly you feel that all-too-familiar tightening in the chest.

What do we do when instead of a decent bank balance, we see that there's next to nothing there? We immediately panic. We hit "go" mode: need to sell fast! Need to make collection calls! Need to pretend the bills never arrived, or send out checks and "accidentally" forget to sign them. When we know our bank balance is super low (I'm talking limbo, "How low can you go?" low), we'll do anything to buy the only thing we can afford: time.

I'm going to go out on a limb and guess that you only look at your income statement on occasion. I suspect you rarely look at your cash flow statements or balance sheet. And if you do, I doubt you review these docs on a daily basis or understand exactly what they say. But I bet you check your bank account every day, don't you? It's OK. If you look at your bank account daily, I want to congratulate you because that means you are a typical—scratch that—a normal business leader; that's how most entrepreneurs behave.

It is our natural desire as entrepreneurs to find problems and fix them. This is how we manage money. When we have enough money in the bank, we think we don't have money problems, and so we focus on other challenges. When we see that we don't have enough money in the bank, we go on red alert and take immediate action to fix our money problems, usually by trying to collect revenue quickly, or selling a big-ticket item, or some combination of the two.

We use the money we have to pay the bills we owe; when we don't have enough to cover everything, we try to get more money through sales and collections. Except that to support new revenue, we now have a host of new related expenses, so the cycle starts all over again. If you haven't relied on it from the start, eventually the only "solution" is to take on debt—a second mortgage on your family home, a line of credit tied to your building, a stack of credit cards three inches high. This is how many entrepreneurs end up operating their businesses check to check and panic to panic.

So let me ask you a question. How confident are you that you could grow your business if you operated this way? Do you think you'd ever be able to get off this roller-coaster ride? Could you dig yourself out of debt using this system? Of course not.

And yet bank balance accounting is human nature. We humans are not big on change. Change is hard. With your very best intentions, changing your human tendencies to operate your business based on how much cash you see in your account would take years. I don't know, you tell me— do you have years to make your own transformation before your very own monster destroys everything? I sure as hell didn't.

This is why, if we are to free ourselves from living check to check and panic to panic, we must find a method that works with our nature, not against it.

Without an effective money management system that does not require massive mind-set change, we get stuck in trying to sell our way out of our struggles. Sell more. Sell faster. Get money any way you can. It is a trap—a dangerous trap that would even have Frankenstein's monster poopin' his panties. It's the Survival Trap.

THE SURVIVAL TRAP

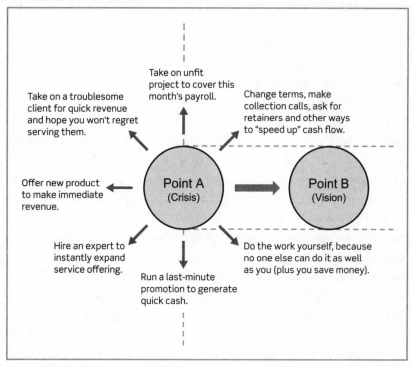

Fig. 1. Survival Trap.

My lawn guy, Ernie, is a good example of someone caught in the Survival Trap. As is true for most lawn guys in the Northeast, Ernie makes good money removing leaves from lawns. Despite this, Ernie is always in need of more revenue. This past fall he knocked on my door and said that he noticed leaves in my gutters and would gladly clean them up. He had a captive client (me), and could now sell me another service. Easy money. When he was on the roof, he noticed my shingles needed repair. He offered roofing services. Why not repair my chimney, too?

Sounds like a smart guy, right? Except that he's an idiot. (Let me be clear: Ernie is a great person. He truly is. Ernie has great goals and ambitions. It's his decision to expand his offering and expand his offering further that is pure idiocy.) Any sale feels like a good sale because sales help to temporarily lift us out of crisis.

Take a look at Figure 1. Ernie is at point A (which is really called crisis) and he wants to get to point B (which is his vision for our future). The thing is, as is the case for most of us, his vision is very vague. Instead of a clear statement of his products or services and the clients he wants to serve, Ernie might have a goal like, "I want a lot of money and need relief from stress." The connection between point A and point B is never defined beyond, "Sell, baby! Just sell anybody anything!" Looking at the figure, you can see that many of the decisions we make around "just selling" in fact take us further away from our true vision. When Ernie offers me a new service, because it will make fast money, he hasn't considered that it has nothing to do with what he wants his company to become or whom he wants his company to serve.

It is very easy to go from being a guy who rakes lawns to a guy who fixes chimneys because of the opportunity for "easy money" with captive clients. The money may be easy, but what about the costs to do it all? Rakes and blowers for yard work are useless when working on roofs or chimneys. Now this guy needs ladders, roofing gear, bricks, and other materials. And most important, he needs the skills to complete the tasks, which means hiring skilled labor or going back to raking, gutter cleaning, roofing, and chimney school. Each new "easy sale" took Ernie further from his lawn-raking business.

The Survival Trap promises fast money, but when we're caught in it, we, like Ernie, rarely think about the massive cost of opportunity; and most of the time, we can't discern profitable income from debt-generating income. Instead of being the world's best at one thing, mastering the process of delivering perfectly and super-efficiently, we end up doing a greater variety of things and becoming less and less efficient at each step while our businesses become harder to manage and costlier to run.

The Survival Trap is not about driving toward our vision. It is all about taking action, any action, to get out of crisis. Any of the actions shown in Figure 1 will get us out of an immediate crisis. But by taking actions like those on the left of the circle, we get out of crisis, sure enough, but we are going in the opposite direction from our vision at point B. We take money from anyone (and I mean anyone) willing to pay us. Money from bad clients. Money for bad projects. Money from our own pockets (if there's anything left in them besides two dimes, a stick of gum, and a wad of lint). In this way, we stay stuck on the roller-coaster ride that is surviving check to check and panic to panic.

Other actions shown on the diagram don't take us in the opposite direction, but they are askew. Only when you stay in the channel of the horizontal dotted lines do you make your vision for your business a reality.

The Survival Trap is deceptive because it fools us into thinking we are at least inching toward our vision, as if our reactionary behavior is actually "smart" or evidence of our good instincts, and will eventually lead us to the promised land: financial freedom. Consider the actions on the right side of Figure 1. For instance, a "just sell" approach will, by pure happenstance, also occasionally move us toward our vision, and we can easily trick ourselves into believing that we're on the right track. Sometimes we make a crisis decision without considering our vision or the path to get there, and we get it right. Happenstance happens. At that point, we say, "See! I'm getting there. Things are clicking. Things are coming together." But this is random chance, resulting from crisis, not focus or clarity, and is therefore false. It is like believing that because you once won on a scratch-off card, the lottery is a good investment strategy. And it is this kind of thinking that quickly lands us back in crisis mode.

The Survival Trap is an ugly beast. It buys you time, but the monster gets bigger and bigger. And at some point it will turn on you and destroy you ruthlessly.

Sustained profitability depends on efficiency. You can't become efficient in crisis. In crisis, we justify making money at any cost, right now, even if it means skipping taxes or selling our souls. In crises, the Survival Trap becomes our modus operandi—until our survival strategies create a new, more devastating crisis that scares us straight or, more commonly, scares us right out of business.

Part of the problem is bank balance accounting—looking at the money in your bank account as one pool from which you can operate your business without first addressing tax issues or your own salary, never mind profit. This leads to top line thinking—focusing on revenue first, last, and always. That thinking is further supported by the traditional accounting method public companies must use and most small businesses elect to use: GAAP (Generally Accepted Accounting Principles).

TRADITIONAL ACCOUNTING IS KILLING YOUR BUSINESS

Since the dawn of time—or shortly thereafter—businesses have kept track of their earnings and expenditures using essentially the same method:

Sales – Expenses = Profit

If you manage the numbers like most entrepreneurs, you start with sales (the top line) and then subtract costs directly related to the delivery of your offering (product or service). Then you subtract all the other costs you incur to run your business: rent, utilities, employee salaries, office supplies, and other administrative expenses, sales commissions, taking your client out to lunch, signage, insurance, etc., etc. Then you pay taxes. Then, and only then, do you take your owner's distribution (owner's salary, profit distribution, etc.).

Let's be honest, entrepreneurs hardly ever take anything close to a real salary, and good luck telling the government that you decided to skip taxes this year so that you could pay yourself. Finally, after all that, you post your company's profit. And if your experience is like the majority of entrepreneurs, you never get to "finally." When you're waiting for the leftovers, at best you'll get scraps.

The traditional accounting methods we use today became formalized in the early 1900s. The particulars are updated regularly, but the core system remains the same: Start with sales. Subtract direct costs (the costs you directly incur to create and deliver your product or service). Pay employees. Subtract indirect costs. Pay taxes. Pay owners (owner distributions). Retain or distribute profit (the bottom line). Whether you outsource your bookkeeping or keep a shoebox of receipts under your bed, the basic idea stays the same.

Logically, GAAP makes complete sense. It suggests that we sell as much as we can, spend as little as we can, and pocket the difference. But humans aren't logical. (One episode of *Bridezillas* pretty much proves that.) Just because GAAP makes logical sense doesn't mean it makes "human sense." GAAP both supersedes our natural behavior and makes us believe bigger is better. So we try to sell more. We try and try and try to sell our way to success. We do everything we can to make the top line (revenue) grow so that something, anything, will drip down to the bottom line. It becomes a relentless cycle of chasing after every shiny object disguised as opportunity (that's "little pumpkins" to my peeps—you know who you are).

Throughout this haphazard, desperate growth process, our expenses are lost in the wash—we just pay as we go. They're all necessary, right? Who knows? We're too busy hunting down sales and trying to deliver on all our promises to worry about the impact of expenses!

We try to spend less without considering investments versus costs. We don't think about leveraging our spending to get way more mileage out of way less expense. We can't. The more variety of stuff we sell, the more our cost of doing business rises. They say it takes money to make money. But no one ever tells us what that translates to in the real world: It takes more money to make less money.

As our monster gets bigger, its appetite gets out of hand. Now we're faced with covering expenses for more employees, more stuff, more everything. The monster grows. And grows. And grows. Meanwhile, we're still dealing with the same problems, just bigger ones: more empty bank accounts, higher stacks of credit card bills, bigger loans, and an ever-increasing list of "must-pay" expenses. Sound familiar, Dr. Frankenstein?

GAAP's fundamental flaw is that it goes against human nature. No matter how much income we generate, we will always find a way to spend it—all of it. And we have good reasons for all our spending choices. Everything is justified. Soon enough, whatever money we had in the bank dwindles down to nothing as we struggle to cover every "necessary" expense. And that's when we find ourselves in the Survival Trap.

A secondary flaw is this: GAAP teaches us to focus on sales and expenses first. Once again, it works against our human nature, which urges us to grow what we focus on. It's something called the Primacy Effect (more on that in the next chapter)—we focus on what comes first (sales and expenses) and actually become blind to what comes last. Yes, GAAP makes us blind to profit.

There is a saying: "What gets measured, gets done." GAAP has us measure sales first (it is the top line, after all), and therefore we sell like mad while expenses are treated like a necessary evil to support—you guessed it—more sales. We spend all that we have because we believe we must. And we use terms like "plowback" or "reinvest" to feel good about it. Profit? Your salary? Mere afterthoughts. Leftovers.

Another problem with GAAP is its overwhelming complexity. You need to hire an accountant to get it right, and when you ask the accountant the details about GAAP, he is likely to get confused. The system changes and is up for interpretation. And we can play games with GAAP: move some numbers around and post stuff in different spots, and the numbers look different. Just ask Enron—they were able to post profits as they were going bankrupt. Yuck!

Before we go any further, I want to make sure you and I are on the same page when I talk about profit. Because the way accountants think about profit can be very different.

Here's what I mean: A couple of years before I wrote *The Toilet Paper Entrepreneur*, I was sitting in my accountant's office, watching him scratch down some notes with a pencil on a legal pad. He erased something, then wrote down another note. Then he looked at his computer, clicked and clacked a few buttons, and the dot matrix printer spit out a report.

"Yep. Just as I thought, Mike," Keith said, peering over his John Lennon wannabe glasses.

"What?" I said.

"You had a $15,000 profit this year. Congratulations, that isn't too bad."

For a second I felt pride. Damn straight there is a profit. I patted myself on the back. Then I had a sinking feeling. Where was the cash? There wasn't a penny in the corporate coffers, let alone in my pocket.

Then, feeling embarrassed that I didn't know the answer, I asked, "Hey, Keith, where is the profit?"

He pointed to the paper report that the printer had just spit out. He circled it on the paper with his fancy-schmancy number 2 pencil.

"Yes, Keith, I can see that profit on the paper. But where is the cash? I want to take it out and celebrate a little. I want that profit for me."

There was a moment of awkward silence. Keith did his best to avoid making me feel stupid. He stared at me. Then he said, "This is an accounting profit. You spent the money in some way already. It doesn't mean there is any money actually there right now. In fact, in your case it's already gone. This is just the accounting of what already happened."

"So are you saying I have a profit, but there is nothing in the bank for me to take as a profit right now?"

"Exactly," said the John Lennon poseur.

"Damn! This sucks."

"Maybe next year," Keith said.

Next year? Why next year? Why not starting tomorrow? I thought.

Accountants define profit differently than entrepreneurs. They point to a fictitious number at the bottom of an accounting report. Our definition of profit is simple: cash in the bank. Cold. Hard. Cash. For us.

At the end of the day, the start of a new day, and every second in between, cash is all that counts. It is the lifeblood of your business. Do you have it or not? If you don't, you're in trouble, and if you do, you are sustained.

GAAP was never intended to manage only cash. It is a system for understanding all the elements of your business. It has three key reports: the income statement, the cash flow statement, and the balance sheet. There is no question that you need to understand these reports (or work with an accountant and bookkeeper who do), because they will give you a holistic view of your company; they are powerful and highly useful tools. But the essence of GAAP (Sales – Expenses = Profit) is horribly flawed. It is a formula that builds monsters. It is the Frankenstein formula.

To successfully run a profitable business, we need a super simple system to manage our cash, one we can understand within seconds, without help from an accountant. We need a system that is designed for humans, not Spock.

We need a system that can instantly tell us the truth about the health of our businesses, one that we can look at and know instantly what we need to do to get healthy and stay healthy; a system that tells us what we can actually spend and what needs to be reserved; a system that doesn't require us to change but automatically works with our natural behaviors.

Profit First is that system.

PROFIT FIRST IS BUILT FOR HUMANS

How many times did Spock stare into Captain Kirk's eyes and say, "That is highly illogical"? Well, just like you, Captain Kirk was a human, and humans are not logical. We are emotional beasts with monkey brains. We like shiny objects; we stuff ourselves when there's free pizza; we buy twelve pounds of cat food just because it's on sale, even though we don't have a cat. (OK, maybe that's just me.) But we also know to trust our gut, go with our instincts, take shortcuts, and be inventive on the fly so we can move on and get more things done.

If you were Spock, the relentlessly logical Vulcan on *Star Trek*, in addition to your pointy ears and awkwardly tight uniform, you would follow all the accounting instructions necessary to pinpoint your numbers. On a weekly basis you would study your income statement, tie it into you balance sheet, and, of course, do an analysis of your cash flow. Next you would run the critical ratios, like the OCR (operating cash ratio), and tie all this into your budget and projections. Then you would evaluate the associated KPIs (key performance indicators). You would do it all, and you would know exactly where your profits stand at any time. But you don't, do you? Not even close. I don't. In fact, I still can't read those documents well. (That's why I employ a couple of Spocks—my accountant and my bookkeeper.) I am a human. And so are you. And I strongly suspect you are a Captain Kirk. And that is a good thing, because you are the perfect person to lead your corporate ship to profits at warp speed.

As a human, you likely have certain tendencies. Chances are you log into your bank account every few days, or maybe a few times a day, to see what your bank balance is. You probably make gut decisions based upon the balances you see. A lot of deposits and you feel good. Business is cooking! Let's take our clients out for bottomless margaritas! Let's buy that foosball table for the office! No money and panic sets it. Need to start making collection calls! Sell the foosball table! Sell the rad vending machines! Sell all the chairs! Sitting is bad for you anyway! All while praying that someone buys *you* a bottomless margarita. This and other normal human behaviors put businesses, unintentionally, into a constant state of flux.

But I have good news, people. I designed Profit First so that you don't have to change yourself at all. This is a critical point. You have always had an opportunity to change yourself and read your financial statements, sync your accounts payable and accounts receivable, make sure you are within budget, and make sure all the financial ratios are right. If you did all that, you would know where your profit stands all the time. But only Spock and accountants (and actually not that many of them) can and do that. Most entrepreneurs revert to checking their bank balance and going with their gut. Why?

As Charles Duhigg explains in *The Power of Habit*, it is human nature to revert to established habits in times of stress. And guess what? The definition of entrepreneurship is constant stress. So we look for shortcuts and quick answers, especially with our finances. The great news is that Profit First is within your natural path. It is directly in alignment with the shortcut of looking at your bank account. It is unavoidable, designed to complement your natural human behaviors; therefore, it works.

Established habits die hard, so why try changing your habits? Instead, use a system that works with your existing habits.

Profit First sits in front of your accounting. It will tell you when you have a red flag and need to dig into the complex accounting stuff (with your qualified* accountant or bookkeeper), and it will show you exactly where your cash stands at any given moment. You'll know your profitability, your reserves for taxes, what you are getting paid, and the amount you have to run your business operations. All that and more.

HAPPILY EVER AFTER

The ending of Frankenstein (spoiler alert) is one of the most heartwarming happy endings in literature. Dr. Frankenstein and the monster talk it out

---

* To find a qualified accountant, bookkeeper, or coach to support your business, I encourage you to visit ProfitFirstProfessionals.com and choose the FIND option. I have vetted the best of the best providers throughout the globe, trained them in the nuances of Profit First, and continually work with them—as they work with their clients—to grow their profit skills. My team will gladly introduce you to a Profit First expert who we believe will be a perfect match for you. And if you act within the next fifteen minutes, you will get a free set of Ginsu Knives. (That's a joke, people. The part about the Ginsu knives, I mean. The Profit First Professionals are very real, I assure you.)

and reconcile their differences, become best friends, and go into business together to create a hugely successful and beloved ice-cream brand, Frank & Stein's. Leaves me in joyful tears every time.

Just kidding. If you've read the book, you know that the monster destroys everything in Dr. Frankenstein's life—his wife, his family, his hope for the future—so he sets out to exact revenge and kill his creation. The hunt for the monster takes a toll on Dr. Frankenstein and he dies a wrecked man, the monster close behind him. Frankenstein is a scary parallel to the extremes of entrepreneurship. Monster businesses have killed marriages, torn apart families, and for some entrepreneurs, decimated any hope for the good life. That miracle of a business we created can end up causing untold suffering; when that happens, the hatred Dr. Frankenstein had for his monster is all too often the chief emotion entrepreneurs have toward their businesses.

But your story doesn't have to end that way. You can have your happily ever after. The good news is that while your business may seem to be a monster controlling your life, it is also powerful. Whether your annual revenue is $50,000, $500,000, $5,000,000 or even $50,000,000, your business can become a profit-generating workhorse.

Never forget the power of your "monster"—you just have to understand how to direct and control it. When you learn this simple system, your business will no longer be a monster; it will become an obedient, pasture-loving cash cow. A damn strong one, at that.

What I am about to share with you is going to make your business profitable immediately and determinately. I don't care what size business you have or how long you have been surviving check to check and panic to panic, month after month and year after year. You are about to be profitable. Forevermore. No more leftovers for you—it's time for you to eat first.

Here's the deal. There is only one way to fix your financials: by facing your financials. You can't ignore them. You can't let someone else take care of them. You need to take charge of the numbers. But there is good news— the process is really, really simple. In fact, you will fundamentally understand it, and implement it, within just a few more chapters.

TAKE ACTION: SEND ME AN EMAIL

It's time to draw the line in the sand and get some accountability. Email me right now (my email is Mike@MikeMichalowicz.com) with the subject line "I've Drawn the Line in the Sand," and tell me that you are committed to profitability. And tell me that you will do what it takes to once and for all become permanently profitable. If you are all in on this, I want to know it. Email me. Commit. Let's do this.

Chapter 2

THE CORE PRINCIPLES
OF PROFIT FIRST

You would think that my daughter presenting me with her piggy bank as a way out of our financial ruin would have compelled me to change.

You'd be wrong.

That Valentine's Day was a defining moment, for sure. The problem was, I had no idea where or how to begin. In reality, wake-up calls are rarely as depicted in the movies. I didn't hear "Eye of the Tiger" playing as the soundtrack of my life, spurring me into an inspired training montage; there was no drinking raw eggs, punching my debt into submission, or running up the steps to raise my fists in the glory of an entrepreneurial turnaround. Instead, I entered a very dark period of depression and insomnia. The shame I felt was overwhelming—ashamed of my idiocy, of my lies of omission, of my lack of courage to tell my wife the truth about how bad I'd made things.

I share this with you not to seek your pity, but because I think you may have your own version of the story, and I want you to know you're not alone. And if you haven't gone to the dark place, know that it can be avoided. I emphatically believe that. Profit First is the solution to pending disaster in business.

Here is how I dealt with depression: I hit the bottle (beer bottles actually . . . and lots of them). I'm really not much of a drinker at all. But I started to rely on it as my escape. That choice just led to more shame, and I hid it as best as I could—if slumping on the couch, watching infomercials, surrounded by Bud Light cans is hiding it. Imagine me in a white undershirt covered with Cheetos stains. It's not a pretty picture. And I don't even *like* Cheetos.

Why was I watching infomercials, when we now have 2,976 channels to choose from? Because when I blew it all, cable TV was the first thing to go. That left me with a rabbit ear antenna (Google it, young padawans) and five network channels that, at three a.m., regress to pitching the latest vegetable pulverizing box or electrocuting belt—all promising ripped abs.

Tired of infomercials, I turned on PBS. A fitness expert was explaining to the studio audience that the quick fixes lauded by late-night diet infomercials didn't work and weren't sustainable. He said that what we really need are simple *lifestyle* fixes that change how we eat without our even really noticing. And his first fix suggestion? Smaller plates.

Now riveted, I watched as the man explained that our natural human behavior is to fill up our plates with food, and because Mom said so, clean that plate by eating everything on it. (I still don't get Mom's logic—there are children starving in Africa, so I need to stuff myself?) The clean-your-plate behavior was instilled in me, and probably in you, too. The message is ingrained. Changing that habit for a day is a no-brainer. But changing it permanently? That's hard. This is why so many people who diet gain the weight back; why people rarely follow through on New Year's resolutions past the end of January; and why it's so difficult to be disciplined with your spending.

As I continued to watch the program, the expert went on to say that when we use smaller plates, we dish out smaller portions, thus eating fewer calories without changing our ingrained behavior of serving a full plate and eating all of what is served.

I sat up straight on the couch, my mind alert with this new revelation. The solution is not to try to change our ingrained habits, which is really hard to pull off and nearly impossible to sustain, but instead to change the structure around us and *leverage* those habits.

It was then that I realized: every penny my company made was going onto one huge plate, and I was gobbling it all up, using every last scrap to operate my business. Every dollar that came in went into one account, my operating account, and I was "eating it all."

It hurts to admit this, but I was never good at money management. While my businesses were doing well, it was easy to think I knew how to manage money well, but looking back, I realize that that was never the case.

I thought I was frugal in principle, or because I was a savvy entrepreneur. But in truth, I was frugal only when it was forced upon me. When I started my first company, a computer network integrator (today it would be called a managed service provider), I had no money. I was able to sell, service, run my office—I found ways to do all that with practically no money because I didn't have any.

As the business grew, I started to spend. The more money came in, the more I spent, and I believed—scratch that, I was convinced—that all expenditures were necessary. We needed better equipment, a better office (an unfinished basement is no place for a business), and more employees to do the work so I could focus on sales. Every step forward in sales growth required an equal step up in my infrastructure, human resources, grade A office space—all fancy terms for expenses.

After losing it all, I discovered that I work with whatever is put in front of me. Give me a hundred dollars and I will make it happen. Give me a hundred grand and I will make it happen. And while it's easier to make things happen with a hundred thousand dollars in hand, it's also way easier to make mistakes. Totally waste a few hundred dollars when you have a hundred thousand at your disposal, and you feel nothing. Totally waste a few hundred bucks, when you only have a few hundo to your name, and you feel that pain fast and hard.

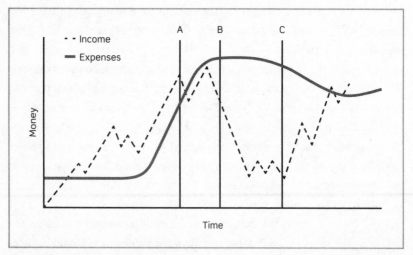

Fig. 2. Income Versus Cost.

Looking back at my companies, I realized that I grew them quickly but still survived check to check, only making the real money when I sold them. As my incoming cash increased (the dotted line in the chart), my expenses increased at a similar rate (solid line). The only time I would have a profit was when income jumped up, and I didn't have time to spend at the same rate (point A). However, I would quickly ramp up my expenses to serve my "new level of sales" (point B). Then sales would settle back down, or drop, while my new level of expenses remained higher (point C), which meant I started to accumulate losses, making me desperate to sell more and sell faster at any cost (which could, in turn, further increase my expenses).

As the PBS show shifted into early morning kids' programming, I muted the television and began to connect the dots (which Count von Count, the vampire on *Sesame Street*, was also doing, literally connecting dots on the screen). If I reduced the "plate size" of my business's operating account, I would spend differently. So rather than try to curb my spending habit, I would create the experience of having less cash on hand than I actually had, and then would find ways to still make things work. How did I know this would work? Because it already works for millions of people with every paycheck—think 401(k) deductions. As Richard Thaler and Cass Sunstein explain in their fascinating book *Nudge*, when people start participating in 401(k)s, they rarely stop. The key is to get started so both the savings accumulate and the lifestyle adjusts to meet their residual pay.

If 401(k)s were like regular savings accounts, people would find it way too tempting and easy to dip into their savings anytime they felt like it. The reason they don't is because investment accounts charge penalties and make it difficult to withdraw money whenever you want. In the same way, I could make myself believe and behave as if I had only my "small plate" money to work with (and not a small plate plus a big Crock Pot at the table).

But what would I *do* with the "other money?" Could I use it to—shock of shocks—*pay myself a salary*? Pay my taxes?

Hey. Hey, wait. Wait one stinkin' minute. Could I actually set aside some of it for profit—*before* I paid bills?

And that's when it hit me—what if I took my profit *first*?

For a guy who built two businesses on top line (revenue-focused) thinking, this idea was a revelation. At six a.m., with beer breath, Cheetos stains covering my undershirt, and hair going in more directions than Einstein's, it sounded like crazy talk. Who would have the audacity to take profit first? I would.

THE FOUR CORE PRINCIPLES OF PROFIT FIRST

Let's take a moment to talk dietary science. No groans, please. This stuff is fascinating.

In 2012, a report by Koert Van Ittersum and Brian Wansink in the *Journal of Consumer Research* concluded that the average plate size in America had grown 23 percent between the years 1900 and 2012, from 9.6 inches to 11.8 inches. Running the math, the article explains that should this increase in plate size encourage an individual to consume just fifty more calories per day, that person would put on an extra five pounds of weight each year. Year after year, that adds up to a very chunky monkey.

But using smaller plates is just one factor. A Twinkie on a small plate is still a Twinkie. There is more to a healthy diet, and it is based on four core principles of weight loss and nutrition.

1. **Use Small Plates**—Using smaller plates starts a chain reaction. When you use a small plate, you get smaller portions, which means you take in fewer calories. When you take in fewer calories than you normally would, you start to lose weight.

2. **Serve Sequentially**—If you eat the vegetables, rich in nutrients and vitamins, first, they will start satisfying your hunger. When you move on to the next course—your mac and cheese or mashed potatoes (they don't count as veggies!)—you will automatically eat less. By changing the sequence of your meals by eating your vegetables first, you automatically bring a nutritional balance to your diet.

3. **Remove Temptation**—Remove any temptation from where you eat. People are driven by convenience. If you're anything like me, when there's a bag of Doritos sitting in the kitchen, it calls out to you constantly—even when you aren't hungry. If you don't have any junk food in the house, you're probably not going to run out to the store to get it. (That would mean putting on pants.) You're going to eat the healthy food you stocked instead.

4. **Enforce a Rhythm**—If you wait until you are hungry to eat, it is already too late and you will binge. Then you are likely to eat too much and stuff yourself. You go from starving to stuffed, and back to starving again. These peaks and valleys in your hunger result in way too much calorie consumption. Instead, eat regularly (many researchers suggest five small meals a day) so that you never get hungry. Without the peaks and valleys, you will actually eat fewer calories.

Though they don't realize it, the folks in the diet industry know quite a lot about growing a healthy business. Let's examine these principles one by one:

1. Parkinson's Law: Why Your Business Is Like a Tube of Toothpaste

In the years since I discovered these four physical health principles, I dug further and further into why they matter. The four principles that the PBS fitness expert shared are all rooted in behavioral science. When you know what makes you tick, it gives you a massive advantage over yourself. Behavioral science gives you the advantage to subdue your biggest competitor, namely, you.

Let's start with small plates. In 1955, a modern philosopher named C. Northcote Parkinson came up with the counterintuitive Parkinson's Law: that the demand for something expands to match its supply. In economics, this is called induced demand—it's why expanding roads to reduce traffic congestion never works in the long term because more drivers always show up in their cars to fill those extra lanes.

In other words, if you went to a Spanish tapas bar that served those tiny plates, you would eat less. But if you went to a Ponderosa all-you-can-eat buffet, where they have plates the size of manhole covers, you would eat until the food was coming out your ears. (It's an all-you-CAN-eat buffet . . . Challenge accepted!)

Similarly, if your client gives you a week to turn around a project, you'd likely take the whole week—but if she gives you just a day, you'll make it happen in a day. You see the more we have of something, the more of it we consume. This is true for anything: food, time, even toothpaste.

How much toothpaste do you use when you have a brand-new tube of toothpaste? A big ol' glop of it, right? I mean, why not? After all, you have a full tube of toothpaste. So you put a nice long bead on that brush of yours. Then before you start brushing, you turn on the faucet to moisten up the brush a little. Then it happens . . . damn it, the paste falls into the sink. But who cares, right? You just opened up that tube, for God's sake! You have tons of this stuff. So you put on another big ol' glop and brush away.

But when you open that cabinet drawer and find a nearly empty tube . . . my oh my, how the game changes. It starts off with an insane amount of squeezing, twisting, and turning. You reach for your toothbrush, momentarily releasing a little bit of your viselike grip on the tube, and with that, like a tortoise's head when a three-year-old comes at it with a stick, the paste shoots back into the tube. You could shout out some expletives at this point, but you can't because you are already onto stage 2 of toothpaste extraction: biting down hard on the tube. With a precarious balance of biting, one hand squeezing and tube twisting, while your other hand somehow tries to get the brush bristles to scoop out toothpaste, you have a victory. One droplet of toothpaste. Which is just enough for that fresh-mouth sensation.

Isn't it funny how much *we* change based upon what is available? Here is what's fascinating: Parkinson's Law triggers two behaviors when supply is scant. When you have less, you do two things. The first is obvious: you become frugal. When there is less toothpaste in the tube, you use less to brush your teeth. That is the obvious part. But something else, far more impactful happens: you become extremely innovative and find all sorts of ways to extract that last drop of toothpaste from the tube.

If there is one thing that will forever change your relationship with money, it is the understanding of Parkinson's Law. You need to intentionally make less toothpaste (money) available to brush your teeth (to operate your business). When there is less, you will automatically run your business more frugally (that's good) and you will run your business far more innovatively (that's great!).

If you first extract your profit and remove it from sight, you'll be left with a nearly empty toothpaste tube to run your business. When less money is available to run your business, you will find ways to get the same or better results with less. By taking your profit first, you will be forced to think smarter and innovate more.

2. The Primacy Effect: Why the *First* Part of Profit First Matters

The second behavioral principle you need to understand about yourself is called the Primacy Effect. The principle is this: We place additional significance on whatever we encounter first. Here's a little demonstration that may help you understand.

I am going to show you two sets of words. One set describes a sinner and another describes a saint. The goal is, as quickly as possible, to determine which one is which. Got it? Good. Now look at the two sets of words below and determine which one describes the sinner and which one the saint.

1. EVIL, HATE, ANGER, JOY, CARE, LOVE
2. LOVE, CARE, JOY, ANGER, HATE, EVIL

At first glance you likely identified the first set of words to be the sinner and the second set of words to be the saint. If you did, that is wonderful news, because it means you are a human being and are experiencing the Primacy Effect. In other words, you will thrive under Profit First. If you tried to figure out the catch as you were going through the exercise, that is awesome news, too; it means you are an entrepreneur and are more than willing to break old systems (like reading left to right only), which also means you will thrive under Profit First.

Now look at the set of words again. You will see that both sets of words are identical, just in the opposite sequence.

So when you see EVIL and HATE at the start of a set of words, your mind assigns greater weight to those words and less weight to the remaining words. When the set started with LOVE and CARE you put the weight there.

When we follow the conventional formula of Sales – Expenses = Profit, we are primed to focus on those first two words, *Sales* and *Expenses*, and treat *Profit* as an afterthought. We then behave accordingly. We sell as hard as we can, then use the money we collect to pay expenses. We stay stuck in the cycle of selling to pay bills, over and over again, wondering why we never see any profit. Who's the sinner now?

When profit comes first, it is the focus, and it is never forgotten.

3. Remove Temptation: Once You Take Your Profit First, Put It Away

My greatest weakness is Chocodiles: Twinkies covered in dark chocolate, filled with cream, and wrapped in love. Fortunately, they stopped making them.* But if one sneaked into my house, even if it had expired in 1972, I would devour that delicious elixir of love and monounsaturated fats. Now I always make sure I have healthy options with me, and the junk is nowhere around.

Money works the same way. As you implement Profit First, you are going to use the powerful force of "out of sight, out of mind." As you generate a profit (which, remember, starts today), you are going to remove the money from your immediate access. You won't see it, so you won't access it. And just like anything that you don't have a reasonable degree of access to, you will find a way to work with what you do have and not worry about what you don't. Then, when Mr. Buffett (ahem, your profit account) releases money to you, it will serve as a bonus.

4. Enforce a Rhythm

Just as it keeps us from starving and bingeing on food, enforcing a rhythm works with money, too. When we get into a rhythm (I will explain in Chapter 6 a twice-a-month method that I call the 10/25 rule), we don't get into the reactive mode of crazy spending when we get big deposits and panicking in the face of big cash dips. I am not saying the money will automatically appear and you'll always have cash at your disposal, but establishing a rhythm will get you out of the daily panic.

In fact, establishing a rhythm will also be a great indicator of overall cash flow. This system is the easiest way to measure cash flow. Instead of reading the cash flow statement (which, honestly, when was the last time you did that?), you can measure your cash flow by just checking your bank accounts, which you do anyway.

---

* For my Chocodile-loving comrades: Supposedly Hostess has reintroduced the product, albeit slightly reformulated. Distribution is sparse, yet I have got my hands on a few. If these are the new formula, they taste like they have been on the shelf since 1972 . . . and they are still delicious.

When you get into a rhythm with your cash management you'll have your finger on the pulse of your business. You will monitor your cash position every day by just looking at your bank account. Log in. Spend two seconds looking at your balances. Log out. You will know where you stand that quickly. Think of your cash flow as waves rolling onto the beach. If the cash wave is big, you will notice and take action (this is when looking at the reports with the guidance of a pro is helpful). When the waves are small, you will surely notice that, too. Most of the time, I expect the cash waves will be normal, and no action will be required. But no matter what, you will always know. Because you will continue to do what you normally do: log into your bank account.

BUT IF I SET ASIDE MY PROFITS, HOW WILL I GROW?

This is a question I get asked a lot. By now I hope I've convinced you that chasing growth for its own sake is how you wind up broke and out of business. But that doesn't mean growth doesn't matter, or that you shouldn't want it.

Growth strategies have been part of my spiel for years. I have now written multiple books on the idea of fast, organic growth (like my book *Surge*). But like most entrepreneurs, I always used to think it was one or the other. Either you could grow or you could be profitable—you surely couldn't do both. I was wrong.

What I've found is that the fastest, healthiest growth comes from businesses that prioritize profit. And it is *not* because they plow money back into their businesses. Businesses that plow back their profits aren't truly profitable; they are just holding money temporarily (feigning profit), then spending it, just like any other expense.

Profit First sparks faster growth because it makes you reverse engineer your profitability. When you take your profit first, your business will tell you immediately whether it can afford the expenses you are incurring; it will tell you whether you are streamlined enough; it will tell you whether you have the right margins. If you find that you can't pay your bills after taking your profit first, you must address all those points and make the fixes.

Taking profit first will help you figure out which of the many things you do makes money, and which don't. Then the direction is obvious—you do more of what is profitable, and you fix (or dump) what is not. You will focus on what makes profit for you, naturally, and you will get better and better at it. And when you get better at what your customers already want and like, they will like you more. All this translates into fast, healthy growth. Boom!

Specialists, such as heart surgeons, know the secret. Keep doing a few things (like heart surgery) really, really well, and you will attract the best customers, dictate the biggest premiums, and see your practice grow to be world renowned. Alternatively, the general practitioner does everything (from hangnails to rashes, coughs, and colds), but never specializes and therefore attracts the general customers. And when things get serious for the patient—that cough is actually indicating heart disease—the general practitioner refers the work to the specialist (who then collects all the premium money for her services). Specialists own the biggest houses in town, while general practitioners can't pay off their student loans.

To grow the biggest and the fastest, you need to be the best at one thing you do. And to become the best at something, you need to first determine what you are best at and do it a whole lot better. To get there, you take your profit first and the answers to being the best at something will reveal themselves.

THE NEW ACCOUNTING FORMULA

Now you know the psychology behind how you work. The next step is to put a system around the normal you. And we start with a simple new Profit First formula:

Sales − **Profit** = Expenses

What you are about to learn isn't anything new (not even to you). It is something I suspect you have been aware of—in full or at least in part—but have never done. It is the concept of "pay yourself first" meets "small plate servings" meets "Grandma's envelope-money management system" meets your preexisting natural, human tendencies.

Here's how you apply the four principles:

1. **Use Small Plates**—When money comes into your main INCOME account, it simply acts as a serving tray for the other accounts. You then periodically disperse all the money from the INCOME account into different accounts in predetermined percentages. Each of these accounts has a different objective: one is for profit, one for owner compensation, another for taxes, and another for operating expenses. Collectively, these are the five foundational accounts (Income, Profit, Owner's Comp, Tax, and Operating Expenses), and where you should get started, but advanced users will use additional accounts, outlined in Chapter 10.

2. **Serve Sequentially**—Always, *always* allocate money based upon the percentages to the accounts first. Never, ever, ever pay bills first. The money moves from the INCOME account to your PROFIT account, OWNER'S COMP, TAX, and OPEX (OPERATING EXPENSES). Then you pay bills only with what is available in the OPEX account. No exceptions. And if there isn't enough money left for expenses? This does *not* mean you need to pull from the other accounts. What it *does* mean is that your business is telling you that you can't afford those expenses and need to get rid of them. Eliminating unnecessary expenses will bring more health to your business than you can ever imagine.

3. **Remove Temptation**—Move your PROFIT account and other "tempting" accounts out of arm's reach. Make it really hard and painful to get to that money, thereby removing the temptation to "borrow" (i.e., steal) from yourself. Use an accountability mechanism to prevent access, except for the right reason.

4. **Enforce a Rhythm**—Do your allocations and payables twice a month (specifically, on the tenth and twenty-fifth). Don't pay only when there is money piled up in the account. Get into a rhythm of allocating your income, and paying bills twice a month so that you can see how cash

accumulates and where the money really goes. This is controlled re-curring and frequent cash flow management, not by-the-seat-of-your-pants cash management.

By the time I started applying this small plate philosophy to my company's finances, I was doing consulting work and speaking on entrepreneurship. I also applied my new Profit First system to my one surviving investment, Hedgehog Leatherworks. I had given up booze and infomercials as coping mechanisms, and my depression had lifted. At the time, I was putting the finishing touches on my first business book, *The Toilet Paper Entrepreneur*, into which I inserted a small section about the concept of Profit First. After the book came out, I continued to refine the system, exploring and living it, and everything changed. I started implementing it with other entrepreneurs. And it worked—for me, for them, and for my readers.

Fueled by my passion for entrepreneurship and my determination to be profitable *now*, not at some indeterminate date in the future, I set about to perfect my system. In that process I discovered other entrepreneurs and business leaders who were running their businesses check to check and desperately needed the Profit First system. But I also found entrepreneurs and business leaders who had been implementing a similar system with great success. People like Jesse Cole, owner of two AAA baseball teams, who, while growing his businesses, paid off nearly $1 million in loans. And Phil Tirone, who, while building his first, highly profitable multimillion-dollar business, continued to rent the same studio apartment until he de-termined that he had secured enough profit to upgrade—to a one bedroom.

In the coming pages, I will share stories about people who are in lock-step with their profits, and stories about other folks, like you and me, who were giving it their all but still ended up breaking even only on their best days—people who now turn a profit every month and enjoy the fruits of their labors. People like José and Jorge, two entrepreneurs who started using Profit First in the first few months of launching their business and have experi-enced not only very respectable growth, but have continually taken in a 7 to 20 percent profit month after month.

LOWER THE BAR

In their book *Switch*, Chip and Dan Heath explain the concept of "lowering the bar." We entrepreneurs are all programmed to "raise the bar." Go bigger. Live bolder. Take on more. But I have found that isn't always the best way to gain momentum. And if you intend to be profitable, it is time we start with a small "low bar" step. I want you to take one small, simple, and easy action that will start you down the path of permanent profitability. There is no excuse because it is so easy.

Right now I want you to set up your PROFIT account. It is the first step in the Profit First system, so do it right now. Call your bank (or do it online) and set up one new checking account. Don't get mired in whether it should be a savings account or a sweep account or any of that. The five seconds you spend thinking about it cost more than the little dribble of interest it will yield. Your goal is just to get started and not to slip back.

After setting up this new checking account at your bank, nickname the account PROFIT, and from this moment forward from any deposit you put into your normal checking account, transfer 1 percent of that deposit into your PROFIT account. Then proceed with your business and processes and money management as you have in the past. Just add to the PROFIT account, and never touch it (until you get to the section of this book where I explain what to do with it).

If you get a $1,000 deposit, I am telling you, starting today, transfer $10 into your PROFIT account. If you could run your business off $1,000, you can surely run it off $990. If you get $20,000 in deposits, you transfer $200 into your PROFIT account. If you can run your business off $20,000 you absolutely can run it off $19,800. You'll never miss that 1 percent. It is a low bar.

But something magical will happen. You will start proving the system to yourself. You won't get rich overnight this way, but you will get a wealth of confidence. You will have a flavor of how powerful it is to reserve your profit in advance. Your job is to stick with this small step for a while. Watch your profit accumulate. Yes, it is notably small, but it is profit nonetheless. The goal here is to win over your *mind*. The goal is for you to realize that this unfamiliar process of taking your profit first isn't so scary after all. Then once you are digging the Profit First vibe, you are set for greater success. Because you will be staged perfectly to do the rest of the system, and your heart will be in it. Big-time.

TAKE ACTION: EASY FIRST STEPS

1. Trust the process. This works, but it is unfamiliar. So you will resist. Commit to, for now, relinquishing your resistance and comfort in doing what you did in the past. First, trust the process. Then prove it to yourself.

2. Open just one new account: PROFIT. For simplicity's sake, make it a checking account. Don't worry about the insignificant interest implications of savings and other accounts. Your goal for now is to get started immediately and decisively.

3. Transfer 1 percent of your current money into the PROFIT account. You have "seeded" the account. Don't touch it. Never transfer it. Just let it sit for now.

Chapter 3

SETTING UP PROFIT FIRST
FOR YOUR BUSINESS

When I was a teenager, my mom had a part-time job working for Lenze Corporation, a German-based company that distributed proprietary machine parts. Every other week, after she cashed her paycheck, she would divide up her money. I can still see her sitting at the kitchen table, placing fives and tens into envelopes labeled "Food," "Mortgage," "Community," "Fun Money," and "Vacation." She had one other envelope labeled in a German phrase, which roughly translated to "In case of emergency." Half of her money went into the "Mortgage" envelope. Then she'd put 15 percent into the "Vacation" envelope, 5 percent into "Fun Money," and 10 percent each into "Food," "Community," and that rainy-day envelope, *Nur für den Notfall.*"

Despite the fact that her hours fluctuated, Mom always had enough money for food. Now let me be clear about something—this did not mean she always had the same amount of money. She always had *enough*. Some weeks she worked fewer hours because she was sick or because she volunteered at my school. (It's totally embarrassing when your mom shows up at your class with German puppets to teach German folklore . . . when you're a senior in high school.) Other weeks she worked overtime. Her income varied (sound familiar?), yet Mom always had enough because once she put money into one of her envelopes, she kept it sealed until she needed it. She never borrowed from other envelopes if she was short. Instead, she drove to the grocery store, and only when she had parked the car would she open the "Food" envelope.

Mom shopped with whatever food money she had that week. If it was a light week, it would be PB&J for lunch and rice and beans for dinner. More money meant cold cuts for lunch and chicken and rice for dinner. And if she was rolling in dough, it was liverwurst all day long. No one but Mom liked liverwurst, so when she was cranking hours and sure to come home with more pay that week, my sister and I would try to get her to spend more time at home so she couldn't afford liverwurst. As an aside, if you never heard of liverwurst, consider yourself blessed, because it means "liver sausage." See? Now you don't like it either.

You might be wondering, "What about the mortgage envelope?" If her pay was light that week, it wasn't as if she could go to the mortgage company and tell them she would have to pay less that month. Mom knew that when she worked a normal work schedule, 40 percent of her pay would be enough to contribute to the mortgage bill. But as we all know all too well, normal ain't always so normal. Things happen. So she intentionally set up a 50 percent mortgage allocation. By always putting in 10 percent more than she needed, there was always a cushion for when "normal" contributions fell short. And when all hell broke loose (which it never did, probably because she was prepared for it), Mom had the *"Nur für den Notfall"* envelope for backup.

The envelope system is not unique to my mom. She is a member of the "greatest generation" and a survivor of the near constant bombing of her town during World War II. Since I published the first edition of *Profit First*, I've received countless emails from readers whose parents or grandparents used similar systems. From envelopes, to jars, to a nifty steel box with different compartments used by a reader in Sweden, many readers adapted these systems for their own use. Profit First is, in part, the envelope system applied to business and modernized by using bank accounts. The system worked flawlessly for my mom, and I suspect it has done the same for someone in your family tree.

How do you apply this system to your business? I've given you a step-by-step process below . . . no envelopes, jars, or nifty steel boxes required.

BANK BALANCE ACCOUNTING

The default cash-management system for most entrepreneurs is what I call bank balance accounting. Ironically, it is what our accountants tell us not to do. "Don't look at your bank accounts," they say. "Look at your accounting system."

Right. Don't you just love looking at your accounting system? Just like those one thousand "beautiful" vacation pictures your friend shows you, with a "funny story" about each one. You could look all day long. Not.

If you follow your accountant's directions explicitly, this is what is expected of you when you review your accounting system to figure out how much cash you have—once you have reconciled all accounts for accuracy, reviewed your profit and loss (P&L) and cash flow statements and then tie the numbers into your balance sheet. Next you'll run the critical metrics, such as your OCR (operating cash ratio), inventory turn, and both the current ratio and quick ratio. Then you'll tie those into your KPI (key performance indicators), and then you will know the health of your business. Oh, and before I forget, do that every week. Then you will have a clear understanding of where your business is. So says the accountant.

There is just one problem: I have no idea how to truly read and tie in all those documents and ratios. In fact, that is *why* I hired my accountant and bookkeeper in the first place. My head is spinning just writing this down. In fact, I may be having flashbacks. It's bad, my friends. Really bad. When I think about financial reporting docs I start to get the shakes, and if I look at numbers too long, I inevitably end up under my desk sucking my thumb (still a hundred times better than eating liverwurst).

So what do I do? What do most entrepreneurs do? We revert to bank balance accounting. What is that? We log into our bank accounts, make note of our balances, and then, based upon what we see, make decisions on how to proceed. When our balance is low, we make collection calls and sell hard. When our balance is high, we invest in equipment and expansion. It works. Kinda.

Bank balance accounting seems to work because it is how we are wired to look at quick indicators (e.g., "Does my bank account have enough money?"). Then we trust our gut and take an action. This system doesn't work perfectly, though, because it seems that we never have enough money left to pay ourselves. That's why I created Profit First.

Profit First is designed so that you can (and should) continue doing bank balance accounting. The system is set up with your bank accounts so that you can log in, see what your balance is, and make decisions accordingly.

This is what you are doing already, so you don't need to change. Profit First just has multiple accounts at your bank so that when you log in, you know what purpose that money is meant to serve. You open your "envelope," see what you have to work with, and make your decisions. Will it be rice and beans or Wiener schnitzel?

With Profit First, we are not going to change your behavior; we are going to put guardrails around it. We are not only going to allow you to do what you always have done; we are also going to encourage it.

THE FIVE FOUNDATIONAL ACCOUNTS

If you've made it this far into the book, I assume you're on board with the idea of Profit First. It's time to take your first step: setting up your envelopes, or plates. Do this now. Don't put it off for later. It's time to get your ass in gear.

What you are about to do is the foundation of Profit First. This is the structure your profits will be built on. All the muscle in the world is useless if it isn't connected to a strong skeletal structure. These accounts are the bones.

Here are the five checking accounts you need to set up:

1. INCOME
2. PROFIT
3. OWNER'S COMP
4. TAX
5. OPEX

Make sure you set these up as checking accounts. The flexibility offered by checking accounts far outweighs any minuscule interest you get by using savings accounts. Call your bank and set up the foundational five accounts. Most banks allow you to assign a nickname to the account that is displayed online and on statements in addition to the account number. Just as Mom labeled her envelopes, name your accounts according to their purpose.

You can use your existing primary bank account as one of the five accounts. Rename it your OPEX account because you are likely paying all your bills from that account. Going forward, we are just going to move deposits to your INCOME account. That should be a no-brainer for check deposits; simply put them into a new account. For other types of deposits, such as credit card or ACH payments, you'll have to update your bank information wherever necessary. The process will take about half an hour—if you have a lot of automated payments, maybe an hour. Make the effort and get this done.

TWO "NO-TEMPTATION" ACCOUNTS

Now that you've set up your five foundational accounts at your primary bank, your next step is to set up two "no-temptation accounts." We are going to get your taxes out of sight and out of mind. And we are going to do the same with your PROFIT account.

You may be thinking, "Why do I need to do this? I already have a TAX account and PROFIT account at my primary bank. Why do I need a duplicate?" The reason we have these secondary accounts is to keep the money that you allocate and reserve for tax and profit out of your sight. Because when something isn't available to consume, you don't consume it.

If something is not readily available, we are unlikely to go through an extraordinary measure to consume it. Your profit is for you, and if you can access it easily, you might be tempted to "borrow" from it to cover expenses. And the tax money? That belongs to the government. We are going to make sure you never borrow (a soft term for "steal") from these accounts.

If you take money from your PROFIT account and put it back into the business, you are basically saying that you are unwilling to find a way to run your business with the operating expenses you allocated for it. If you take money from your TAX account, the money you have reserved to pay the government, you are stealing from the government. And I suspect you already know this, the government doesn't like that too much.

Find a new bank that you have never worked with before. In this case, you will not be moving money too much, and you will rarely bring the two accounts to a zero balance (unless you are short on tax). So with this bank, you can be less concerned about any minimum balance fees they have.

At the second bank set up two savings accounts (this is where you will collect interest because your money will pool for a while). The two accounts are PROFIT HOLD and TAX HOLD. Then link these two accounts to the respective PROFIT and TAX accounts at your primary bank so that you are able to transfer money.

I will explain shortly when to transfer money and how often you will do it. But for now, I want to address one question you may have. You may be thinking, "Why should I set up PROFIT and TAX accounts at both my primary bank *and* my no-temptation bank? I'm an entrepreneur! I like shortcuts! Can't I just transfer money from my primary bank's INCOME account to the PROFIT HOLD and TAX HOLD accounts at my no-temptation bank?" While technically speaking you can do that, it is a bad idea for two reasons.

1. Transfers from one bank to another are not instantaneous. It can take three days or longer (weekends and holidays add time), and when you log into your primary account, the money looks as if it is still there.

2. The goal with Profit First is to give you instant and accurate knowledge on where your cash stands. When you move money from one account to another at the same bank, the transfer usually happens instantaneously. By first moving money from your INCOME account to the PROFIT and TAX accounts (along with the other accounts), you will instantly see where your money stands, on their respective plates. Now that your money is clearly on the right "plate" at your primary bank, initiate the transfer to the PROFIT HOLD and TAX HOLD accounts at the second bank. Now, anytime you log into your primary bank you will know exactly where you stand, even if the transfer to your no-temptation bank hasn't completed yet.

TWO FREQUENTLY ASKED QUESTIONS

I speak about Profit First at roughly thirty major conferences a year, as well as a number of smaller conferences, webinars, and lectures. Inevitably, when the Q&A part of my Profit First speech starts, one or two questions always come up:

1. "I haven't ever been profitable in the past, so how can I take my profit now?"

People have difficulty accepting the notion that they can start taking profits right away because it seems like some kind of woo-woo accounting trickery. It's not (in fact, it's regular accounting that employs trickery). By taking profit first, you're fundamentally changing the way you run your business. When I hear this question, I always explain Parkinson's Law: you spend every penny you have available and stretch every dollar in the lean times to keep your business moving forward. I'm simply asking you to remove the profit first, and operate on less. You've done this already, and you've found a way. There is a saying: "Nothing changes if nothing changes." If you don't change the way you take your profit, you will never *take a profit*.

2. "Can't I just do this on a spreadsheet or in my accounting system? Why do I need to do this at the bank?"

I answer this question by asking a question: How has that served you so far? Aren't you already following your cash flow every day on a spreadsheet? Are you not checking your accounting system daily, reviewing the numbers? No? Exactly. So setting up Profit First in your accounting system is only a slight modification over something you are supposedly "doing" already and failing at.

No matter what those spreadsheets or monthly reports say, your current bank balance is always going to be a stronger determinant of your behavior. The reason you *must* set up your Profit First accounts at your bank is because it is the only way to insert the system into your normal path of behavior. By setting it up at your bank, you cannot miss your allocations when you log into your bank.

PICKING THE BANK

When choosing your banks, focus on convenience options for one and inconvenience options for the other. At your primary bank, you want easy access to view your accounts (plates or envelopes). You want the easy ability to transfer money from INCOME to your other accounts. And you want to be able to pay bills out of OPEX. At your secondary bank, you want no convenience options. Remember: out of sight, out of mind. What we can't see or use, we don't worry about. You work with what you have here and now.

Peter Laughter, a longtime friend of mine, knew the power of removing temptation. When he set up Profit First for his company, he went to a new bank and asked the branch manager for assistance in setting up the accounts. The manager was more than excited to talk with Peter because a good chunk of money would be deposited into the bank. In his salesman-like way the manager shared all the wonderful convenience options that Peter would get with his new bank accounts: online banking, starter checks, and that shiny new ATM card.

Peter looked at the branch manager and said, "I don't want any of that. I am seeking the most inconvenient options you have. In fact, the only way I want to withdraw money from this bank is if I visit this branch and ask you to write out a certified bank check to me. And when that day does come, just to make sure I am only using it for the right reason, I want you to slap me in the face a few times when I ask you to write the check."

For the Gene Wilder fans out there, this is like the scene in *Young Frankenstein* when Dr. Frankenstein locks himself in a room with his monster and says, "No matter what you hear in there, no matter how cruelly I beg you, no matter how terribly I may scream, do not open this door or you will undo everything I have worked for."

The bank manager was befuddled, but he agreed to make things as inconvenient as possible for Peter.

Banks won't always work with your needs. Back in 2005, when I had my forensics business, I deposited (and more often, withdrew and borrowed) millions of dollars every year. I was doing a lot of business with a certain bank, but they weren't flexible and wouldn't accommodate my needs. Then Commerce Bank came along. They were doing what was, up until that time, unheard of: they were open late at night every weeknight, and they were open on weekends. They were available to do business when I was doing business, which was after business hours. I went to my bank branch and told them I wanted to close all of my accounts because I wanted to switch to Commerce Bank. The manager came out and asked me why. She cackled like some villain in a movie and said, "You'll be back." She literally said that.

I have never been back, nor has my money.

You have the ability to change banks, too. Their job is to serve you. Just like you wouldn't risk botulism and accept undercooked chicken from your local restaurant, why should you accept a poisoned relationship with a bank?

Feedback from so many people who are implementing Profit First demonstrates that some (but very few) large banks will work with you by cutting out the fees. But many regional and local banks and federal credit unions will be thrilled to work with you, and in many cases (like my own experience), they don't have all those crazy fees in the first place. Small banks and credit unions are plug and play for Profit First. Select big banks are, too.*

Here's how to proceed: if you like your current bank, tell them that their requirements for a "minimum balance" and "transfer fees" and all those rules they have don't work for you. Ask them to wave the minimum balance requirement and other fees. Yes, you can ask that. Your bank will either comply with your request, or they won't. If they do, kudos to you. If they don't, move on to a new bank.

You've already taken three steps toward a profitable business: you emailed your commitment to me (Chapter 1), you set up one Profit First account, and you transferred 1 percent of your current money. You have the momentum; now it's time to kick Profit First into gear and experience the simple, yet powerful transformation for yourself. I won't say it works like magic, but it is pretty friggin' amazing to watch your profit *and* your business grow day by day, deposit by deposit. Don't stop now. Take action.

TAKE ACTION: GET YOUR BUSINESS PROFIT-READY

Step 1: Set up the five foundational accounts: an INCOME account, a PROFIT account, an OWNER'S COMP account, a TAX account, and an OPEX account.

---

* I do my best to keep an updated list of Profit First–friendly banks at MikeMichalowicz .com/Resources.

In most cases, you will already have one or two accounts with your bank. Keep the primary checking account you already have as your OPEX Account, and set up the remaining accounts: INCOME, PROFIT, OWNER'S COMP, and TAX. For simplicity's sake, set them all up as checking accounts.

Some banks may charge fees or have minimum balance requirements. Don't let that deter you. Ask to speak to the bank manager and negotiate the fees and requirements. If the manager is unwilling to negotiate, find a new bank.

Step 2: Set up two more external savings accounts with a bank other than the bank you use for daily operations. One account will be your no-temptation PROFIT HOLD account. The second will be your no-temptation TAX HOLD account. Set them up with the ability to withdraw money directly from the respective checking accounts at your primary bank.

Step 3: Don't enable any of the "convenience" options for your two external no-temptations accounts. You don't need or want to view these accounts online. You don't want checkbooks for these accounts. And you definitely do not want a debit card linked to those accounts. You just want to deposit your profit and tax reserves and forget it . . . for now.

Chapter 4

ASSESSING THE HEALTH OF YOUR BUSINESS

fter I finished writing *Profit First*, I put out a call for volunteers to help me edit my book. My professional editing team is composed of aces, but I find it invaluable to also get detailed feedback from entrepreneurs who have read my other books. Business coach Lisa Robbin Young was one of my volunteer "editors." She actually started implementing Profit First as she was reviewing the book. "It was too good, too useful, and made too much sense to wait," she said. (Lisa is my kind of go-getter—she took action not only before she finished reading the book, but before the book was even *published*.)

It wasn't all unicorns and rainbows. Let's just say I'm glad I wasn't in the room when Lisa completed her Instant Assessment. "Within minutes, I was angry!" Lisa told me. "I mean, really pissed off that I had been overspending on what I thought was important and necessary infrastructure for my business."

In the years since I published the first edition of *Profit First*, countless readers have shared their initial reactions to completing the first step in the process, the Instant Assessment. It's not uncommon to hear from readers who were shocked and overwhelmed, and like Lisa, downright pissed after completing this step. This is when you get real about your financials. It's a simple process, but damn, facing the truth hurts like a mother.

If you're coming to this book at a point of financial stress, you may not want to face the Instant Assessment. Because you know, right? You know seeing the cold, hard truth is going to suck—big-time. As hard as it is for struggling entrepreneurs to complete this task, it's even more sobering for entrepreneurs who *think* they're doing OK because they are not prepared for the bad news.

Or you could put this book down, tell yourself your business is doing great, and keep doing what you're doing. Denial is a wonderful thing; it lets you ignore reality until reality punches you in the face. Don't get punched in the face; don't get caught unaware. The sooner you accept the truth about your business, the faster you can do something about it.

At the time Lisa completed her Instant Assessment, she was in business transition, and though she had a five-figure cash flow, her money was all over the map. "The only feelings I had around my financials were numbness. I was overspending, but didn't realize it, because there was still more inflow than outflow, but it never felt like I was making any progress. Then *Profit First* helped me understand why."

After some initial resistance, Lisa accepted the reality of her Instant Assessment and started implementing Profit First, step by step. In the two years since she opened her first PROFIT account, Lisa's business experienced significant change. "My 'profit' used to be something I realized at tax time. You know, when the IRS gave me a refund of four or five thousand dollars," Lisa explained. "Now I get a quarterly bonus that I can 'feel,' plus regular payroll. I've also increased the withholding profit to 10 percent, because my overhead is substantially lower now that I've reduced my expenses and developed systems that serve the business." She also spends much less time on her business. "I was practically killing myself before, and now I'm only working a few hours a week. I was able to focus on the big obstacles blocking my path rather than put out countless fires."

Once Lisa set out on the Profit First path, she realized she wasn't working to her best potential or serving her best audience. Like her money, her services were spread out all over the map. Lisa shifted her business audience and formed Ark Entertainment Media, a business incubator for creative entrepreneurs.

Lisa's revenue has doubled every month so far since she made the shift. I've known for a while that Profit First triggers growth because it requires us to focus, streamline and innovate, but every confirmation is exciting. When I heard about Lisa's explosive growth, I punched the air like the dork I am.

Is Lisa getting punched by reality? Nope. Her business is kicking ass and taking names.

"Nearly two years in, after a business restructure and audience shift, the Profit First approach has made it all effortless. I finished my taxes earlier this year than I have in the past five years, and I had plenty set aside; no scrambling. And I had profits! Say what?! That was pretty awesome."

Running the Instant Assessment is easy. Facing the truth about your business financials, on the other hand, is right up there with root canals and colonoscopies. But it is a necessary step that will set you on a path toward profit, growth, and (gasp) work fulfillment. So buck up, bucko, and get 'er done.

THE (ALMOST) INSTANT ASSESSMENT

Whether your business is simply not as profitable as you would like it to be or is in full cardiac arrest, you should be willing to keep your eyes wide open. In order for Profit First to work, you need to come to this with no blinders on. Now it's time to get down to the nitty-gritty. It will help if you have a few documents available to complete this next phase. But if you don't have the documents (I list them in step one below) or can't get them, that's OK. We can get close enough without them.

Profit First is a cash-management system. We don't do anything on accrual or any of that funny-money stuff. It is really simple: Did you get the cash or not? And did you spend the cash or not? That's it. Nothing else really matters unless cash happens. So that is why our focus is exclusively on cash. If you are wondering how Profit First addresses depreciation or accounts receivable, you are still thinking funny money. We are only going to measure actual cash transactions. Money in. Money out. Real money. Period.

As you complete the Instant Assessment, remember that different businesses have different setups. I'll help you get to the perfect numbers for your specific business in the next chapter. For now, know that in this chapter I provide ballpark numbers that I pulled from surveying a mix of fiscally elite (very profitable) companies.

Before you start the Instant Assessment, get your P&L from your last full year in business. Get the tax returns for each owner in the business for the tax period for that year. Get your balance sheet for the year-end of that year. Your accounting software (if you use one) can spit this stuff out easily;

everything but your tax returns. If you don't have access to a balance sheet or your P&L, that's OK; we can still get darn close.

Are you ready? You have no excuses. You must proceed with this. Get ready for the ice bucket challenge, Profit First style.

Figure 3 is the Profit First Instant Assessment Form. Complete the form right now! You can write directly into this book (or if you are on an iPad or Kindle or some other reader and don't want to replace the screen, you can download a printable copy from the Resources section at Mike Michalowicz.com.). Go to the back of the book (Appendix 2) for a full-page version of the Instant Assessment form.

	ACTUAL	TAP	PF$	DELTA	FIX
Top Line Revenue	A1				
Material & Subs	A2				
Real Revenue	A3	100%	C3		
Profit	A4	B4	C4	D4	E4
Owner's Comp	A5	B5	C5	D5	E5
Tax	A6	B6	C6	D6	E6
Operating Expenses	A7	B7	C7	D7	E7

Fig. 3. Profit First Instant Assessment Form

A1

1. In the Actual column, cell A1, enter your Top Line Revenue for the last twelve full months. This is your total revenue from sales, and should be the top line (or near it) on your P&L statement. One of the common labels for the top line is Total Income, Total Sales, Revenue, Sales, or Net Sales.

A2

2. If you are a manufacturer, retailer, or more than 25 percent of your sales are derived from the resale or assembly of inventory, put the cost of materials (not labor) for the last full twelve months in the Material & Subs cell, A2. This is *not*, I repeat, this is *not* the same as Cost of Goods Sold. This is only for materials, and only if your materials cost 25 percent or more of your sales.

3. If subcontractors deliver the majority of your service, put the cost of the subcontractors for these twelve months in the Material & Subs cell, A2. (Subcontractors are people who work for you on a project basis, but have the ability to work autonomously and have the ability to work for others. You don't pay them on payroll; you pay them their project fee, commission, or hourly rate, and they handle their taxes, benefits, etc., themselves.) In some cases, you will have both materials and subcontractor costs (think home construction). In that case, put the cumulative amount of these two costs into cell A2. Remember to put only your materials and subcontractors here, but not the labor of your own people.

4. If you are a service company and the majority of your services are provided by your employees (yourself included), put $0 in cell A2.

5. If your material or subcontractor costs are less than 25 percent of your Top Line Revenue, put $0 in cell A2. (We will account for these expenses in Operating Expenses in a little bit).

6. If you are unsure of what to put in the Material & Subs section, put $0. Do not overthink this. And do not use it to make nominal adjustments. The goal here is only to adjust your company's revenue to represent what it really makes as revenue if the majority of cost is for materials, supplies, or subcontractors. Again, if you are even a wee bit unsure, put $0 in Material & Subs (cell A2). It will serve you better in the long run by making you more critical of your costs.

7. Now subtract your Material & Subs number from your Top Line Revenue to calculate your Real Revenue. If you put an n/a in the Material & Subs section, just copy the Top Line Revenue number to the Real Revenue cell A3.

8. The goal here is to get you to your Real Revenue number. This is the real money your company makes. For the other stuff—subs, materials, etc.—you may make a margin, but it isn't the core driver of profitability because you have little control over it. This can be a real wake-up moment for entrepreneurs. The real estate agency that does $5,000,000 in annual revenue and has a couple dozen agents (subcontractors) taking $4,000,000 in commissions is really a $1,000,000 business that manages real estate agents making $4,000,000, not a $5,000,000 business. The $3,000,000 a year staffing firm that bills out subcontractors to do work, and pays those subs $2,500,000, is really a $500,000 business. The architectural firm that bills out $2,000,000 in annual fees and has an in-house staff that does practically all the work has Real Revenue of $2,000,000 a year. The Real Revenue number is a simple, fast way to put all companies on equal footing (their Real Revenue numbers).

Real Revenue is different from gross profit, in that Real Revenue is your total revenue minus materials and subcontractors utilized to create and deliver the service or product. Gross profit, on the other hand, is an accounting term calculated as total revenue minus materials, subcontractors, *and* any of your employees' time utilized to create and deliver the service or product. It is a subtle difference but a critically important one. Gross profit includes a portion of your employees' time and your time. But the important thing is this: you will generally pay your employees for their time regardless of whether you have a bad sales day or good one. You will likely pay them the same if they fix a car transmission in four hours or five. So to simplify things, we categorize any employee that you have, full- or part-time, as a cost of the business operations, not as a cost of the goods sold. Plus, gross profit can be manipulated by moving numbers around. What good is that? We want to make clear sense of your numbers. So avoid using anything but the cost you incur in materials and subs when calculating Real Revenue for the Instant Assessment.

A4

9. Now that we know your Real Revenue, let's start with profit first. (See how that works?) Write down your actual profit from the last twelve months in the Profit cell A4. This is the cumulative profit you have sitting in the bank, or have distributed to yourself (and/or partners) as a bonus on top of—but not to supplement—your salary. If you think you have a profit, but it is not in the bank and was never distributed to you as a bonus, this means you don't really have a profit. (If it turns out that you have less profit than you thought you would, it's likely you used it to pay down debt from previous years. Or maybe you are attempting an Enron remake.)

A5

10. In the Owner's Comp cell A5, put down how much you paid yourself (and any other owners of the business) these past twelve months in regular payroll distributions, not profit distributions.

A6

11. In the Tax cell A6, put down how much tax your company has paid on your behalf. This is critical: This is *not* how much you have paid in taxes. This is how much money your company paid (or reimbursed you) in taxes. Tax is both the income tax of all the owners and any other corporate taxes. The likelihood that your company paid your taxes for you is very low (we'll fix that, too). So chances are you will put a big fat $0 in that section, too. If your income taxes got deducted from your paycheck from the company, or at the end of the year you had to scratch together cash out of your pocket, the company definitely did not pay your taxes and a big $0 goes in cell A6.

A7

12. In the Operating Expenses cell A7, add up the total expenses your business paid for the last twelve months—everything except your Profit, Owner's Comp, Tax, and any materials and subcontractors that you have already accounted for. The expenses are listed on your income statement. Now, here is where people get confused. It's okay if the numbers don't match up perfectly. This is not accounting, and you don't need to reconcile to the penny. This is simply a system that gets us in the ballpark of where we are, and then tells us where we need to start going. The goal is *not* to have perfect numbers; it is just to understand roughly where we stand now. And with that understanding we can start working on a profit plan for your business. This is simply a starting point. As we implement Profit First over time, we will automatically adjust and nail the perfect numbers for your business. Just get started.

Double-check your work by adding up your Profit (A4), Owner's Comp (A5), Taxes (A6), and Operating Expenses (A7) to see if you get your Real Revenue number (A3). If you don't get this number, something is off. Double-check your numbers to see if you missed something. Once you make sure all the numbers are as accurate as possible, adjust the Operating Expense number up or down to get the Real Revenue to balance. This makes many accounting professionals squeamish, but again, the goal is just to get in the ballpark; we aren't looking to master accounting here. Now add your Real Revenue to the Materials & Subs costs and you should get the Top Line Revenue number. Make sure it all squares out. Now that we have the hard work done in the first column, we can plug in the easy stuff.

B4–B7

13. Next, enter the Profit First percentages in the TAP column based upon your Real Revenue Range (fill in cells B4 through B7). Use the percentages in Figure 4. I call these percentages TAPs (Target Alloca-

tion Percentages), the percentage of each deposit that will be allocated to different elements of our business. TAPs are *not* your starting point; TAPs are the targets you are moving toward. For example, if your Real Revenue for the last twelve months is $722,000, you should use column C from Figure 4. If your business has $225,000 in Real Revenue, use column A. If you run a division (or have your own company) that does $40,000,000, use column F.

C3-C7

14. In the PF $ column, copy the Real Revenue number from your actual column (cell A3) to the PF $ Real Revenue cell (C3). Then multiply that Real Revenue number by the TAP for each row and write down the number in the corresponding PF $ cell. For example, to determine your PF $ Profit, multiply C3 (Real Revenue) by B4 (the Profit TAPs) to get C4 (the Profit First dollar target for Profit). Do this same process to calculate each cell in the PF $.* These are your target PF dollar amounts for each category. Welcome to the moment of truth. (I hope we can still be friends.)

D4-D7

15. In the Delta column, take your Actual number and subtract the PF $ number.† This is very likely to result in a negative number for Profit or Owner's Comp or Operating Expenses or all three. It is your Delta, the amount you need to make up. Negative means you are bleeding money in these sections. Sometimes it is just one category with a problem, but in most cases businesses are bleeding out in the Profit, Owner's Comp, and Tax accounts and have a positive number (meaning

---

* To get PF $ Profit (cell C4), the formula is C3 x B4 = C4. To get the PF $ Owner's Comp (C5), the formula is C3 x B5 = C5. To get the PF$ Tax (C6), the formula is C3 x B6 = C6. And to get the PF $ Operating Expenses (C7), the formula is C3 x B7 = C7.

† To get the Delta for Profit (D4), the formula is A4 – C4 = D4. To get the Delta for Owner's Comp (D5), the formula is A5 – C5 = D5. To get the Delta for Tax (D6), the formula is A6 – C6 = D6. To get the Delta for Operating Expenses, the formula is A7 – C7 = D7.

excess) in Operating Expenses. In other words, we are paying too little in Profit, Owner's Comp, and Taxes, and paying too much in Operating Expenses.

E4–E7

16. The final column (cells E4 through E7), Fix, will have no numbers, only the word *increase* or *decrease* next to each category. If the number in the Delta section is a negative number, put *increase* in the corresponding Fix cell, because we need to increase our contribution to this category to correct the Delta. Conversely, if it is a positive number in the Delta section, put *decrease* in the Fix cell, since this is a category where we need to spend less money in order to fix it.

	A	B	C	D	E	F
Real Revenue Range	$0–$250K	$250K–$500K	$500K–$1M	$1M–$5M	$5M–$10M	$10M–$50M
Real Revenue	100%	100%	100%	100%	100%	100%
Profit	5%	10%	15%	10%	15%	17%
Owner's Comp	50%	35%	20%	10%	5%	3%
Tax	15%	15%	15%	15%	15%	15%
Operating Expenses	30%	40%	50%	65%	65%	65%

Fig. 4. Target Allocation Percentages (TAPs).

What Do These Percentages and Numbers Mean?

The numbers in Figure 4 are typical ranges that I have found while working with countless companies over the years and in running my own. And they represent what I have found to be very healthy numbers. But here is the deal: the percentages aren't perfect, but they are an excellent starting point.

When you run your Instant Assessment, chances are you will find that your actual percentages are nowhere near the numbers in Figure 4, but that is okay because these percentages are only your targets, what you will move toward. We are going to approach these targets in small steps. More on that soon, but here are the details behind the percentages.

In determining these Target Allocation Percentages, I sorted companies into six tiers:

1. When a company is doing less than $250,000 in revenue, it typically has one employee: you. You are the key employee and usually the only employee (with some contractors, part-timers, or possibly one full-timer). Many freelancers are at this stage, and if they elect to stay (just them and no employees), they should be able to increase the profit and pay percentages even more than what I have listed because they don't have the expense of employees or the need to incur the expenses necessary to support multiple employees.

2. At $250,000 to $500,000, you likely have employees. Basic systems will be necessary (like a shared CRM* for your team), equipment, etc., plus you will need to pay your people, so Operating Expenses increase. Owner's Comp adjusts down (and will continue to) as you take your first step in being a little less employee and a little more shareholder, when other people start to do the work, and you get the benefit of the profits via your distributions.

3. At $500,000 to $1,000,000, the growth trend and patterns continue with more systems and more people. Focus on increasing profits because, for so many businesses, the growth from $1,000,000 to $5,000,000 is the hardest. You want a little reserve.

4. From $1,000,000 to $5,000,000, systems are no longer added because they are nice to have; now systems become absolutely mandatory. You can't keep it all in your head anymore. Often the biggest investment into the business needs to happen at this time, as all the knowledge in your head needs to be converted to systems and processes and

---

* CRM refers to customer relationship management tool.

checklists. This means larger allocations must be put toward Operating Expenses. This is when you are no longer doing most of the work; this is when, if your business is to grow, a significant portion of your time is spent working on the business (not in it), and the rest of your time is spent selling the big projects.

5. At $5,000,000 to $10,000,000, typically a management team enters a company to bring it to the next stage, and a clear second tier of management starts to form. The founder starts more and more to focus on her special strengths. The owner is on a consistent payroll, and the majority of her take-home income is from the profitability of the company, not the salary she takes.

6. At $10,000,000 to $50,000,000, a business will often stabilize and achieve predictable growth. The founder's income is almost entirely made up of profit distributions. Owners' salaries are relative to their roles, but typically are insignificant. Businesses of this size can leverage efficiency in big ways to maximize profitability.

Example of a Completed Instant Assessment

	ACTUAL	TAP	PF$	DELTA	FIX
Top Line Revenue	A1 $1,233,000				
Material & Subs	A2 $0				
Real Revenue	A3 $1,233,000	100%	C3 $1,233,000		
Profit	A4 $5,000	B4 10%	C4 $123,000	D4 ($118,000)	E4 Increase
Owner's Comp	A5 $190,000	B5 10%	C5 $123,000	D5 $67,000	E5 Decrease
Tax	A6 $95,000	B6 15%	C6 $184,950	D6 ($89,950)	E6 Increase
Operating Expenses	A7 $943,000	B7 65%	C7 $801,450	D7 $141,550	E7 Decrease

Fig. 5. Completed Instant Assessment for Law Firm.

Figure 5 is a completed example from a law firm to which I just introduced this process: the Instant Assessment reveals a few (painful) things. This business is not nearly profitable enough—it should be filling the profit coffers by an additional $118,000 (cell D4) every year. At $5,000 in the Profit Account (cell A4), this is basically a break-even business. One bad month and this company will go down.

The two owners are taking a combined salary of $190,000 (cell A5), which is way too much for a business of this size. The owners are likely living a bigger lifestyle than the business can afford, and they need to cut their salaries by $67,000 (cell D5).

As the business gets healthier, the taxes are likely to increase (cell C6). (More taxes, as painful as they are to pay, are a sign of a healthy business— the more you make, the more you pay . . . until you make so much you lobby politicians and pay nothing. Don't get me started.) And those Operating Expenses are too high, to the tune of more than $141,000 (cell D7).

Looking at this Instant Assessment, it's obvious what this company's leaders need to do to make their business healthy: Cut owners' salaries (cell E5) and cut operating costs (cell E7), possibly including staff. This will free up cash flow for profit, which we need to improve (cell E4), and allow us to reserve more cash for the owners' and business's tax responsibilities (cell E6). It will require courage, and it is going to be painful.

The Instant Assessment brings clarity fast, and it can be a rude awakening. No more putting things off. No more hoping that big client, big check, or big anything will save you from the day-to-day panic. We know exactly what we need to do.

A financially healthy company is a result of a series of small daily financial wins, not one big moment. Profitability isn't an event; it's a habit.

DON'T PANIC!

You might remember that during my "rebuilding" period, I wrote my first book, *The Toilet Paper Entrepreneur*; the foundation of which was a series of principles I used to start my businesses. Chief among these principles was frugality—I wholeheartedly believed that any entrepreneur could start a business with little or no seed money and grow that business no matter what they had in the bank. The book is full of tips for saving money while launching and running a business, and since its original publication I've heard from thousands of entrepreneurs who followed the advice (or a variant thereof) while starting or operating their own businesses.

And let me tell you, I didn't just spout off about frugality. After my spending craze, after my come-to-Jesus moment (if Jesus were another name for "near bankruptcy"), I went back to my roots. Way back. Not because I had to, this time, but because I wanted to. I made it my mission to get what I needed for my business on the cheap and took pride in doing so. My office space cost a mere $1,000 per month—peanuts compared to my previous $14,000 a month digs. I got my gently used conference room furniture for a whopping 75 percent discount. My dry erase board was homemade, with white board material used to make showers, dental floss, and some car wax. (Top that, MacGyver!)

So imagine my surprise when I ran my own assessment on my business and discovered that despite my frugal superpowers, I was still bleeding out. It is not an exaggeration to say I was shocked to discover this. "How much cheaper can I get this stuff?" I thought, beyond frustrated.

Then I realized—duh. It wasn't how much I was spending on expense line items. The problem was, I shouldn't have been spending *anything* on some of those line items. For example, I didn't really need an office space. I wasn't seeing clients or greeting customers. I was writing a book and building a speaking career, which meant I spent a lot of time alone, on the road, and in phone and Skype meetings. My subcontractors could just as easily do their work from home.

Truth was, I wanted an office space because it made me feel legitimate. And after my piggy bank moment, I needed to feel that. But the bottom line was, I couldn't keep it up if I wanted to turn a profit every month. So I sublet my office space and found a sweet deal at a cookie factory—free office and meeting space from a trusted longtime friend. I cut expense line items across the board until I stopped the bleeding and watched my business and profit grow. An added bonus was free cookies. And when I say added bonus, I mean a bonus of about five pounds around my waist. So . . . not really a bonus, after all.

In the years since I had that realization, cutting costs has become an almost enjoyable strategic challenge. But to enjoy the process, you first have to face some harsh truths. I have applied the Instant Assessment to countless businesses, and the reactions vary from "Really? I can do that?"

to "Who the hell do you think you are, Mike, telling me where my business should be? You know nothing about my unique industry!" to buckling knees and tears streaming down people's faces. It's hard to face the harsh reality that your business is worse off than you thought it was. But now you know, and knowledge is power. Now we can fix it.

You are not a fool. You have done nothing wrong, and you have nothing to be ashamed of. You have this book in your hands. You are discovering the truth and another way to get where you want to go. You are no longer asking, "How can I make my business bigger?" You are asking, "How can I make my business better?"

IF YOUR BUSINESS IS BRAND-NEW

How does Profit First work if you just launched your business and have no revenue? Should you wait until you have some to start using Profit First? Heck, no. Starting with squat, with your whole business future ahead of you, is actually the best time to start using Profit First. Why? Because it allows you to form a powerful habit right from the get-go, when your business is forming and, perhaps more important, prevents you from developing bad financial habits that can be difficult to break.

Also, in the early stages of building a business, you need to spend as much time as possible on the selling and the doing; systems and processes come later. For these reasons, it's best not to worry about getting the exact right percentages for your business.

Simply use the percentages in the Instant Assessment for your target allocations, but start at 1 percent allocation for the PROFIT account (Why 1 percent? You'll find out in the next chapter), 50 percent for OWNER'S COMP, and 15 percent for the TAX account. Use quarterly adjustments to step up to higher percentages and nudge your business closer to the TAPs recommended in this book. And as for the advanced Profit First strategies I share in the end of the book—don't worry about any of that until your business has been active for at least a year. The goal for new businesses is to form the basic core of the Profit First good habit and then spend every other waking second getting your baby off the ground.

TAKE ACTION: COMPLETE THE INSTANT ASSESSMENT

Step 1 (the one and only step): This entire chapter is really one big action step, so if you have not yet completed an Instant Assessment on your business, do it now. Can you get a lot out of this book if you table this exercise for when you have more time or feel up to facing reality? Sure. Will you get the most out of reading this book and see results quickly if you don't? Nope. So stop right now and do it. I'm waiting. Do it now.

PLEASE READ THIS

If you are feeling overwhelmed, bad about yourself and the choices you've made, or angry about the numbers you came up with in your Instant Assessment, there is something I want you to know:

You are normal. Totally, completely, 100 percent normal.

If you are having trouble facing the rest of this book right now, that's okay. Stop now and come back to it when you feel ready to face it. But do this one thing: set up a PROFIT account at a separate bank, and every time you make a deposit, move 1 percent into that account. I know it's "peanuts," and you may think the amount is too small to make an impact on your business, but that is the reason you're going to keep the profit allocation percentage low. You can run your business as you always have, and you won't feel a thing, but you will start the habit that will change your business forever. Soon enough, the feeling of being overwhelmed, the anger and frustration, will fade as your new profit habit builds. Then you can crack this book again and dig into the rest of the Profit First system.

Chapter 5

ALLOCATION PERCENTAGES

Years ago a colleague shared a powerful story with me about hitting financial targets. An up-and-coming motivational speaker went to a speaking boot camp. During one of the sessions, the instructor explained how to make back-of-the-room sales. He said, "When you follow this method, eighty percent of the audience will buy your product at the end of an event."

With pages of notes and tons of enthusiasm, our up-and-comer set forth on the speaking circuit. Initially, she closed only 25 percent of her audiences. Reaching for that 80 percent, she tweaked and improved her strategy and pitch, constantly reviewing her notes. Over time her close rate rose to 50, then 60 percent. After another year, she was consistently selling 75 percent of the room after her speech. She had achieved outstanding results, but not to the level her instructor had promised.

One morning she sat down to breakfast with a few colleagues, and her old instructor happened to be there. She couldn't wait to speak with him and get direction about what could help her get that last, elusive 5 percent. What was the secret to finally breaking 80 percent? When she told her story to her instructor, his jaw dropped. "Eighty percent? You thought I said eighty percent? I said eighteen."

I tell you this story to illustrate something I believe to be true because I've experienced it—no matter what the number is, if you work toward it and believe it's a possibility, you will not only achieve it, you will blow past the "reasonable" numbers others have set.

Profit First works on so many levels. It begins with setting allocation percentages, the amount you will transfer to PROFIT, OWNER'S COMP, and TAX accounts, which we will sort out in this chapter. By the end of this chapter, you'll have a customized assessment of your business. If you'd rather jump right in and start implementing Profit First, turn to Chapter 6. You can always come back to this chapter later and tweak your percentages. Either way, as long as you're actually working the Profit First system, you're winning.

TWO COMMON PROBLEMS

The Instant Assessment is based on ranges. Every business is slightly different (though your business and your industry are not nearly as unique as you may think). The numbers you came up with in the Instant Assessment won't be perfect, but they are probably close to what you'll end up with after a more detailed assessment.

Before we dig in, I want to address two common problems entrepreneurs face when they decide to start following the Profit First system—and they do not go hand in hand.

1. **Don't Get Bogged Down in the Details:** First, some entrepreneurs make the mistake of getting trapped in the details, spending hours, days, weeks or longer perfecting their percentages before they do anything. Worse, some entrepreneurs who get stuck in the minutiae never get around to doing anything. It's our old nemesis: analysis paralysis. In this chapter, we get down to the nitty-gritty, but if at any time you think you are lost in a research- and percentage-tweaking rabbit hole, stop and move on to the next chapter. Perfectionism kills every dream—better to just start.

2. **Look Before You Leap:** On the other hand, if you're like me, you might make the common mistake of taking action too big and too fast. I'm the type who starts before I have all of the information because most of the learning occurs in the doing anyway. But I put success at risk when I go into a situation ill prepared. In those cases, my ego blames the system when mistakes were simply due to the fact that I didn't put in the necessary preparation.

I've seen entrepreneurs kick-start their Profit First system by taking a profit percentage of 20 percent immediately. They say, "This is so simple. I get it. Bammo! Twenty percent! I'm done. Next problem." Not so fast, chiefy. This is a classic mistake—one I've made myself. Going full throttle into Profit First on the first day is like donating five gallons of blood at your first blood drive. You know what would happen if you tried to do that? You would die. The body has less than two gallons of blood pumping through it, so you'd keel over way before you reached your five-gallon goal anyway. However, there is a way to reach your goal in a safe way. If we donate small amounts over time, eventually we will donate five gallons—cumulatively.

The Target Allocations Percentages, which we call TAPs, are simply the targets you are moving toward. To be clear, TAPs are, *not*—I repeat, are *not*—your starting point. I derived the TAPs from surveys and evaluations of approximately one thousand of the most fiscally elite companies, across all industries and of all sizes, as well as an analysis of some of the thousands of companies who have implemented Profit First and, as a result, *joined* the fiscally elite. Aspire to move toward the TAPs. At this point, you may be thinking, "Mike, you don't know my industry. I could never hit those numbers." This is when I have to bring out the big guns, people like Henry Ford, who said, "If you think you can or think you can't, you're right." Be optimistic when you assume profit capabilities for your business or your industry. In other words, think you can.

Your business may currently have better numbers than the TAPs. If that's you, congratulations! This does not mean you can slow things down, however. You still need to push yourself. Try to become the elite of the elite.

CURRENT ALLOCATION PERCENTAGES (CAPS)

Current Allocation Percentage (CAP) is where your business is today. This is the number you will adjust slowly but consistently over time to get closer and closer to the TAPs. For example, the Profit TAP for your size business may be 20 percent, but your historical profit allocations may have been 0 percent. (If that is you, don't fret; it's common.) If you haven't made profit allocations until now, then your profit CAP is 0 percent.

For your company to join the fiscally elite, you will slowly, deliberately, and consistently move toward the TAPs. What you will do is move from

0 percent profit CAP to 1 percent. Then, next quarter, you will move your CAP to 3 percent, and then next quarter, 5 percent.

Some people hear what I just shared about CAPs but still think, "I have been told to 'go big or go home,' so I am going all in and taking every stinking penny for my profit (and me)." If you hoard most of the food at the table for yourself, you're not leaving any fuel for your business. Remember, your business, not you, is now living off the leftovers. But your leftovers have to be enough for your business to continue to thrive.

The key to successful Profit First implementation lies in stringing together a series of many small steps in a repeating pattern. So take it easy.

While you slowly start to build up your Profit First muscle, we are also going to get you into a simple, repeating pattern. Entrepreneurs typically manage their money in an erratic, noisy rhythm that causes confusion and panic. But by the end of the next chapter, we will get you into a simple rhythm that will give you clarity and control over your financials.

Let's dig in.

YOUR PROFIT TARGET ALLOCATION PERCENTAGE (PROFIT TAP)

The Instant Assessment is a starting point for all of your Target Allocation Percentages (TAPs). If you're the analytical type, you can refine the TAPs to be even more specific to your industry. This is not necessary, by the way, because TAPs are simply targets. As you move along and adjust your CAPs, you will naturally find what works for you.

Now you need to do a little bit of research to set more specific target numbers. There are a few ways to approach this:

1. Research public companies: look at the financial reports public companies are required to make available. Do a quick Internet search using the term *financial market overview*, and you will find dozens of Web sites that report the financials for public companies. Look up at least five companies in your industry or a similar industry. If you don't find your niche, try expanding. For instance, if you find no public DJ companies, expand to entertainment companies and select five that come close. (Tip: My preference is Marketwatch.com for these re-

ports, because the site is easy to navigate. You might also try Yahoo! Finance and Google Finance.)

For our purposes, look up the income statements for the last three to five years. If you really want to dig in, check out the balance sheets and cash flow statements for these companies, too.

For each year, divide the net income (profit) number by the total sales/ revenue number.* Then come up with the average. This is how you find the profit percentage for any public company. Do this for each of the five public companies you look at, and you will find the overall industry profit average. Use that overall industry profit average as your Profit TAP.

2. Review your tax returns for the last three to five years and determine your most profitable year—based on percentages, not on dollar amounts. Why do we want the percentage? Because a billion-dollar company that reports only a million dollars in profit is in big trouble. Even if it had only one bad day, a million bucks wouldn't be enough to bail it out. But a five million-dollar company that reports a million in profit is kicking butt and taking names. That li'l ole company spits at bad days.

3. Or, the easiest way, just pick your profit percentage number based on your projected revenue for this year, using revenue for the last twelve months from the Instant Assessment form you filled out for Chapter 4. (You did fill it out, right?) Remember, the form is also available for free, downloaded from the Resources section at MikeMichalowicz.com.

Perhaps you will never quite reach the TAPs to which you aspire. But they will force you to constantly think about what you are doing and how you are doing it, so that you can get *closer.* Or maybe you can beat the TAPs.

---

* If more than 25 percent of the stuff your company sells comes from materials rather than labor or software—as happens with manufacturers, restaurants, and retailers—use the gross profit (sometimes called gross income) as the Real Revenue number. Gross profit is calculated somewhat similarly to how I suggest you determine your Real Revenue, and you need to evaluate your business based on that. Whenever you run the numbers for your business, or evaluate others, you will always base it on Real Revenue (gross profit).

Maybe you can become the new industry standard for TAPs. That would be badass. When you do surpass your TAPs, tell me about it. I want to tell everyone else to elevate his or her game.

Because at this point your PROFIT account will fund your profit distributions and serve as your rainy-day fund, you'll want your CAP to grow past 5 percent quickly. If you save 5 percent of your company's annual income, for example, that represents about twenty-one days of operating cash, which would help you keep your business afloat if your income were to plummet. (If your income dried up, you would stop contributing to your PROFIT account and TAX account and stop profit distributions to owners.) Three weeks is not much time to fix the problem, but Armageddon rarely happens. More often, revenue slows down over time, and you'll have at least something coming in during lean times. Kinda like a "Hangnail-ageddon" instead of an Armageddon. (It's a bad joke, I know, but I like it. So it stays.)

If your sales were to stop completely, with not a single deposit coming in, here's a good longevity rule of thumb:

1. 5 percent profit allocation = 3 weeks of operating cash.
2. 12 percent profit allocation = 2 months of operating cash.
3. 24 percent profit allocation = 5 months of operating cash.

Why is it that as the profit allocation percentages basically double, business longevity almost triples? The math doesn't seem to make sense at first glance. But it does make sense. The bigger your profit allocation percentage, the more efficiently you are running your business, which means less in operating expenses. So not only do you have more saved up with a higher PF percentage, you spend less, which affords you even more time.

FAT MARGINS DRAW STIFF COMPETITION

The goal is to make your profit allocation percentage as high as possible. However, super high profit percentages are not sustainable. At least not for long, and definitely not if your revenue stays stagnant. The reason for this is that if you can pull off consistently fat profits—

say 50 percent allocated to Profit and only 10 percent of revenue to your Operating Expenses—your competitors will figure out what you're doing. Then, to get more business, they will drop prices (they likely have the profit margins to afford it). When that happens, you will have to drop prices, too, in order to stay in business. For competitive sharks, fat margins can be like blood in the water. The only way to keep big margins is to milk them for all they're worth when you have them and keep innovating to find new ways to bump up profitability.

OWNER'S COMP TAP

Gone are the days when you paid everyone but yourself and had to support your life with credit cards and loans from the in-laws. Remember, your business is supposed to serve you; you are not in service to your business! No more leftovers for you!

Owner's Comp is the amount you and the other equity owners take in pay for the work you do. I suspect you are familiar with the term *owner operator*, which means you own the business (have equity) and you operate the business (work as an employee for the company). Owner's Comp is the money we reserve for you and any other owner operators of the business to get paid for the work you do for the company. (Equity members of your company who do not work in the business just get a profit distribution.) Your salary should be on a par with the going rate for the work you do, in other words—the salary you would have to pay your replacement.

There are two options to consider when choosing your Owner's Comp TAP number. Either

1. Take a realistic look at the work you do. If you have a small company with, say, five employees, you may call yourself the CEO—but that's just the title on your card. It's likely you are doing a lot of other work. You probably spend a lot of time selling, completing projects, handling customers, and dealing with human resources (HR) concerns. In reality, around 2 percent of your time is spent actually doing the job of CEO: vision planning, strategic negotiations, acquisitions, reporting

to investors, addressing the media, etc. Determine your salary based on what you are doing 80 percent of the time, and what you would reasonably pay employees to do those jobs. Then evaluate pay for all equity owners who work in the business.

Add up the salaries that represent your Owner's Comp draw. The percentage of revenue that you set as your Owner's Comp TAP must, at minimum, cover Owner's Comp draw. Remember, you will likely get raises—maybe even a bonus for a job well done. So make the percentage one and a quarter times the amount you determine for your salaries, so you can adjust for revenue fluctuations. Say you work with four equity owners in a business with a revenue of $1,000,000, who draw a salary of $50,000 each, you need to set your Owner's Comp TAP to at least 25 percent.

Or,

2. Pick the percentage I suggested in the Instant Assessment, based on your Revenue Range. (Refer to Figure 4.) The money that is transferred into this account is divided among all equity employees. It does not have to be split up equally, nor does it have to be split up based on your equity percentages. The Owner's Comp is a negotiated agreement.

Why should you have a separate account if you and the other equity owners working in the business are just employees? Because you are the most important employee. If you had to fire people, I suspect you would fire everyone else before you fired yourself. Think about your very best employee. I'll bet you take extra steps to ensure that you are taking care of that person. I'll bet you would do everything in your power to keep your best employees happy, including paying them what they're worth, right? Well guess what, bucko! You are your best, most important employee. We must take care of you.

When it comes to pay, different business formations require you to take Owner's Comp in different ways. An S Corporation is different from an LLC (limited liability company) or a sole proprietorship, which are both treated way differently than a C Corporation. The Owner's Comp allocation still works the same way; you just need to work with your accountant to make sure the money flows out properly and legally. I strongly recommend an accountant who is a certified Profit First Professional, who knows exactly how to support your Profit First business.

Don't Underpay Your Most Important Employee

I was having dinner with my friend Rodrigo when he told me how his business generated $350,000 in annual revenue, but he was living on below-minimum wage.

As a thunderstorm approached in the distance, I took the napkin with the fewest salsa stains and jotted down Rodrigo's numbers. Multiplying his $350,000 in Real Revenue by 35 percent (from the Instant Assessment), I came up with just over $122,000.

"How many partners work in the business?" I asked.

"Me, and one other," he replied.

Dividing by two, the amount for Owner's Comp was a little more than $61,000 each, but that was if they were doing the same work, warranting a fifty-fifty split. As we discussed in the previous section, Owner's Comp should represent the work you do.

When I asked Rodrigo for more details about his own pay, he said, "I take roughly $30,000 a year, and my partner left to get a full-time job, so he takes zero now. We have three full-time employees at $65,000 each per year, and I manage them."

I'd like to say I was shocked, but this scenario is all too common. How was Rodrigo supporting himself and his family on below-minimum wage? I figured he was using credit cards, family loans, and possibly a home refinance to supplement his paltry income.

"If all three of your employees decided to leave on the same day, what would you do?" I asked.

"I would do all of the work myself and my partner would come back."

"So why don't you do that?" I asked.

"Because then I would be stuck doing the work, and it would not be able to grow," Rodrigo explained. "I don't want to do the work; I want to grow the business."

Rodrigo had the right idea, but he was executing it in the wrong way.

Michael Gerber, in his classic must-read book *The E-Myth Revisited*, explains that we should work on our business, not in it. This "on versus in" philosophy is spot-on, and yet most entrepreneurs have trouble executing it. Working on the business does not mean hiring a bunch of people to do the work and then spending all the livelong day answering their never-ending questions about how to do the job (the job you used to do). Working on your business is about building systems. Period.

However, what Rodrigo and so many entrepreneurs miss is that growing a company is not an overnight switch from doing all of the work to none of the work. The transition from working in the business to working on the business happens over time—slowly, deliberately, one small step followed by another small step. (Are you starting to see the theme here?) This is the reasoning behind the Owner's Comp percentages in the Instant Assessment—larger percentages for owners when the company is tiny and smaller percentages as the company grows.

In the early days of a company, when annual revenues are below $250,000, you are not only the most important employee; you are likely the only employee. If your annual revenue is under $500,000 and you have an employee or two, you are still the key employee. And that means you must be doing 90 percent of the work. You're bringing home the bacon and frying it up in the pan.

The other 10 percent of the time you spend recording everything you do so that you can systematize it for your other few employees or contractors to do the work without your input. Basically, you are a true entrepreneur (building systems) 10 percent of the time, and a hardworking, hard-selling employee of your own company 90 percent of the time.

This is why you get such a big salary in the beginning. No more of this "bottom of the bowl" stuff. You can't live on a minimum wage or less. Say it again, once more with feeling: my business serves me; I do not serve my business. Paying yourself next to nothing for hard work is servitude. Always start with CAPs—where you are now—and increase by 1 percent each quarter.*

As your annual revenue grows past $500,000, you will transition to

---

* Sometimes you can (and should) adjust your CAPs more aggressively. Other times you should be more cautious. Making quarterly adjustments to your CAPs is a great example of where an outside expert is of tremendous value. Go to ProfitFirstProfessionals.com and choose the FIND option, and you will be connected with an expert who can help you with the CAPs adjustments.

spending more time building systems. Now you're a systems developer 20 percent of the time, a manager 10 percent of the time, and an employee 70 percent of the time. (Note that the better you are at creating systems, the less management is required because the recipe for how to get things done is consistent.) As annual revenue grows past $1 million, your salary percentage will drop even further because you will be working less and less *in* the business and more and more *on* the business.

However, remember that it is likely you will always work in your business. Because even if you are a master of building systems and spend 80 percent of your time in that magic zone, you'll still spend roughly 20 percent of your time handling the big sales. Almost every entrepreneur-to-CEO is in charge of the big sale. You bet your bottom dollar Jeff Bezos is in the room when Amazon is closing a hundred-million-dollar deal. And when your big deals are on the table, you will be right there, sitting at its head.

Ironically, getting back in your business is the best way to create systems. And as you put the systems in place and your revenue increases to accommodate them, you can slowly plug in great people to implement those great systems.

The bottom line is this: don't cut your salary to make the numbers work. The goal of every business is health, and that is achieved through efficiency. Your martyr syndrome is not doing anyone any favors; making yourself the sacrificial lamb does not promote efficiency; it hinders it.

YOUR TAX TAP

Greg Eckler loves tax time. Greg, the owner of Denver Realty Experts, LLC, read an early draft of *Profit First* and started applying it to his business. We are close friends from college and were in the same business fraternity, Delta Sigma Pi, so he was kind enough to read the draft and give me feedback. And to blackmail him to get the job done, I told him that if he finished reading it and implemented Profit First, I would never reveal his fraternity nickname, which was Elk Turd. Oops. Sorry, Greg.

Back to Greg and his bizarre love of tax time. I mean, who loves tax time? Good ol' Elk Turd, that's who. And why does he love tax time? Because one of the benefits of using the Profit First system is that Greg no longer worries about having enough money to pay his taxes.

"I have all my docs to my accountants by January fourth because I can't wait to hear back from them about what I owe. I had $30,000 in my TAX account at the end of the 2015 and only needed $10,000 to cover my bill. Woo-hoo! Bonus time!"

Greg told me he has stuck with Profit First since it started, and he sees no reason to stop. "It's the peace of mind knowing that everything is taken care of with a quick glance on my bank app . . . log in . . . peace."

Profit First is not about accounting to the exact penny. That's what your bookkeeper and accountant do. It is about handling your accounting quickly and easily with numbers that are as close to accurate as possible. We work percentages off the Real Revenue number, and this is true for all your "small plate" accounts.

The Tax plate, so we are clear, is designed to pay the direct Tax liabilities of the business and (this is the big one), the *personal income taxes of the owners*. Let me say that again because this often gets missed: your company (assuming you own it) will reserve *your* personal income tax liability for you, and then pay it. Here's the deal: you started your business in part to achieve financial freedom. So if that is true, shouldn't your company pay your taxes for you? Hellll, yeah. So that is exactly what is going to happen.

When your taxes are due and you submit your quarterlies, the company will send the payment in for you. Don't get stuck in the micro details here. This system also works if you have taxes drawn from your paycheck (maybe you don't take distributions as you would from an LLC, but take a paycheck from an S-Corp or a C-Corp), then the company will reimburse you for your taxes. All taxes (including, scratch that, *especially* yours) are paid by your business, not you. Got it? Good.

The first step in getting to your Tax TAP is to determine your income tax rate. Taxes range all over the place, depending on your amount of personal income and corporate profit and the area you live in. As of this writing, many entrepreneurs have an average income tax rate of 35 percent or so; for others it will be less, and in some countries it can be 60 percent or more.

One goal of the Profit First system is that the company takes care of all forms of Tax responsibility. It's mandatory that you talk with your accountant so she can advise you on all the ways you and your business will be taxed.

Here are three different approaches for determining your Tax TAP:

1. Look at your personal and business tax returns. Add up your taxes and then determine the percentage of taxes you paid compared to your Real Revenue. Do this again for the prior two years. Looking at your taxes as a percentage of Real Revenue for the last three years will give you a good sense of your ongoing tax responsibility.

2. From your accountant get your estimated tax responsibility for your business, year to date (YTD), and then determine your Tax percentage of your YTD Real Revenue.

3. Or simply use 35 percent for U.S.-based businesses, and if you have a business in another country, simply use the average prevailing rate of taxes for an individual at your income rate as your Tax number. It may not be perfect, but it's usually pretty effective. And while the optimal number will have you neither paying additional taxes at the end of the year nor receiving a refund, it is better to guess a little too high, get a refund and consider what to do with the extra cash than to get a call from your accountant, Keith, because you don't have enough money, and have to ask your daughter if you can borrow from her piggy bank. Trust me.

But hold on: If the tax rate is 35 percent (again, for U.S. citizens with higher levels of income), why would I only reserve 15 percent for taxes (as noted in the Instant Assessment I shared earlier)? Let's do a little simple math.

A Little Simple Math

Now we are going to determine the percentage that stays in your OPEX account after you move money to your PROFIT account, your OWNER'S COMP account, and your TAX account. The amount left over for expenses is likely going to be somewhere between 40 percent and 60 percent. This is the money you have available to pay all your expenses.

Next, subtract that percentage from 100 percent. So if your total OPEX account is at 55 percent, you're left with 45 percent. That 45 percent is the amount you will be taxed on. (More often than not, expenses are not taxed. This is why some accountants encourage you to buy equipment or make other large purchases toward the end of the year.) Now multiply your non-operating percentage (in this case, 45 percent) by your taxable income percentage (in this case, 35 percent). You end up with a percentage of approximately 16 percent, which is your Tax percentage.

Now that you have a more accurate picture of your actual percentages, you're ready to get started. In the next chapter I'll take you through the first year of Profit First, and beyond, and outline everything you need to know from day one. Congratulations! You survived. Send me a selfie.

I can sense your hunger to put this into practice in your business. Wipe that drool off your chin, and let's start doing it.

TAKE ACTION: APPLY YOUR ADVANCED KNOWLEDGE

Step 1: Following the steps detailed above, determine your custom Profit, Owner's Comp, and Tax percentages based on your industry and other factors. Set these as your TAPs, your targets. This is the X on the map of where we are heading, but it is not where we are starting.

Step 2: Because you chose to get down to the nitty-gritty and determine your exact Profit, Owner's Comp, and Tax percentages, stop now and adjust the numbers in your Instant Assessment chart.

Step 3: Set your CAPs. For the remainder of this quarter, set your CAPs 1 percent "better" than what you have done historically—meaning increase your Profit, Owner's Comp, and Tax all by 1 percent and cut your Operating Expenses by 3 percent. Every quarter we will push the CAPs to an even better percentage. Over time you will continue a relentless march toward a healthier and healthier company, and a fatter and fatter wallet.

Chapter 6

PUTTING PROFIT FIRST INTO MOTION

Jorge Morales and José Pain unofficially stand as the first business owners to implement Profit First after reading my book. Not this one, but *The Toilet Paper Entrepreneur*, which had a short section outlining the Profit First idea. After I released that book, I held a meet up for my early readers in Newark, New Jersey (a popular vacation spot, up there with North Korea). Jorge and José made the trek up from South Florida to attend. They had paid for their trip up to New Jersey out of their PROFIT account. But this wasn't just a business trip; they brought their spouses and toured New York City (once they had finished their extensive sightseeing in Newark) after the event. Jorge and José had gone all in on Profit First, even based on the meager two paragraphs that I wrote about it, and they were seeing results.

When Jorge Morales and José Pain started Specialized ECU Repair in 2007, they dreamed of one day enjoying what they perceived to be the big perk of owning a business: profit, or extra money to spend on their own interests, all while working less.

Here's where many seasoned entrepreneurs chuckle knowingly because they think Jorge and José are naive dreamers. Don't they know that entrepreneurship is about personal sacrifice? The only reason free time exists is so that you can use that time to work more. And unless they're exceptionally lucky, it will be a long time before they earn enough extra cash to indulge in their little hobbies, right?

Wrong.

Two years into operating their own business, Jorge and José had decided that the only way they could reap the benefits of entrepreneurship would be to increase their salaries a little bit each year. (They were already better off than most entrepreneurs in that they *did* have enough to pay their own salaries, and hadn't fallen into the death trap of debt.)

Then they read the small section on Profit First in *The Toilet Paper Entrepreneur*, and began applying the system almost immediately. Over the next few years, Jorge and José tweaked Profit First to suit their rapidly growing business, adjusting their PROFIT account percentages and allowing Profit First to control that growth so that they never ended up underwater because of large purchases or a ridiculously high payroll.

In 2013, they surpassed their accountant's revenue projections. Every year they have increased their sales revenue, and they are on track to break $1 million in annual revenue within the next two years. Their staff has tripled in size, but thanks to their shrewd and careful planning and the Profit First system, they are not struggling under the weight of too-high operating expenses. More important, their business is serving them, with salaries appropriate for their positions and the work they do at Specialized ECU Repair, and with significant PROFIT account disbursements that have enabled them to live the lifestyle they envisioned when they started the business. The dream all entrepreneurs have—that our business will *improve* the quality of our lives, not destroy it—is being lived by Jorge and José. They do not serve their business; their business serves *them*.

As I wrote this revised and expanded version of *Profit First*, I checked in with Jorge and José to find out how Profit First was working for them a few years later. Jorge excitedly talked about his kitesurfing and snowsurfing trips—he's an adventurer at heart. Then we got down to business.

"We have six employees now, and we pay well above industry average," Jorge said. "We were able to pay cash for expensive equipment that, over time, will help us streamline and earn more profit. And we increased our profit percentage to nine percent." (Let me remind you that this 9 percent profit is above and beyond the nicey-nice paychecks they pay themselves every couple of weeks.)

Jorge explained that following the Profit First system means they always have enough cash on hand to take advantage of deals that save them money, such as discounts for paying an entire year's worth of services in advance. And once it was up and running, Profit First enabled them to quickly make purchasing decisions without worrying about whether or not they could afford it.

While he wasn't on board initially, their accountant is now convinced Jorge and José aren't just lucky guys; they are using a system that bakes profit into every transaction. Their accountant is now fully on board and supporting them each step of the way.

Profit First works. Period. Whether you use the percentages I provided for you in the Instant Assessment or choose the path of assessing all the nuances of your business and industry (see Chapter 5) and arrive at your own perfect Target Allocation Percentages, it will work. How can it work with different percentages, you ask? Because your Profit, Owner's Comp, and Tax TAPs are simply targets—you aren't going to start with them, you are going to build toward them. And as you build, you will transform your business into a lean, mean efficiency machine that generates profit on every deposit, no matter how small.

In this chapter, I will teach you exactly how to implement Profit First, step by step, day by day, month by month, and so on. Your Profit percentage may seem steep or out of reach, but by the end of this year you will be closer to it than you thought you could be. You may even leave it in the dust.

DAY ONE

1. Tell Your People

Jorge and José included their financial professionals in the implementation of Profit First right from the start. "When we first learned about Profit First, it made sense to us," Jorge told me, in one of our many phone calls about their progress. "I pulled the numbers and then, with our bookkeeper and accountant, we did a projection for the year. Then we worked in the PROFIT account percentage we wanted to start with."

With buy-in from their accountant on the principles and processes of Profit First, Jorge and José have been able to systematically apply the method to their business with great success. Their accountant helps them meet their Profit First goals and stay the course.

But not every accounting professional will get it. You may tell them about the system, and they'll say, "Phooey." I'll tell you how to address them in a bit. Just know you can be successful going it alone, or better yet, get the support of another accounting professional who does get it.

To make your life easier, I have compiled a list of accountants, book-keepers, financial planners, and others who not only understand Profit First, but are doing it for themselves. Imagine a stockbroker who says you should go all in on XYZ stock, and then doesn't go all in on it himself. I mean, does he really believe in the stock? Clearly, not enough to put his life savings into it. I wouldn't invest in the advice of someone who isn't taking his own advice. Our recommended professionals not only get Profit First, they use it for themselves and they use it with their existing clients. To get the list of financial professionals who specialize in Profit First, go to ProfitFirstProfessionals.com and we will get you a perfect match with an individual (or a team if you prefer) who can get up to speed within a few minutes. And help you for as long as you need it.

Get Your Accountant/Bookkeeper on Board

When your "money" people hear about Profit First, be prepared for them to scowl a little. On the other hand, your accountant or bookkeeper may get it. She may be enthusiastic and ready to support you. Unfortunately, from my experience, most won't.

To your accountant or bookkeeper, the mere suggestion of taking your profit first may cause her head to spin in circles, like in the scene from *The Exorcist*. You need to understand her perspective. Your accounting profes-sional has grown up under the laws and rules of the past. Accounting is the way it is today because that's how it has always been. If you want to manage cash flow, the old established rule is to budget accordingly and stick with it. Just do what your accountant says and never deviate and you will be profitable.

If you have a progressive accounting professional, she will be all over Profit First. She will thirst for ways to support you better and make your job of making a profit easier. Tell her to pick up this book to get started, and definitely tell her to check out Profit First Professionals so that she can gain access to the special training and/or tools for accounting professionals.

But what if your accountant or bookkeeper stands her ground and tells you not to implement Profit First? Do this: Ask her whether she has hands-on experience implementing Profit First (or a similar pay-yourself-first system), and if she does, ask her to explain why it doesn't work. Prepare yourself for a blank stare. Because if she has properly implemented pay-yourself-first plans, she will know it does work, every time.

If your accountant or bookkeeper then tells you that "no one else does this," you should slap her (figuratively speaking, of course). Because the fact that she has not told her few dozen clients about it, doesn't mean the whole world follows suit. Quite the opposite; more and more businesses are doing Profit First every day.

If your accountant or bookkeeper continues to act like a stubborn ox, ask her, "How many of your clients are consistently profitable under your direction? All of them? Half? Any?" Wait for her to mumble. Or cry. Or commit hara-kiri.

Most accountants using the old GAAP method of cash management are lucky to have a handful of profitable clients. Almost all of the remaining clients are likely struggling to stay afloat. This should be their wake-up call.

Ask yours to read *Profit First* cover to cover and support you in the process. If they are unwilling to listen to you (remember, you are the client, and their job is specifically to support you in maximizing your profitability), find new accounting professionals who not only support Profit First but are trained in it. (If you don't know where to start, check out Profit FirstProfessionals.com.) And as you leave your old fuddy-duddy accountant, give her a copy of *Profit First* as your parting gift and a poster-size picture of me sticking my tongue out.

2. Set Up Your Accounts

Before we begin, you better have already set up your foundational five accounts at your primary bank (INCOME, PROFIT, OWNER'S COMP, TAX, and OPEX) and the two accounts at your new no-temptation bank (PROFIT HOLD and TAX HOLD). If you haven't done it yet . . . what are you waiting for?! I mean how are we gonna make progress together if you aren't doing your part? Do *not*, I repeat, *do not*, try to make a "shortcut" and just do this in a spreadsheet or in your accounting system. And absolutely do not try to do all of this in your head. Don't wait another second. Set up those accounts, damn it!

Now you are going to add to the nickname for each account by adding the CAP next to the account name and also put your TAP in parenthesis. For example, if you are nicknaming your PROFIT account, and the CAP is 8 percent and the TAP is 15 percent, nickname the account "PROFIT 8% (TAP 15%)." This allows you to quickly identify which money is going where currently, and the ultimate allocation percentage you are trying to achieve. Within seconds of logging into your bank account, you will be extremely clear on which money is available for what purpose, how much you are allocating, and the target you have set for your cash flow.

The final setup of your accounts at your bank should look something like this (of course, with the correct CAPs and TAPs you have designated for your business):

INCOME *8855

PROFIT 8% (TAP 15%) *8843

OWNER'S COMP 20% (TAP 25%) *8833

TAX 5% (TAP 15%) *8839

OPEX 67% (TAP 45%) *8812

CAPs—Start Out Easy

We are making progress now, baby! We have the accounts set up at your bank and we are getting super practical with the nicknames. We have determined the Target Allocation Percentages (TAPs) for each account during the Instant Assessment phase. But TAPs are simply the vision. TAPs are where we are headed. TAPs are *not* where we start. We're going to start with a manageable profit, a doable Owner's Comp, and a reasonable Tax reserve that will allow adequate time to cut down on expenses, start finding profit opportunities within your business, and adjust to the new system. The percentages we are about to assign to each account are going to be called your CAPs (Current Allocation Percentages).

For your CAPs, we'll start at our Day Zero* contribution levels for each

---

* Day Zero contribution levels are the historical percentages you were allocating to each category before implementing Profit First.

account and then add 1 percent, bringing us to Day One* of your Profit First implementation. This may mean your Day Zero is zilch for a few of the accounts. If your business has never had a profit, or if you have sometimes had a profit and sometimes a loss, your profit has been zero. Therefore, our easy Day One start for the PROFIT account will be 1 percent CAP (that's 0 percent historically plus 1 percent, starting today), and we will bump it up as we start getting into our quarterly rhythm.

	DAY ZERO	ADJUST	DAY ONE
Profit	0%	+1%	1%
Owner's Comp	17%	+1%	18%
Tax	5%	+1%	6%
Operating Expenses	78%	-3%	75%

If your company historically has paid taxes[†] of 5 percent of your total revenue, we are going to set up your tax CAP reserve at 6 percent by simply adding 1 percent to your Day Zero Tax allocation of 5 percent. If your pay represented 17 percent of your income, we add 1 percent to your 17 percent and you have 18 percent Owner Compensation CAP. And so on. Even if our targets are much higher, we start with what we've got, plus 1 percent for Profit, Owner's Comp, and Tax. We then reduce the Operating Expenses by the cumulative of the percentage adjustments we made to the other three accounts.

Why start with small percentages, when we likely could do more? The primary goal here is to establish a new automatic routine for you. I want

---

* Day One is your first-ever adjustment to your new CAP for each account. Day Zero is prior to Profit First, and Day One is your first day of designated allocation percentages.

† Remember, this is how much your company has directly paid in taxes for both the business and the owners' personal income tax liabilities and/or reimbursed the owners for the taxes they paid (or had automatically withdrawn from their paycheck).

the amounts to be so small you don't even feel them. The goal is to set up these automatic allocations immediately, and then adjust the percentages each quarter until we are aligned with our target distribution percentages. Take small easy steps and you will gain powerful momentum.

Practical to the core, Jorge and José started out with a modest Profit First percentage of 2 percent. Because their decision was made more than five years ago, before I finessed this system, their number was not based on the 1 percent rule I've just shared with you. They chose an allocation of 2 percent because initially Jorge was reluctant to begin implementing Profit First—even though he knew it made perfect sense.

"I think by going slowly, I was able to see how Profit First could work," Jorge explained. "What it really came down to was I realized that at two percent, there was no excuse not to try it. Because if your business can't afford to set aside two percent of your revenue, it's probably not a business worth pursuing."

Start slow. Real slow. Put the percentages at a level where there is *no excuse not to try*.

These starting CAP percentages you set are your quarterly allocation percentages. We are going to use them for the rest of this quarter, whether the next quarter begins next week or in ninety-one days.

Most businesses have never taken a profit before and just pay the owner as close to a regular salary as possible. In this case, Day Zero Profit will be 0 percent. Don't get upset about that; most companies have no historical profit. You are among friends here. In other cases, owners take money out of the business whenever there is any sitting around and they aren't sure whether those dollars are considered Owner's Comp or Profit. The answer is simple: all of it is Owner's Comp and none of it is profit. In this case, your Day Zero Profit percentage is 0 percent. Then there are circumstances where your income statement says there is a profit, but you only took money out to support your personal lifestyle as best you could. For our purposes, this is again a situation of no profit. Set Day Zero Profit to 0 percent.

Your Day Zero Owner's Comp is the pay that you received from the company this year, either in paychecks or distributions and has not been classified as profit already (as I explained in the prior paragraph). And to be super-duper clear, you likely had no profit, so the Owner's Comp will be all the pay you took. Divide your Owner's Comp by the Real Revenue of your company, and you will have your historical Owner's Comp percentage.

If you are still a little unclear on what goes to Profit and what goes to Owner's Comp, simply do this: Put 0 percent to Profit and put any money you (and any other owners of the business) have received into the category of Owner's Comp and figure out the historical percentage of Real Revenue. By the way, if you look at the income tax returns for each owner in your business, you can find the Owner's Comp there. Just add it up.

Your Day Zero Tax is the amount of Tax that your business (not you personally) has paid in taxes. Has your company paid taxes directly to the government? Yes? Then add up that amount. Has the company paid the government directly taxes on your behalf? Meaning did you get a tax bill for personal income, and then have the company write out a check to pay it? Yes? Then add that in. But did you get distributions or paychecks from your company, and then pay the tax man out of your own pocket? In that case, you paid your own income taxes and your business did not, and you would not add this into your calculation. In most cases, businesses have never paid taxes on behalf of their owners (even though they should), so the calculation here is easy. You put the Day Zero Taxes to 0 percent, or possibly a very low percentage to account for the corporate taxes paid.

The norm for most businesses, and therefore yours, I suspect, is that the business neither paid a profit to the owners nor paid taxes on their behalf. So in this case, we set profit to 0 percent and tax to 0 percent and Owner's Comp to the total payments to the Owner's Comp, divided by Real Revenue. And if this totally confuses you, do not worry at all. The Profit First system is self-correcting. Just set Profit and Tax historical to 0 percent and figure out the percentage for Owner's Comp.

The Operating Expense historical percentage is everything else. It should be reflected on your income statement. It includes all your expenses, from cost of goods sold to SG&A* and every cost in between. (The only exception is whether or not you made an adjustment for Real Revenue, as I explained earlier in the book.) Then your expenses are all expenses, except what you adjusted to get to Real Revenue. If you are still confused, it is OK—we will make it really simple; just put all your expenses in here. Then

---

* SG&A refers to sales, general, and administrative costs.

divide Real Revenue into the expense number (your Real Revenue and total income will be the same number), then go with this percentage.

These numbers do not need to be perfect. If you are the accounting type, you are going to want to get this figured out to the penny. But that is not necessary, not possible, and not even helpful. The goal here is to get to a rough starting point. The Profit First system is designed to just get started now—that's the primary goal—and will, over time, be tweaked and adjusted to get to the perfect percentages.

After going through these steps, your Day Zero percentages may look something like this:

INCOME *8855

PROFIT (0%) *8843

OWNER'S COMP (4%) *8833

TAX (0%) *8839

OPEX (96%) *8812

From these percentages we can see that the company had no historical profit, had paid the owner (or Owner's Comp) of the business 4 percent of the income (Real Revenue), and 96 percent of the income that came in went to pay bills. In fact, this is more than an example; these are the exact CAPs of one of my prior businesses from years and years back. Just for a hoot I decided to look at my old business, Olmec Systems, from the late nineties, before I had developed Profit First. At this time, the business was running check to check, from one bank account. In 1999, the business did just over $1 million in revenue, my business partner and I took home $40,000, and the company blew through $960,000 in expenses. Not much of a hoot. That was ugly, and I had no idea. It is as if someone had tied my hands behind my back, blindfolded me, jammed a ball gag into my mouth (I am not suggesting that I have ever experienced this), and then put me into one of those machines that blows money all around. Kinda like a human-size snow globe of money, without the ability to catch any with my hands.

Those percentages were my reality, and I wouldn't be surprised if they are yours.

Now that we know your Day Zero percentages, we are going to ease into Profit First. To do this, simply add 1 percent to your Day Zero Profit, 1 percent to your Owner's Comp, and 1 percent to your Tax, and reduce your Operating Expenses by 3 percent.

In my example, for my old company, the Day Zero Profit was 0 percent, so adding 1 percent, the new profit CAP is 1 percent. My Day Zero Tax allocation was also 0 percent, so I add 1 percent, and my Tax CAP becomes 1 percent. My Owner's Comp was 4 percent, so now I set it to 5 percent. My Operating Expenses were 96 percent, so it now gets adjusted down by three percent points, so now it is 93 percent. The accounts will look like this:

INCOME *8855

PROFIT 1% (TAP 10%) *8843

OWNER'S COMP 5% (TAP 10%) *8833

TAX 1% (TAP 15%) *8839

OPEX 93% (TAP 65%) *8812

Hopefully, you see the immediate implications on my then $1,000,000 business. My business partner and my compensation will immediately go from $40,000 annually to $50,000, we would have $10,000 of profit at the end of a full year, and we would also have $10,000 reserved in taxes to help cover our personal tax bills. And we are now forced by my company to run the business off $930,000 a year, instead of $960,000. I am sure we could (and can) find a way because now it is crystal clear what I must do.

3. Make Your First Distributions

You know that saying "Today is the first day of the rest of your life." I love it. To me, it represents the profound realization that we can change our lives (and our businesses) in a moment. Now is the time. This very *moment* we will make a profit for your business, and we will be profitable every day going forward. Please don't just read this and then move on to the next chapter. I want you to take action now.

Right now, this moment, look at your bank balance in your original primary account, which we have renamed your OPEX account. Then subtract any outstanding checks and payments you have from that account. Transfer the remainder of the money into your INCOME account.

Now we are going to do our first allocation. Divide up the money in the INCOME account into all the other accounts (PROFIT, OWNER'S COMP, TAX, and OPEX) based on the CAPs you set. This is your first-ever "allocation" and will be the only thing you ever do with the INCOME account, besides receiving future deposits from sales.

Let's do the allocation right now. Say you had $5,000 in your old primary bank account. You have renamed that account OPEX and determined that you have $3,000 in checks and payments still waiting to clear. That means you have $2,000 currently available. Transfer the $2,000 to the INCOME account. Then transfer all the money from the INCOME account to the respective accounts based on percentages.

Run your percentages on that $2,000 and move that money into the accounts. Continuing my example, it would allocate the $2,000 as follows:

INCOME *8855 → This account, which had the $2,000, goes to $0 as all the money gets allocated to PROFIT, OWNER'S COMP, TAX, and OPEX, based upon the CAPs we have set.

PROFIT 1% (TAP 10%) *8843 → $20 goes here

OWNER'S COMP 5% (TAP 10%) *8833 → $100 goes here

TAX 1% (TAP 15%) *8839 → $20 goes here

OPEX 93% (TAP 65%) *8812 → $1,860 goes here

As you see the numbers allocated, you will see that while the percentages aren't pretty, it is obvious that a huge portion of your money is going to expenses. It feels good to know you now have a system and have clarity, but the immediate picture is ugly. And that is kind of what we want because over time you will be motivated to make the allocation percentages better and better. You will be motivated to reduce expenses, and perhaps even more important, you will find ways to increase your profitability (via innovations, thinking up new, better, and more efficient steps). This system will make it undeniably clear on what money you have and what purpose it is being used for. And with this clarity, you can make much better decisions to improve the health of your business.

Now that you've seen an example, do you have any deposits to make today? If so, tally up the deposits, put them in the bank, and then *immediately* distribute the money to all the other accounts. Do this for every deposit going forward. (If you have lots of deposits, don't worry, you don't need to do this every single day or multiple times a day. We are going to get you into a twice-a-month rhythm shortly that will make this process manageable.)

4. Our First Day, Our First Celebration

Congrats! I am not saying that lightly. You've just taken a big step. This is likely the first time in your entire business life that you have deliberately accounted for your profit first. Before anything else, you made sure you addressed your profit, your personal income, and your tax responsibilities. That's a big deal. And it is a big step to a very, very healthy business. Kudos to you. Enjoy a nice margarita tonight; that is, unless you don't like margaritas. In that case, tell me and I'll drink one in your honor.

WEEK ONE: CUT EXPENSES

Now that we are moving money into our PROFIT, OWNER'S COMP, TAX, and OPEX accounts, we need to get the money from somewhere. There are only two ways to do that: by increasing sales and cutting expenses. Increasing sales is very doable (you did read *The Pumpkin Plan* and *Surge*, right?), and is the key for colossal profitable growth. But it takes time and it won't happen overnight. Cutting expenses is generally a very quick process and is usually very easy. From all the businesses I have met, it is pretty easy for most of them to cut 10 to 20 percent of expenses overnight, such as frivolous costs like unused recurring membership fees, office space that impresses no one, that expensive car that is "justified" because it is an expense, and perhaps even extra staff who aren't helping your cause much. Cutting unnecessary expenses might bring you some psychological pain, but it's a whole lot easier than trying to conjure new sales out of nothing.

Jorge and José run their business based on what they can afford to do today, not what they hope to be able to afford someday. This means that they sometimes have to wait to hire someone or make a high-ticket purchase. "When big expenses showed up," Jorge explained, "we would sit down and ask ourselves, 'Do we really need this?' If we determined it would hurt our profits at the end of the year, we didn't buy it."

Here we have just accounted for at least 3 percent (1 percent in each of the PROFIT, OWNER'S COMP, and TAX accounts) of our income, so we need to cover that by cutting three percent from our expenses. To do that, I need you to print out two things:

1. Your expenses for the last twelve months.
2. Any recurring expenses: rent, subscriptions, Internet access, training, classes, magazines, etc.

Now add up all the expenses and then multiply that number by 10 percent. You must cut costs by 10 percent. Now! No if, ands, or buts!

So why cut by at least 10 percent, when we "only need 3 percent?" Because cutting costs doesn't mean the bills go away overnight. It may take a month or two to pay down balances owed on expenses we eliminate. More important, we need to start building cash reserves because by the start of the next quarter, we are going to move another 3 percent to your PROFIT, OWNER'S COMP, and TAX accounts, and then another 3 percent the quarter after that. So we will be accounting for that money quickly.

You can easily find your first 10 percent in cuts by doing the following:

1. Cancel whatever you don't need to help your business run efficiently and keep your customers happy.
2. Negotiate every remaining expense, except payroll.

I share a lot more about cutting expenses in the coming chapters. You are about to become a frugal (not cheap) entrepreneur. You will learn to use only what you need and not be wasteful. You will pay fairly for what you use, but you will use less. And you are going to *love it.*

TWICE A MONTH: THE TENTH AND TWENTY-FIFTH

Many years ago I explained the Profit First system to my friend Debra Court-right. Debra runs DAC Management, a bookkeeping business. (I'll give you one guess at her middle initial.) Since the day she integrated the Profit First system into her own business, Debra has used it to save one company after another. Actually, she has more than just saved companies; she consistently turns them into cash cows.

When I first taught her how to use Profit First with her clients, I drove down to her office in Fairfield, New Jersey, to spend the day going over all of the advanced strategies. Just an hour into our training day, she had not only mastered the concepts; she was on the phone with one of her clients, helping her set up a PROFIT account.

I always have my mobile office with me (backpack with laptop, other electronic gadgetry, and critical lifesaving essentials, like Milano mint cookies). So while Debra went over the basics with her client, I knocked out a few tasks on my to-do list. I knew I had some bills due, so I went into my online bank account to look at the OPEX account and ensured that all of the disbursements were current. Yep—PROFIT account was up to date. TAX account looked good. OWNER'S COMP account—check. Other advanced accounts we'll discuss later in the book—all good. Now it was time to pay my bills from the OPEX account.

"Why are you paying your bills today?" Debra asked, startling me. I had no idea she was behind me, looking over my shoulder at the screen, and I practically spit out some coffee. If you met Debra, you would never guess that she is a fully trained super ninja. She must be because she has an ability to appear next to you without your noticing, especially when you're on the verge of doing something stupid with your finances.

Confused, I replied, "Um . . . because I have time, and they're due."

Debra said, "Well, that's dumb." (Ninjas don't mince words.)

That's when Debra taught me the tenth and twenty-fifth cash flow rhythm, that is, paying expenses twice a month, on the tenth and the twenty-fifth. And that was the day that process became integral to Profit First. Thanks, Debra! (If that is your real name.)

I implemented the process in my business immediately. I let the bills come in and I deposited income, but that was it. I no longer did accounting when I had time or when someone called to check to see if I'd received an invoice. I got into a rhythm. I did my accounting every tenth and twenty-fifth (or the business day prior if the tenth or twenty-fifth fell on a weekend or holiday).

First, I tallied all the new deposits that had gone in over the last few weeks, and did the Profit First allocations, moving money into each account. Then I tallied up all the bills and put them in the system.

A little bit of magic started to happen. I became less and less reactive about bills. I didn't immediately look at the bank account when I got a big bill and wonder why I'd spent so much, and when I could pay this one off. Instead, I started to feel more in control. By looking at my bills and my deposits two times a month, on the same days each time, I could see a pattern. I noticed that 80 percent of my bills were due at the beginning of the month, and that few were due in the second half. And I saw how my deposits were pretty equally dispersed over the month.

I realized that I had many "small" recurring bills that added up to a lot of money and were unnecessary expenses. I started to see trends, and understand my cash flow. I didn't start to stack bills, paying what I could and then putting the ones I didn't pay back in a stack. I started to manage bills and cancel unnecessary stuff. I started to pay bills on time. Every bill.

Liz Dobrinska, the graphics guru who designed my Web site told me, "I don't know what happened, Mike, but you now pay on time every time. I wish all my customers were like you."

Before I started following Debra's advice, I paid Liz inconsistently. Sometimes I paid the bill the day it arrived. At other times, I sat on it for sixty or ninety days. It wasn't because I was trying to take advantage of her; I was simply in reactionary mode. My method of bookkeeping was not an effective way to understand my cash flow or to keep my critically important vendors happy. The tenth and twenty-fifth rhythm changed all that.

Here's how to get started:

Step One: Deposit all revenue into your INCOME account.

Step Two: Every tenth and twenty-fifth day of the month, transfer the total deposits from the prior two weeks to each of your "small plate" accounts based on your CAPs and add it to any money (if any) that is already in there. For example, let's say you have $10,000 in total deposits for the past two weeks. Based on the following example percentages, here's how you would allocate the $10,000:

INCOME *8855 → This account, which had the $10,000, goes to $0 as all the money gets allocated.

PROFIT 1% (TAP 10%) *8843 → $20 was here + $100 allocated = $120

OWNER'S COMP 5% (TAP 10%) *8833 → $100 was here + $500 = $600

TAX 1% (TAP 15%) *8839 → $20 was here + $100 = $120

OPEX 93% (TAP 65%) *8812 → $1,860 was here + $9,300 = $11,160

Step Three: Transfer the full account balances for both your TAX and PROFIT accounts to the respective accounts at your second (no-temptation) bank.

INCOME *8855 → $0

PROFIT 1% (TAP 10%) *8843 → $120 transferred to PROFIT HOLD account

OWNER'S COMP 5% (TAP 10%) *8833 → $600

TAX 1% (TAP 15%) *8839 → $120 transferred to TAX HOLD account

OPEX 93% (TAP 65%) *8812 → $11,160

Step Four: You have $600 in the OWNER'S COMP account from which to pay yourself. Take only what you have allocated as your biweekly salary, and leave the rest to accumulate. For this example, we'll say your biweekly salary is $500. This would leave $100 in the account.

Before we continue, I know you are looking at these percentages and dollar allocations and thinking, "What the hell?! No one can live on these numbers. All the money is going right out the window." *Exactly!* This system will bring immediate clarity on how much money pours right through your business. Just like a bucket full of holes. We will adjust these percentages soon, and relentlessly over time. But for now, even if it is painful, revel in the clarity (albeit *painful* clarity).

Step Five: With the remaining $11,160 in the OPEX account, pay your bills. For this example, we'll say you have $10,000 in expenses this pay period (which should make you a little sick to the stomach. We are going to cut that down). Leave the remaining $1,160 in the account.

At the completion of this process the accounts would look like this:

INCOME *8855 ➜ $0

PROFIT 1% (TAP 10%)*8843 ➜ $0

OWNER'S COMP 5% (TAP 10%) *8833 ➜ $100

TAX 1% (TAP 15%) *8839 ➜ $0

OPEX 93% (TAP 65%) *8812 ➜ $1,160

And at your no-temptation bank, which received its first-ever deposits, your accounts will look like this:

PROFIT HOLD *99453 ➜ $120

TAX HOLD *9967 ➜ $120

PROFIT HOLD and TAX HOLD accounts are to hold the money that will be accumulating at your second bank. As new deposits come in, you will deposit them in the INCOME account, and on every future tenth and twenty-fifth you will repeat these same five steps.

A big note here: there is a possibility that you will not have enough money in your accounts to pay bills or to pay yourself what you need to make. This should be a major wake-up call. When you don't have enough money to pay your bills, it is your business screaming at the top of its lungs, warning you that you can't afford the bills you are incurring. Or if there isn't enough money to pay your salary adequately, it is your business shouting out that you can't run your business the way you have been running it; otherwise you will continually compromise yourself. Implementing Profit First didn't cause the crisis—it just helped you notice there is one. You are spending more money than your business can support. But don't panic. By using CAPs, you will adjust to the tenth and twenty-fifth rhythm as comfortably as possible. Even if you can't pay everything on those dates, you must get into this rhythm because it will allow you to get a sense of the accumulation and flow of money. As a heart pumps blood rhythmically, forming a heart-beat, the lifeblood of your business, money should flow in a similar rhythm, not in a random, panicky pump here and there whenever you have funds.

QUARTER ONE

Quarterly Distribution

The new quarter has arrived. Yippee! You are about to take your very first-ever quarterly profit distribution check. That's right, baby. Your business is serving *you* now. You are going to take a profit distribution check every quarter. Every ninety days, profit will be shared to you. This is where your Frankenstein monster starts to become a powerful, lovable beast and serves you a fine meal on a silver platter with a perfectly matched California pinot noir. Don't you just want to pinch those chubby monster cheeks?

The profit distribution is an award to the equity owners (you and anyone who invested in the business with money or sweat) for having the courage and risk tolerance to start the business. Don't confuse the profit distribution with Owner's Comp, which is pay for working in the business. Profit is a reward for owning the business. Just as you get a profit distribution when you own shares in a public company, for which you didn't do squat work-wise, so you get a piece of the profit from your own company. Profit is a re-ward for equity owners, and Owner's Comp is the pay for people who are owner operators in the business.

The calendar quarters* of every year are as follows:

Quarter 1—January 1 to March 31

Quarter 2—April 1 to June 30

Quarter 3—July 1 to September 30

Quarter 4—October 1 to December 31

---

* Some businesses elect to establish fiscal quarters that do not coincide with the calendar year. In that case, sync your profit distributions and other quarterly Profit First activity to match your fiscal year. In either case, consult with a Profit First Professional on which quarterly schedule is best for your organization.

On the first day of each new quarter (or the first business day afterward), you will take a profit distribution. Remember, the PROFIT account serves a few purposes:

1. Monetary reward for the equity owners of the business.
2. A metric to measure growth.
3. Cash reserve for emergencies.

Tally the total amount of profit in the account (don't add any quarterly distribution percentages from deposits you received this day, yet) and take 50 percent of the money as profit. The other 50 percent remains in the account, as a reserve.

Regardless of the day you start doing Profit First, take a distribution for the current quarter on the first day of the new quarter. For example, let's say you decide to implement Profit First on August twelfth. You allocate to your multiple accounts from that day forward. Then on October first, or the first day of the new quarter that you do your bookkeeping, you distribute the profit in the PROFIT Account. Whether you start this process on July third or September thirtieth, the next quarter still begins as of October first; so you distribute profits for the prior quarter that day. It doesn't matter when you start doing Profit First; what matters is that you get into a quarterly rhythm.

Welcome to the big leagues. You will now take a distribution every quarter, just as you would from a large public company. These companies announce their quarterly income and then distribute a portion of the profits to shareholders. And that's exactly what you are going to do (see, you are all grown up now). Quarterly is a great rhythm, by the way. It is a long enough time between distributions that you start looking forward to them, anticipating them. But it isn't so frequent that they come to feel like a normal part of your personal income.

Every quarter, you will take 50 percent of what is in the account and leave the other 50 percent alone. For example, let's say you have saved $5,000 in your PROFIT account during the first quarter of implementing Profit First. On the first day of the new quarter, you will take $2,500 as a distribution to the equity owners and leave the other 50 percent intact.

If your company has multiple owners, the distributed profit is divided up based on the percentage owned by each equity owner. According to the above scenario, if you own 60 percent of the company, another partner owns 35 percent, and an angel investor owns 5 percent, the distribution would be $1,500 (for you, the 60 percent owner), $875 (for the 35 percent person) and $125 (for the investor).

The key is this: the profit distribution can *never* go back to the company. You can't use fancy terms like *reinvest, plowback,* or *profit retention.* No term you use will cover up the fact that you are stealing from Peter to pay Paul. Your business needs to run off the money it generates in its operating expenses. The plowback of profit means you aren't operating efficiently enough to run off the operating expenses. And if you give the profit back, you won't experience the very important reward of your company serving you. You'll just be letting the monster loose again. So always take your profit, every quarter, and use it for your own purposes. It's celebration time!

Celebration Time!

When you take your profit distribution, the money is to be used only for one purpose: for your personal benefit. Profit is intended to be your reward for having the guts to invest in your own business. Use it for whatever gives *you* personal joy. Maybe you go out for a nice dinner with your family. Maybe you feel joy in building up a fortress of money in your retirement fund. Maybe you get that awesome new couch you have your eye on. Maybe you go on a dream vacation.

In the five years since Jorge and José started implementing Profit First in their business, they have taken several dream vacations—Bermuda, Europe, Central America, Australia, Newark, New Jersey (What? OK, it's the *Garden* State)—and have gifted those vacations to their loved ones as well. These guys know how to celebrate!

"Before we started using Profit First in our business, we were a little bit lost, and wondered when the business would take off and improve our lifestyle," Jorge told me. "I don't think anyone wants to work just for the paycheck. You need more incentive. Now, at the end of the quarter, we really look forward to planning what we're going to do with the extra money."

Whatever it is, you *must* use your profits on you! Why? Because this is how you turn Frankenstein, that cash-eating monster, into a cash cow that keeps giving to you and supporting you. Every quarter, with every profit you celebrate, you will fall more and more in love with your business.

Pay Uncle Sam

Every quarter, you will also pay your quarterly tax estimates.* Your accountant will probably give you estimates of how much you owe in taxes each quarter; this is when you pay them. You will actually reduce some of the pain you feel when paying estimates because on this very same day each quarter, you also will take that profit for yourself, above and beyond your salary.

One Small Step

Each quarter, you need to evaluate your current percentages and move them closer to your TAPs. You can move any percentage you want to get to your TAPs, but know this—the goal is to never take a step back. I would much rather you take a small step closer to your target profit percentage than take a big leap toward it only to step it back a month later.

If you are adjusting and tweaking your percentages conservatively, I suggest that you account for three percentage points each quarter. Meaning you could move your PROFIT account from 5 percent to 8 percent. Or you could move your TAX account from 11 percent to 12 percent, your PROFIT account from 5 percent to 6 percent, and your OWNER'S COMP account from 23 percent to 24 percent.

If you can adjust further, go for it, by all means. Just remember, you can't "undo your percentages" because that will undermine this new habit you have established. And don't forget, at the start of the next quarter, you will be doing this all over again. Think about what you're doing for a second. You are now distributing profits quarterly, which forces you to find ways to operate more efficiently. Isn't that friggin' cool? Your little company is now

---

* Some business owners, based upon the structure of their company, will have their taxes withdrawn directly from their paycheck. In this case, on a quarterly basis, the business "reimburses" the business owner for the taxes they had automatically withdrawn by transferring the monies in the TAX HOLD account to the owners.

doing the same thing as the big kahunas in the industry. While Bloomberg Radio babbles on about "higher than expected" quarterly profits and shareholder distribution by such-and-such public company, you can smile and feel pity for the public stock shareholders and the measly portions they get because *you* own *a lot* of stock in your company. Oh man, does that feel good.

YEAR ONE

Because you're in the quarterly rhythm of evaluating and moving closer to your Target Allocation Percentages (TAPs), celebrating your profit disbursement and reassessing your expenses, there isn't much of anything special you need to do on a yearly basis. The only thing you need to add to your financial management at year-end is the finalization of your taxes.

Determine how much you owe and how far off you were in your estimates. If you owe more than you have in your TAX account, a few things likely went wrong. You probably didn't save a big enough percentage in your TAX account, and/or you didn't check in quarterly with your accountant to see how you were doing throughout the year with your tax reserve.

If you owe taxes at year-end and don't have the money in your TAX account, this is the one time you can pull from your PROFIT account for a reason other than profit distribution. In fact, you have to. You won't go to jail if you don't have profits to distribute to the owners, but you will go to jail if you don't pay your taxes. (Unless you decide to go on the lam and play catch-me-if-you-can with the IRS, which I do not recommend. Shoot, even Martha Stewart couldn't get away with that). In this instance, pull the money you have from your TAX account and your PROFIT account to pay the taxes. Then adjust percentages in your TAX account to ensure you will have enough for the next year.

When you adjust your Tax percentage, reduce your profit percentage by that amount. Yes, you are taking a hit on profits, but next quarter you will work on getting those profits up again. The key now is to make sure you are fully prepared for taxes.

If you have too much money left in your TAX account, congratulations— you can move that money to your PROFIT account and take a profit distribution. You may also be able to reduce your TAX TAP and increase your profit allocation percentage by that amount. Just check with your financial expert first.

Rainy-Day Fund

As your profits accumulate in your PROFIT account, and you only take 50 percent as a profit distribution, the remainder will act as a rainy-day fund. You sort of become your own bank. This is a good thing, but too much cash on hand can be a liability (sadly, people like to sue deep pockets), and money should be invested, not allowed to sit and stagnate month after month and year after year. This is a simple analysis of what to do with your rainy-day fund.

Remember a little while ago, when I mentioned the ideal three-month cash reserve for your business, the place where you have enough cash saved to operate your business unscathed for three months if all sales came to a screeching halt and not another penny came into the business? Well, the PROFIT account is where this reserve accumulates, just for that circumstance. If you see that the money in it is in excess of a three-month reserve, you know this is a good opportunity to put money back into the business, to make some appropriate capital investments that will bring a lot more growth and a lot more profit, or to fund the VAULT account (that's a little teaser for what you will be learning in a little bit).

PROFIT FIRST IS A WAY OF LIFE

Jorge and José are living the American dream. Just ask them—they'll tell you they are most definitely living the life they set out to experience when they first opened the doors of Specialized ECU Repair. If you follow the steps outlined in this book, you, too, will look back on your first Profit First year with awe and appreciation.

As I was wrapping up my call with Jorge the other day, I asked, "Do you think you'll ever outgrow the system?"

There was a pause. (Pretty sure it was the pregnant kind.) And then Jorge said in a raised voice, "What are you talking about? No. Why? Profit First is a way of life. For all of life."

A way of life. I love that.

"After you get your idea for a business, Profit First should be the very next thing you do. You have an idea, you fall in love with it, but at the end of the day, you have to survive. You have to at least meet your expectations of what kind of life you want to live."

Well said, Jorge. I love you more than you would probably find comfortable. When you hit that million-dollar revenue mark, I'm flying down with my wife, Krista, to go kitesurfing with you and to throw back some killer margaritas in José's gorgeous kitchen, which he renovated with his profit distribution.

TAKE ACTION: GET READY FOR A GREAT YEAR!

Step 1: Start a "celebration list": Come up with ideas for how to spend your quarterly owner's distribution. Include small treats and big indulgences. Post the list where you can see it, for inspiration and motivation; and as a reminder when the quarter comes around and you convince yourself there are more practical uses for the money. If one of those treats is a trip to meet up with me at an event and tell me your Profit First success story, that would be pretty cool. But if it's flying me down to see you so we can go kitesurfing together, that would be really, *really* cool.

Step 2: Block out the tenth and twenty-fifth on your calendar into perpetuity. You will need about five minutes to do the core process of checking the balances of your foundational five accounts to see where you stand, do the allocation of funds, and to transfer PROFIT and TAX to the no-temptation accounts. If you have a bookkeeper, she can do the other elements like pay bills, reconcile accounts, and applaud you for being a profit-making machine.

Chapter 7

―――

DESTROY YOUR DEBT

YOU CAN'T CRASH-DIET YOUR WAY OUT OF DEBT

Well-dressed poverty is still poverty. Just because your business is making lots of money doesn't mean you're hanging on to it. Too many entrepreneurs believe the top line is what defines success, and then they behave accordingly. Another big client comes on board, and the entrepreneur expands the office. A big sale rolls in, and with it a fancy dinner. It's like putting Frankenstein's monster in a tuxedo and having it dance and sing to "Puttin' on the Ritz" (shout-out to Mel Brooks). The monster may look like it has its act together, but it doesn't. One tiny bit of faulty wiring—as when the big client decides not to pay his bills—and the monster goes on a rampage, and everything falls apart.

As I was writing the first version of *Profit First*, my cell phone rang with a call from my friend Pete. I was expecting the call—we had plans to have dinner in New York City that weekend, and because Pete is a resident of the Big Apple he knows all the hot spots. I figured he was calling to confirm plans. The call was not what I expected.

"I'm sorry, Mike, I can't do dinner this weekend," Pete said, his voice strained.

"Damn, that sucks. I was really looking forward to it. But no problem, brother. Let's reschedule," I said, looking at my calendar. "What's going on? Heading out of town?"

"Yeah, kinda. Well, not really," Pete replied. Then he sighed and said, "I, uh . . . I'm broke, Mike. I'm broke."

Pete explained that his bank had called his line. If you aren't familiar with this experience, here's how it works: you get a revolving line of credit from the bank. It's a bank account that functions like a credit card, in that you can draw as much money from it as you want, up to your credit limit, and pay it back over time. As long as you pay your interest and make your minimum percentage payment every month, you're good.

Except there's this pesky little rule in the fine print that says the bank can call back the entire loan at any time. Even if you've paid your monthly percentage on time every month, even if you're not carrying a high balance, the bank can yank your line of credit without warning. And once the bank notifies you that they're calling your line, you have just thirty days to pay back every single penny.

Pete got the call. His line? A million bucks. The amount he had drawn from the line? *A million bucks.* The amount in his company's cash reserves that he could tap into? Zero. Needless to say, dinner in Manhattan was off.

Struggling to get the words out, Pete said, "Mike, can you help me? I'll follow your lead. I'll do anything. If you told me to run naked in the streets, I'd do it."

Of course I agreed to help him find a way to dig himself out of this massive debt. A naked romp through the streets of New York might get him some attention and give me enough razzing fodder for years to come, but it surely wouldn't address his debt (especially not with the fines for lewd and lascivious behavior). So we spent two hours on the phone that night, going over Profit First in detail.

At first Pete was confused—why was I talking about profit when he was so far in the hole? You may be feeling this way, too. I get it. It's awfully hard to think about profit, let alone plan for it, when your situation is as dire as Pete's. You may not have a million dollars in debt, but I'll bet that whatever debt you're carrying feels at times as if it might as well be a million dollars.

This is the ultimate survival moment. If you focus all of your energy on paying down debt, that is all you will ever achieve. You'll still be caught in the trap of top line thinking, which will likely result in more debt.

We can trace almost every major change to a pivotal moment when the pain of staying a certain way is greater than the effort to make aware-ness of it go away. Call it a turning point or a wake-up call, the choice is the same. Will you fix the crisis or the root of the problem?

When life "calls the line," we take action. The problem is, most of the time the action we take is a reaction, a narrow, driving focus on the alleviation of immediate pain. We move heaven and earth to bail ourselves out of a jam with little thought of creating permanent change. Why do so many people who have lost weight gain it all back (and then some)? Because as soon as they reach their goal, they revert to old habits. Sure, people don't want to drink a gallon of water and eat grapefruit every morning for the rest of their lives, or spend so much time with the ThighMaster that they're going steady with it. The pain of being fat is gone—what's the point of taking another SoulCycle class?

Once the pain is gone, the action we decided to take in that pivotal moment falls away. Grapefruit is replaced with grape jelly beans. Water turns to soda. And the ThighMaster is tossed into the basement where all good intentions go to die. Is it any wonder that when the weight comes back, it's with a vengeance? After all, your mind now knows you can lose weight in a pinch. Who cares if you gain a few pounds? You can always crash-diet again, right? Try out for *The Biggest Loser*? And of course there's always "the surgery."

What my friend Pete intended to do was the same deal, different crisis. He had had the equivalent of a financial heart attack. As soon as his big moment hit, he became a man on a mission—crush that debt immediately! His actions (or reactions) were the equivalent of a crash diet. He wasn't giving any thought to how to make his business *permanently* healthy.

If Pete manages to survive this crisis in crash-diet mode, what are the chances he will find himself in a similar situation—or worse—a few months or years from now? The chances are high—so high I would say it's a sure bet.

Even when you and your business are in debt up to your eyeballs, you must establish a habit of putting your profit first. You must still (and always) pay yourself first. When you get into the habit of fiscal health based on this system, you will fix the problem permanently. Financial crises will be a thing of the past, because if someone calls your line, you'll have the cash to cover it.

Here is what I told Pete: "If you have debt, be it one thousand, one million or somewhere in between, you need to kill that debt once and for all while still slowly and methodically building profit."

The Profit First system I'm teaching you will keep your focus on a super healthy business, working in your sweet spot to produce goods and provide services for ideal clients. This laser focus will automatically keep your costs down, allowing you to pay off debt faster and eventually increase your Profit percentage. The tweak is, when you distribute profits, 99 percent of the money goes to paying down debt. The remaining 1 percent goes toward rewarding yourself. This way, the debt gets hit just as aggressively, but you still strengthen your Profit First habit.

In short, if you wait to implement Profit First until after you pay down your debt, you are less likely to ever build the business efficiencies that will permanently eradicate your debt and create a perpetual profit stream. Start the habit now, and eventually that 99 percent will go toward building up your cash reserves and your own owner distribution.

ENJOY SAVING MORE THAN YOU ENJOY SPENDING

I was channel surfing one Sunday morning when I saw Suze Orman explaining personal financial strategy to a group of about fifty people. In the middle of her lecture, she stopped, looked around the room, and said, "The solution to debt is this simple: If you want to get out of debt, you must get more enjoyment out of saving your money than you do spending your money."

These words turned a lightbulb on in my head. I put down my coffee and stared out the window. Suze continued to speak, but I was so caught up in my aha moment, I heard nothing. I just kept repeating what she'd said about saving versus spending over and over in my head. *That's it*, I thought. Wealth is a game of emotion. Business success is a game of emotion. Profit First is a game of emotion. It all comes down to the story we tell ourselves about what we're doing. "Is what I'm doing making me happy or not?"

When something makes you happy in the moment, you'll keep doing it. If spending makes you happy, you'll spend more. And that spending could be on anything from a new pair of pants to a new hire to new mountains of debt. If saving makes you happy, you'll look for any opportunity to save more. Coupons, sales, bargain bins—heaven. Saving 100 percent because you eliminated the expense entirely? Nirvana!

Listening to Suze that day, the whole "pain and pleasure" motivation that Anthony Robbins has talked about for years finally made sense to me.

The pain moment is the kick in the ass, when you finally say enough is enough. Pain gives you a big shove out the door. For me, the pain moment was my daughter sliding her piggy bank toward me, trying to save our family from absolute financial ruin. For Pete, it was a call from the bank. But pain just gets you to take enough action to get out of immediate pain. Then it stops working. Suze was teaching me the other half: pleasure. (Don't do it. Don't let your mind go there. And . . . there it went. Pervert.)

The premise is simple—we avoid pain and move toward pleasure, putting a significant emphasis on the moment and very little emphasis on the long term. Immediate pain gets the ball rolling, but pleasure keeps it moving. You probably picked up this book because of pain, and you will likely see results quickly because your efforts will reduce the pain. But the only way you will be able to make this work forever is if you get immediate pleasure each time you exercise your new habits. Just as at the gym, the pain of seeing your muffin top in the mirror will only motivate you to work out so much before you decide it isn't worth the effort. The only way to turn it into a sustained habit is to start enjoying your workouts.

Give yourself more joy when you choose *not* to spend money than you do when you choose to spend it. Give yourself more joy when your bottom line grows (not just the top line). Give yourself tons of joy when your profit percentage grows.

When you opt not to spend money, acknowledge it. Give yourself a pat on the back. Do a happy dance. Celebrate every time you save—whether it's ten bucks or ten thousand. Put on your favorite music and crank it, get really happy. Embarrass your kids at the mall. Heck, embarrass yourself. Over time you will train your mind to equate happiness and celebration with choosing to save money over spending it.

PREPARING FOR YOUR WORST MONTH

We entrepreneurs are an optimistic bunch. We have to be. It takes a lot of courage, and more than one pair of rose-colored glasses, to do what we do. That optimism serves us until, well, it doesn't. The trap we fall into is believing our most recent best month is our new normal. Then we start running the business according to that "normal." When the next month, or the month after, we come up short, things drop and we are caught off guard.

To prevent shortsighted behavior but stay optimistic, always look at your twelve-month rolling average income (and related numbers). When comparing figures, compare your current month to the same month in the prior year. Comparisons and rolling averages will give you a much clearer picture of where you truly stand.

Until your best month becomes your average month, it's not the norm; it's the exception. When you base decisions on your best revenue month, you will run out of cash—quickly. Debt will start to pile up. And you will go back to your old standby, "Sell more—grow, grow, grow!" Acting as if your best month is the norm is one surefire way to keep yourself locked in the Survival Trap.

In fact, accountants have an inside joke about this. I had a call with Andrew Hill and Gary Nunn, the founders of Solutions Tax & Bookkeeping in Frisco, Texas, about the spending habits of entrepreneurs, and they told me an accountant's inside joke. Whenever a client approaches them about a windfall of new money, the client will inevitably say, "I don't even know how I would ever spend all this money."

Each time, Andrew and Gary have the same response: "Oh, you'll find a way. And you'll probably figure it out within the next month."

Maybe that insider's joke isn't ROTFLMAO (Rolling on the Floor, Laughing My Ass Off) funny to you, but it is to Andrew and Gary. They hear the same comments from entrepreneurs all the time, and in every case, by the next month, the money is gone.

That's why percentages are such a valuable tool. As an entrepreneur, your income varies. Some months are great; some months suck, and most are average. But it is typical behavior for entrepreneurs to look at their best month and tell themselves, "This is my new normal"—and then start spending and taking from the business accordingly.

Percentages are based on real results—the cash in the bank. No games, no hypotheticals, no "We'll make it up next month." Projections are an opinion. Cash is a fact.

The percentages put a varying sum of money into your different accounts, such as OWNER'S COMP, every tenth and twenty-fifth; and then you draw your owner's salary from that account based on the pay you allotted. If you have more money in the account than you take in salary, the difference in money stays, and accumulates. This way, when (notice I didn't say *if*) a slow month happens, money has accumulated in your OWNER'S COMP account and your salary stays consistent. If the money in the OWNER'S COMP account is not enough to pay your salary, you can't take it. You need to make a hard decision about cutting other costs, and you'd better kick ass on growing the top line with great clients, too.

So how do you predict the owner salary your company will likely support? Look at your slowest three months and average them out. That is the lowest your revenue will likely ever go. Then determine the percentage of this income that will be allocated to Owner's Comp (35 percent, for example, times the average monthly revenue for the three worst months). Every quarter we will do a salary raise based upon how much money is in the salary account and whether it is accumulating faster than we are withdrawing it. Take the bump that you can reasonably take based upon your twelve-month rolling average. As long as the account accumulates more cash or stays even, you are taking a healthy salary (one that your company can healthily support).

THE DEBT FREEZE

I've taught you how to ensure your business is profitable immediately—from your very next deposit. Now I'm going to teach you how to immediately stop accumulating debt, and to destroy the debt you currently have. I call the method you are about to learn a Debt Freeze. It will guide your business through a rapid pay down of accumulated debt and a freeze of new debt, all while continuing your Profit First habit.

Now, don't panic. I'm not asking you to sell everything and move into a van down by the river. I'm not even asking you to stop spending entirely. That can irreparably damage your business. I am simply asking you to commit to a spending freeze that will free you from debilitating debt.

The goal here is to cut cost, not to compromise the business. You can fire all your people, shut down your Web site, refuse to pay a penny to anyone, and, seriously, move into a van down by the river with your new roommate, and struggling motivational speaker, Matt Foley . . . but you'll be out of business. You want to cut the fat out of your business, the stuff that is not generating or supporting income for your company. But you don't want to cut out the muscle, the stuff that you absolutely must do to deliver your product or service.

For those of us who get happy when we save, the Debt Freeze is a rave party. Here are the steps to getting your party started. You will need just a pen:

Print and Mark Up Docs

1. Print out your current income statement for the last twelve months, as well as your current accounts payable report, your credit card statements, loan statements, and any other statements related to debt, and your last twelve months of payments made from any of your business bank accounts. If you do not have an income statement ready, just gather the other documents.

2. Go line by line through each expense (past and present), even if you are not incurring the expense anymore, and with the pen, mark the expense with a P for any expense that directly generates (P)rofit; R for any expense that while necessary, can be (R)eplaced with a less expensive alternative; or U for any expense that is (U)nnecessary for delivering your offering.

3. Review every expense, including salaries, commissions and bonuses for employees, rent for the office, equipment, health care, raw goods, your office Spotify subscription. *Everything.* If money goes out of the business, we need to categorize it as a P, R, or U. I realize these things can get very subjective, so slant toward sharpening the pencil. Also, consider outside help to get you through this process.*

4. Now circle any expense that is recurring (even if it happens to be in a different amount), meaning it will happen again at least once in the next year or more frequently, such as monthly or weekly. As an FYI, this is why we categorized all of your expenses, including ones that you haven't incurred in a while; they are indicators of what may be coming down the pike.

---

* Hint: A Profit First Professional.

Now Let's Do Some Math

1. Add up all the expenses for the year. This includes everything you labeled and/or circled. Exclude any tax payments and owner's distributions or salaries. Now divide that number by twelve to determine your monthly "nut"—the total amount you have decided you need to cover each month.

2. Determine the difference between your current monthly operating expenses and the number it *must* be according to your Instant Assessment. For example, if you currently have $52,000 in average monthly expenses and your Instant Assessment has your monthly expenses at $30,000, you need to cut your operating expenses by $22,000. There will be no justifying past spending mistakes, no saying, "But I need everything." You don't. Your healthy, booming competitor has figured it out. You need to put on your big-girl panties and accept that you spent too much, and today is the day we fix it. (Kinda creepy that I know *you* wear big-girl panties, isn't it?)

3. Band-Aids come off more easily when you tear them off. Work a plan to cut expenses until you are operating at 10 percent below the target number on your Operating Expenses TAPs in the Instant Assessment. Start by cutting the U expenses first. Then find ways to reduce the R expenses with replacements or alternatives. And evaluate the P expenses to see if you can structure the expense more favorably.

But why work a plan to cut an extra 10 percent beyond our Operating Expenses TAP? Because when you cut expenses, you may realize that something has a negative effect on your business, and you can't replace it with a timely alternative. You may need to take back a few expenses. I call this expense "bounce-back." It happens—we just need to prepare for it.

Build a Leaner Team

Labor costs are typically the most expensive part of operating any business. Your labor costs, when totaled, may get a P expense rating. Of course you need some of those people, but probably not all. So evaluate your labor costs on an individual basis and separate the P's from the R's and U's.

If your company is racking up debt, it is all too often because labor cost is too high. The problem with cutting labor costs is, our minds quickly come to defend and justify why people should stay: I own the company, I can't do the work; I need to direct my team to do the work. Plus, they need a job (which is true); they are integral to the company (probably also true); the company will tank without them (super unlikely); and if I get rid of them, I won't have people to do the work (hardly ever true).

Overstaffed entrepreneurs have either tried to get themselves out of doing work as quickly as possible (they like to think they are managers now, or better yet, they need to spend extraordinary amounts of time on the corporate "vision"), or they believe that systems aren't core to a business (which they are). You need to let go of people. And you have to realize that switching from working *in* the business to on the business is not like flipping a light switch. It is gradual. Often the most underutilized employee in an overstaffed company is you, the owner. It's time you got back to actually doing the work, and in the future we will slowly transition you from *in* to *on*.

Now, back to your overstaffed company. Evaluate each person and determine if her role is mandatory for operations to continue (not the person, but the role). If a person wears multiple hats (for example, is your receptionist also the in-house salesperson?), ask yourself whether each role is mandatory for operations to continue.

Next, evaluate your staff members. If they aren't a P rating, they need either to be moved within your business to help it become more profitable, or they may need to be removed from the company. Now it is time to plan the layoffs. Before I get into this, I want you to know that I know how devastating this is. I know how much you will want to resist ever doing this, because I did. There was a day when I had to lay off ten people out of my twenty-five-employee company. It was the most difficult day of my professional life. I had to lay off nearly half my staff, not because they did anything wrong, but because *I did*—I mismanaged the numbers; I hired quickly and often and unnecessarily.

I also want you to know that no matter how devastating this is, laying off people is necessary. Trying to keep a few employees your company cannot afford will only put it under, thereby ensuring that *all* the employees lose their jobs. And because you prioritize the layoff of poorly performing staff and people who fill roles that are not a core need for your company, you are not just saving the cost of keeping these people on; you are also building a more efficient infrastructure.

Keep in mind that in letting these people go, you are freeing them to find jobs that are a better fit. Yes, it sucks that you need to fire the people you hired on good faith, but it would be worse if you kept them in a dead-end job. I know this firsthand. Just this morning I looked up the LinkedIn profiles of the ten people I had to lay off that terrible day. All of them have better jobs now.

When you do layoffs, choose a second person (perhaps your business partner; your HR director; or if you don't have anyone in-house, bring in your attorney—this is one of the few costs you do want to incur*) to witness the layoffs and help you explain the situation in your meeting with each employee. With the approval of your attorney, (1) explain the reason for the layoff to your employee, and (2) provide support that you can afford, such as circulating his résumé or even providing some severance.

Once each person is laid off, call a staff meeting with all your remaining employees. Share what you have done, and why you did it. Explain how difficult it was to have to do it, and that you take responsibility for both the financial problem you got the company into and for fixing it. Assure your team that everyone remaining is there to stay, and that you have taken action to immediately stabilize the company.

Absolutely do not ask people to take a pay cut. I did this with dire consequences. Asking all your people to continue to work just as hard or harder than ever for less money is worse for the emotional welfare of your company than letting just one more person go. When I did this, it disheartened the entire team. Nearly half of my remaining employees started looking for a new job with a more stable company. All of a sudden there were a lot of sick days, and one of my key remaining guys decided to take a job elsewhere.

---

* For a list of lawyers who are also Profit First Professionals, go to ProfitFirstProfessionals .com and click the FIND button.

Time for More Cuts

Now the hardest part is over, call your bank to stop all automatic withdrawals from all of your accounts, except for any expenses you have labeled with a P. Then notify your vendors that you are stopping the withdrawals and will pay by check going forward. I am not suggesting in any way that you should not pay what you owe or break a commitment. I simply want you to be acutely aware of every payment you make.

Call each of your credit card companies and ask that you be issued a new card with a new number. Tell the credit card company that no payments that were being processed on your old card should transfer to your new one. (Many credit card companies do this for you as a convenience, and this is a convenience that you do not want.) You need to do this because your cards have been compromised—by you. This step will stop automatic charges. Then, just as you did in the previous step, notify each vendor that you are moving off automatic charges. It is a simple and effective way to catch any expense you may have missed when labeling the P, R, and U.

Those recurring fees can be insidious. I got trapped in a recurring gym membership fee. I would see it on my credit card, and because it was "only twenty-nine dollars" a month, I let it go. I wasn't going to the gym anymore, but I told myself, "I'll keep the charge because I'll go to the gym sometime this month."

Then one day my credit card was replaced because of suspicious activity. (Maybe my credit card company was suspicious about how I could be a gym member for so long *and* such a regular McDonald's customer). The day the card was canceled, the membership payment for the gym stopped.

But the story doesn't end here. This is when I realized I wasn't working out nearly enough, so I called some friends and started exercising with them. One of them has a membership at the same gym and can bring a free guest once a week. Guess who goes with him? I am averaging fifty-plus workouts per year at the same gym now, at no cost. And he is working out more, too, because he has a motivated workout partner.

The point is this: cutting costs is something that is very easy to put off for another day. It's the mañana syndrome—I'll get to it tomorrow. And for me (and you, too, I suspect) those days of putting things off pile up to a year or more very quickly. You will be unable to put off cutting costs anymore simply by getting your credit cards reissued.

Here's what *can* wait for one more day: that purchase you were planning to make today. Remember the story about how I lost my first fortune by becoming the Angel of Death? You might remember that in the end, all but one of the companies I invested in went belly up. The lone survivor was Hedgehog Leatherworks. The owner, Paul Scheiter, is an amazing guy. I consider him my best friend.

A few years ago, on one of my trips to visit him down in St. Louis, Missouri, we drove by a Home Depot on the way to his leather shop. As we passed it, Paul said, "Oh, I need to get some electrical stuff for the office." Then he smiled and kept driving.

"Why don't we pick it up?" I asked.

"I will," he replied. "In just one more day."

The next day we drove by the same Home Depot. Paul looked at the sign, grinned from ear to ear, then looked away and drove on. I said, "Don't we need the electrical supplies?"

"Absolutely we do. Just one more day."

This pattern went on for the entire week. At the end of my visit, as Paul drove me to the airport, I asked him why he hadn't yet bought the electrical supplies he needed. That's when he shared his "just one more day" technique.

When Paul needs to purchase something, he challenges himself to go just one more day without the item. Every time he passes up an opportunity to buy whatever he needs, he gets pumped. He gets a high from going without for one more day.

Sometimes, while playing this game, Paul discovers that he no longer needs the product or service he intended to buy. Playing the game opens up other possibilities and truly tests how badly you need something. Sometimes you can't get around it—you have to spend money on something because you actually need it. But by waiting "just one more day," you are not only keeping operating cash in your account for one more day; you are giving yourself another day to come up with alternatives.

1. Cut any U expense listed. If you doubt whether you can really cut it, cut it. An expense is always easy to add back. For the R expenses,

it is time to negotiate. When something can be (R)eplaced, it puts you in a position of negotiating strength. And everything is up for negotiation—your rent, your credit card rates and debt, your vendors' bills, your software license, your Internet bill, your weight, your height, your age, everything. Your job now is to contact every vendor and get your costs reduced in the most significant way possible without hurting the relationship. But don't just call, do some research first. Find alternative, less expensive providers and be prepared to go to the alternatives.

2. Start by negotiating the small, necessary expenses. You want to build your negotiation muscle.* Build your way up to the bigger expenses. Negotiation is a whole topic of its own, but for now, realize that being a hard-ass isn't always the most effective approach. Being informed, firm, and willing to concede so both sides win is the best method. The goal is to get the same results at a lower cost. It doesn't mean that you need to stick with what you have and get it more cheaply; you can also find alternatives—perhaps a different thing, more cheaply. For example, some hotels charge for Internet in the room and others don't. If you can't get a hotel to remove or reduce the in-room Internet charge, get the lobby password and work there.

3. For every expense you are able to permanently drop, put a squiggly line through it. For every expense that you reduce, put a straight line through it. Now add up the total savings to see if you got to your number. Remember the goal is 10 percent less than the Operating Expense TAP. If you are not there yet fully, that is OK. We'll be back. For now, job done. And if you made it to your target expense reduction without going on a bender, I say job *well* done. Breathe for a few moments. Feel the stress of overwhelming expenses leaving you. This was a hard day, but by completing it, you have staged yourself for major profits.

---

* To build your negotiating muscle, start by negotiating the small (R)eplaceable expenses first. Build your way up to the bigger expenses. Negotiation is a whole topic of its own, and I suggest you read *Getting to Yes* by Roger Fisher, William Ury, and Bruce Patton. That is, until I write a book on the subject, then I'll suggest that one.

Now you're ready to grow your business in an efficient way.

Cutting costs is embarrassing. You have a reputation. You always pay for dinner or drive the nice car. You are the "nice" boss who throws pizza parties and gives sweet holiday bonuses. Let me assure you, the relief you feel once you complete the Debt Freeze is way more powerful than the embarrassment you fear.

No matter how much debt you have, know there is a way out. More than that, know that you are not the first person to be there. Many people have recovered from dire financial situations, and the key to doing that is in your hands.

The new definition of success is not about the most revenue, employees, and office space but the most profit, generated through the fewest employees and with the least expensive office space. Make the game of winning based upon efficiency, frugality, and innovation, not on size, flair, and looks. We are on a mission to change the perspective of successful business from "make a lot" to "save a lot." We are on a mission to eradicate entrepreneurial poverty, and to achieve that, a Debt Freeze is always in order.

IF YOU OWE THE BANK A MILLION DOLLARS

There is a saying in the banking industry: "If you owe the bank a thousand dollars, it's your problem. If you owe the bank a million dollars, it's their problem." Remember Pete? After our call, he started a PROFIT account, cut expenses like mad, and then called the bank. Almost everything is negotiable, and when you owe a bank a million bucks and don't have it, they'll listen to your ideas. Pete worked out a very doable payment plan, and within three months had already whacked out 5 percent of the debt and turned a profit. And he joined an accountability group. Mine. We have been keeping each other in check for many years now, and while I am vowed to confidentiality about Pete's progress, let me just say this: it's been massive. Pete was, understandably, a quivering wreck when he called me that night many years ago. Today he is the epitome of confidence. And Pete did it by implementing the power of small actions, a series of consistent small steps bringing about big results.

Pete is far from the only one who was able to pay down a million-dollar debt using Profit First principles. As I was finishing the revision of this book, I received a letter from Jesse Cole, owner of the Savannah Bananas, a Minor League Baseball team. Jesse included his baseball card; in the picture he was wearing a bright banana-yellow suit. I was psyched. Jesse is clearly my people.

Jesse's note explained that he'd read *Profit First* a year ago, and following the system he has taken his franchise to a new level. Because I had only four days left before my book was due to my publisher, I called Jesse for an interview. I had to include his story in my book. Profit First saved a baseball team? That's more than a big deal. I mean, I'm puffed out with pride right now just thinking about it.

As the owner of two teams, the Savannah Bananas and the Gastonia Grizzlies, Jesse had revitalized them by shifting their focus to entertainment. While most of the considerably older team owners work on building better baseball teams, Jesse changed the goals so that the team was not just playing baseball; they were also entertaining the fans. He brought in a choreographer to teach the players dances to perform on the field in between innings. He set up granny beauty pageants, and brought in interesting food, including every variation you could think of for fried, baked, boiled, smashed, sliced, and diced bananas. Within months the franchise went from filling maybe two hundred seats to selling out four thousand seats.

At this point, Jesse and his wife opted to get out from under more than a million dollars in debt, which they had accrued over a mere two years.

"We thought about our quality of life, the stress we were under, the fact that we got only a couple of hours of sleep a night, and decided we would use the Profit First system to get rid of our debt," Jesse explained. "It worked. We've paid down a huge chunk of it, and within two years we will have paid $1.3 million dollars to the previous owners of the Grizzlies and the Bananas. We'll be 100 percent debt free."

Now, I want to stop right now and make a strong argument for choosing profitability even when you have debt. In fact, when you have debt, you need to be more profitable than ever. Some people say they can't be profitable until they are out of debt, but that's not true. The only way to get out of debt is by being profitable. Debt accumulates because you have more expenses than cash to pay for them, so you borrow. You get a loan, a line of credit, a stack of shiny plastic credit cards. And yet the only way to have more money than you are currently spending is to be profitable.

To be clear, Jesse and his wife run two profitable baseball franchises. The distinction here is that they are using their profit distribution to eradicate debt. They are not spending out of their means. In fact, they are reaping perhaps the biggest benefit of Profit First—innovation by necessity. For example, most ball clubs automatically purchase a ticketing system that runs around $30,000 for the season, plus kickbacks to the company for every ticket sold. Though they had the money to follow the status quo, they are Profit First entrepreneurs, and they knew they had to find an alternative to the pricey ticketing system.

"We ended up buying a hundred thousand printed tickets shaped like bananas for six thousand dollars," Jesse said. "It was easy, it's on brand, and it cost a fraction of the other system." The tickets serve another purpose— they are souvenirs. The ultimate in innovation is to extract more benefit from less-expensive resources.

For every expense, Jesse asks himself whether it fits with who they are as a brand—entertainment over baseball—and whether he absolutely needs it. If he does need it, he finds a way to trade for it, or he gets it at a deep discount.

Jesse's success is outstanding—through his innovation and ingenuity he rescued two struggling baseball franchises. If like Jesse, debt reduction is your main deal right now, then at least take a small portion of the profits for yourself. Most of the profit distribution will go to crush debt, but a small portion (1 percent) will go to reward you. Perhaps a delicious banana split.

LEAST EFFORT, BIGGEST RESULTS

You, too, must utilize the power of small actions. What is the biggest bang for the buck with the least effort? When it comes to fixing things, we need to build emotional momentum. Similar to going to the gym. If you go back to the gym for the first time in ten years and work out like a mad dog, you may feel great that first day; but within a day or two, you will be so sore and in so much pain, you will likely never go to the gym again. Momentum rarely occurs after one crazy effort. Momentum builds slowly but relentlessly. Small, repetitive, continuous actions, chained together, build momentous momentum (say that one ten times fast).

In his extraordinary book, *The Total Money Makeover*, Dave Ramsey explains the Debt Snowball. It's contrary to logic, but it plays exactly into the psyche of all of us human beings. Ramsey tells us that logic would say to pay off our debts with the highest interest rates first, but that doesn't build emotional momentum. It is getting to tear up a statement—any statement, because it is fully paid off—that gives you a sense of momentum and gets you charged up to tackle the next one. Ramsey explains that you should sort all your debts from smallest to biggest, regardless of interest rates. Only when two debts are a similar amount should the one with the highest interest rate be paid first.

Ramsey tells us to pay only the minimum on all the debts, except the one at the top of the list—the smallest one. Then put all your financial power into crushing that first debt as fast as possible. Once that first debt is wiped out, then tackle the next one on the list by adding to the minimum payment with the money you were using to pay the first debt. Once the second debt is paid off, go for the next, adding all the money being used to pay the second debt to the minimum of the third. See how the snowball grows? And see how your enthusiasm and excitement about eradicating debt grows? You will get more and more pleasure from not spending than you once did from spending. Suze and Dave would both be so proud of you.

But the trick to Ramsey's method, and Suze's, and mine (and anyone with one iota of sanity) is this: you cannot add new debt as you pay off old. That is just shifting money around, paying down one debt while building another. You need to get your Debt Freeze on first. And then destroy it, once and for all.

TAKE ACTION: DOWN WITH DEBT!

Step 1: Start the Debt Freeze. Stop any recurring payments and kill off anything you don't need. Do whatever it takes to get your "monthly nut" down to 10 percent lower than your Instant Assessment suggests it should be.

Step 2: Use 99 percent of your profit allocation toward wiping out your debt. With that remaining 1 percent, you still need to celebrate. I know it doesn't amount to much, but you can still reward yourself. Even if you are strapped with debt you are eradicating, you still need to celebrate during the process, and a cash profit distribution to you, however small, helps you do that.

Step 3: Start the Debt Snowball. Pay off your smallest outstanding debt first. As you wipe out each bill with recurring payments, use the freed-up payments to tackle the next smallest debt.

Chapter 8

FIND MONEY WITHIN YOUR BUSINESS

Your company has more money than you realize. You just don't know where to find it. *Yet.*

After delivering a keynote on Profit First, I was invited to a dinner with board members of Vistage, an organization for business owners, presidents, and executives; they call themselves the World's Leading Chief Executive Organization. It was a unique situation because instead of standing in front of a few hundred people, speaking for sixty minutes, and then exiting stage left, now I was sitting at a round table for a few hours to address an onslaught of questions about Profit First.

One executive, the only consultant at the table, stated why he believed Profit First wouldn't work. To protect his name, I'll call him Mr. Wrong. He made all of the classic nonsensical arguments. "If you don't have profit already, you can't suddenly start taking it," Mr. Wrong scolded, looking around the table for approval. "Profit has to be the bottom line," he argued. "Start-ups can't hold back on spending if they want to grow." Blah. Blah. Blah. Wrong. Wrong. Wrong. That last myth really annoys me because it is that kind of thinking that prevents business owners not only from benefiting from their hard work and ingenuity, but it also stunts growth.

Then another gentleman—I'll call him Mr. Innovator—had a lightbulb moment and without thinking, blurted out, "Split the truck. Split the truck. Split the truck." Everyone looked at him as if he were a bit off, and then he explained.

He said, "I grew a fifty-million-dollar company by doing my own version of Profit First."

Mr. Innovator explained that his company delivered oil to two primary outlets: businesses that stored hundreds of gallons at a time, like Jiffy Lube, and retail stores that put quart containers on the shelves, like Walmart. They delivered the oil using two types of trucks: a tanker to deliver to the Jiffy Lubes of the world and a shelf truck to deliver to Walmart. Nearly every aspect of their business was duplicated. Two trucks, two drivers, two customer service teams—two of everything.

"The costs were too high. We were barely surviving," he said.

Mr. Innovator knew he had to cut costs in order to achieve his profitability goals. So he challenged himself to cut his costs by at least one third while still servicing the same number of customers. He kept asking himself that bigger, better question: How can we keep doing what we're doing for one third of the cost?

Then one day it hit him. "What if we took a box truck and divided it in half?" he recounted. "One side for a tank and the other side for shelves." Now his company could deliver oil to both the Jiffy Lubes and the Walmarts of the world using one type of truck, operated by one driver. Mr. Innovator put the idea in motion and ended up surpassing his goal, cutting expenses *nearly in half*. This simple shift enabled him to grow his struggling business to a $50 million company with a sweet bottom line.

Mr. Wrong never uttered another peep. And Mr. Innovator picked up the check for the entire table with a smile.

Money is everywhere.* Money can always be found through streamlining and innovation, and that begins with asking the big questions. The impossible questions. The questions no one else would ever dare to ask. No one else but *you.*

IT'S SMARTER TO DIG A WELL THAN MAKE IT RAIN

I have yet to meet an entrepreneur who hasn't wanted to hire a rainmaker, that magical salesperson who, like the companies that say they can give you access to your great-grandmother Sally's unclaimed fortune, will save the day by bringing in big sale after big sale. Never mind the fact that we, the

---

* "Money is everywhere." I didn't believe the statement myself, until I met Becky Blanton. I share her story in *Surge.*

owners and leaders who love our companies and what we do, are the ultimate rainmakers; it is this top line approach to solving a cash flow crisis that holds companies back. Cranking up the sales team in order to make it rain is not going to help your company if you don't have efficiencies in place, because, ultimately, whatever new client revenue you generate will have corresponding costs. And these are likely to go unchecked.

If you want to increase profitability (and you'd better friggin' want to do that), you must first build efficiencies. Focusing solely on increasing sales is like setting up a bunch of rain barrels next to your house and doing some frantic rain dance in a loincloth while ignoring a massive water source beneath your feet.

Take Idaho, for example. Idahoans enjoy an average of seventeen inches of rainfall each year, twenty inches under the national average. Hence, 95 percent of the state's water supply comes from underground. The 135-mile-long Big Lost River collects water from the Rocky Mountains as it winds through Idaho and then just disappears as it goes subterranean. The water from the Big Lost River, the Snake River, and other underground water sources collects in the Snake River Aquifer, which measures 400 miles wide. That is enough water to serve the majority of Idaho's agricultural needs. So that Idaho spud you're munching on is thanks to an underground water supply—not some rain dance Idahoans learned on the Internet (albeit Idahoans know how to get their funk on).

Why should you care about Idaho and its underground lakes? Because 95 percent of your company's profitability is contingent on what goes on beneath the surface (after the sales), not what happens in the sky (the sales themselves). And it is what's going on "underground" that will help you "find" gobs of money.

THE PROFIT SQUEEZE

A few years ago I was asked to keynote the Global Student Entrepreneur Awards in Washington, D.C., where leading collegiate entrepreneurs from all over the world gather and are recognized for their incredible impact. At breakfast on the morning of the event, I ended up sitting next to Greg Crabtree. Greg is the author of *Simple Numbers, Straight Talk, Big Profits!* Greg caught my attention immediately, talking with another gentleman at our table about college football. I inserted myself into their discussion ("Go Hokies!"), and soon enough the conversation drifted to entrepreneurs and profitability. I remember thinking: "Hold on—we are talking about college football *and* profitability. There is a God!"

After Greg recounted some information he shares in his book about how to maximize profitability, I asked, "Is there such a thing as too much profit? Is there a ceiling?"

"You always want to expand profit," Greg replied. "In fact, you must, because there are outside forces that will continually take your profitability away—your competition. As you find ways to increase profitability, or even if you don't, your competition is doing the same. Everyone is trying to become more profitable. And as businesses become more profitable, the competitive pressure sets in and prices drop to attract more customers.

"When you figure out a big leap in profitability, the competition will sniff it out, and it is just a matter of time before they do the same thing. Then someone drops prices to get more clients, and everyone else, including you, has to do the same to stay in business. This is how profits get squeezed."

We've seen the phenomena Greg outlined over and over. Consider flat-panel televisions, for example. They became commercially popular in the early 2000s but were still a luxury item until around 2005, when the cost of big-screen TVs started dropping 25 percent each year. By the end of the decade, vendors had dropped the prices so significantly that it seemed re-tailers were practically giving them away. Then, because manufacturing televisions got easier and easier, profits jumped, but only for a short time. It wasn't long before everyone started dropping prices again to capture demand, to the point where it now seems as though a retailer needs to pay you to take a small or last year's flat-panel model. James Li, the chief exec-utive of Syntax Groups Corporation, maker of the Olevia brand of flat-panel televisions, said of his competitors, "If they go to $3,000, I will go to $2,999."

Profit is a slippery animal. When profit margins are big, usually in ex-cess of 20 percent, people sniff out and almost immediately start to dupli-cate what you're doing, and they look for ways to do it better, faster, and above all, cheaper than your company. I'm not, in any way, saying that you should stop investing in efficiency and thereby (temporarily) increase profit. I'm saying that even if you think you're good with profit, you're not.

The competition will squeeze you eventually, and soon, so keep finding ways to do what you do better, faster, and cheaper. The nice thing is that as you keep your profit allocation percentage consistent, you will automatically be forced to find ways to make it happen. For example, when competition sets in and prices drop, your profit allocation will feel the squeeze, which means it's time to innovate again.

TWO TIMES THE RESULTS WITH HALF THE EFFORT

By now you've figured out that focusing solely on top line thinking (sales, sales, sales!) does not lead to profitability. In fact, more sales, without efficiency, lead to further inefficiency. In other words, more sales make you less profitable. It's a vicious cycle. So you may need to slow down or halt your selling while you look for new efficiencies—before you can focus on sales, you must first nail Efficiency 101. Remember the toothpaste analogy? Think of this process as like switching your regular-size tube of toothpaste for one of those travel-size tubes. How are you going to make it last? Remember, Parkinson's Law is your ally. A full tube of toothpaste can last four weeks, and so can a tube that is nearly empty. It just requires the balance of frugality (using conservatively) and innovation (twisting, turning, and squeezing your ideas) to pull off what no else even considered before.

Efficiency increases your profit margins, or the amount of money you earn as profit on each product or service you offer. Increased profit margins will boost your company's profits without the need for increased sales. And then, when you kick the selling machine back into gear (which we will discuss later), profits will skyrocket. So the method is simple: achieve greater efficiency first, then sell more, then improve efficiencies even more and then sell even more. Over time, speed up the back and forth between efficiency and selling until the two happen simultaneously.

Making your company more efficient is about more than just nixing extra coffee breaks and redlining your expenses. To tap into the river of profit flowing just under the surface of your company, you need to look at efficiency in every aspect of your business. Serving the same types of (great) clients with the same or very similar problems and perfecting your solutions so you can use them consistently to fix their problems are two routes of efficiencies. You want to duplicate your best clients, those who have a consistent need; and in turn, you want to reduce the variety of things you do to the fewest that will best serve your best clients' needs. Think McDonald's. That company is a moneymaking machine because they feed hungry people—who don't care, at least in the moment, about their health as much as their hunger—with a few products: fries, hamburgers, and breaded chicken. The fewest things you can do repetitively to serve a consistent core customer need—this spells efficiency.

I want you to set a massive goal for yourself. Look at every aspect of your business and determine how to get two times the results with half the effort. That's a biggie, so I will say it again:

How do you get two times the results with half the effort?

Effort is financial cost and time cost (your time, your people's time, your software's time, your machine's time). For example, if you own a snow-plowing company and currently plow one parking lot per hour, I would ask you to figure out how to plow two parking lots (two times the results) in thirty minutes (half the time).

Your first thought might be, "Easy for you to say! That's impossible, Mike! You don't know my business! You're nuts!" I'm not offended by criticism, not even from those who spouted off without ever cracking open the book, because I know most naysayers are just scared. Maybe you're scared, too. Maybe you've made personal sacrifices for your business, sacrifices you may no longer be able to justify, because you *will* have time for your family and friends. Maybe you're afraid that doing more in less time will make your role less significant. Maybe you're worried that your customers may not want to pay you as much if it appears you can do more with less.

Whatever the reason, if you believe that it's impossible to increase efficiency in this way, you are trapped in "let the other guy figure it out" mode. The thing is, my friend the other guy *will* figure it out. It's only a matter of time.

If instead you say, "Hmm. . . let me think about that. Let me find a way," you will set your company on the path to skyrocketing profitability. Why? Because innovation occurs in small steps, big leaps, and everywhere in between. To double the results with half the effort is a big goal that forces big thinking, and it brings about small and big progress—all of which goes to the bottom line.

Doing more with fewer resources has had a significant impact on my businesses. I am very active in Hedgehog Leatherworks, and employing Profit First triggered degrees of innovation that I strongly suspect no one else in the leather industry has ever achieved. Removing our ability to buy the traditional expensive equipment used in the leather industry forced us to find new cheaper ways to get the same (and in many cases, better) results. It's amazing what you can pull off when you're scrounging Home Depot, Hobby Lobby, and random junkyards to *make* what you need. (A little duct tape goes a long way, pal.) We invented new systems that achieved better results than industry standards at 1/100th the cost. Because we took Profit First, we made hundreds of innovations—tweaks, hacks, brand-new systems and everything in between—all because *we had to*. My editor begged for details about what we discovered, but because our process is proprietary, I had to leave him hanging. Sorry, Kaushik—don't want you leaving the book industry to start a competing leather business!

Most entrepreneurs focus only on tiny improvements—"How do I do this a couple of minutes faster?" Small questions yield only small answers. You want both the incremental improvements and the landslide discoveries, and you'll find both of those with big questions.

Snowplowing a parking lot five minutes faster is not going to make much of an impact on your bottom line. Neither will skipping your coffee break or just "holding it" when you need to go to the bathroom.

But the more you focus on substantially improving efficiency, such as a snowplow that can move snow twice as fast, the closer you'll get to achieving double the results with half the effort. And you'll discover all the small steps that collectively get you closer to the big win. This gain in efficiency is amplified the more you sell. That is the power of percentages. Because you now plow every parking lot more efficiently, every new account is an opportunity for increased profit.

Remember Mr. Innovator? He asked, "How can I cut costs by one third and still service the same amount of customers?" *Split the truck. Split the truck. Split the truck.*

Here's another truck story: Did you know that United Parcel Service (UPS) trucks almost always take right turns? In 2006, UPS dared to ask the efficiency question about fuel costs. They discovered that the less time UPS drivers spent in left turn lanes, the less fuel they burned waiting at lights and to cross traffic, and the less idle time there was for each driver. UPS is now experiencing a savings of $6 million a year from the change.

The "brown truck" company didn't stop with their first efficiency discovery. Next time you see a driver delivering a package, look at him and try to spot his keys. Let me give you a hint: They are not in his pocket (that's a banana). UPS drivers found that fumbling for their keys in their pockets when they got back into the truck cost them five to ten seconds (or more) every time. UPS figured out that it is more efficient to keep their keys hanging from their pinky fingers. Now, a UPS driver makes a quick flip of his wrist and the keys are in his hand. Multiply that saved five to ten seconds by fifty stops a day and five gazillion drivers and you have a very huge savings indeed.

And they didn't stop there either. UPS also found that they could save millions by washing their trucks once every two days rather than every day. Over time, this gave them huge savings in time, energy, and water—and the trucks looked just as shiny.

Look, it may seem impossible when you first hear my challenge, but if you've never seriously asked yourself, "How can I get two times the results with half the effort?" how do you know that you can't? You might be missing your own no-left-turn, pinky-flip, don't-wash-yourself efficiency miracle and not even realize it.

CHIP AWAY AT EXPENSES

Wesley Rocha didn't take a raise in ten years. The founder of LinkUSystems, a company that provides marketing services, tools, and Web site design for the real estate industry and small businesses, Wesley watched his company grow and his own income remain stagnant. "I didn't understand why it seemed like even though we would make more money, we never had any left over. I felt stressed about finances all the time."

Wesley finished reading *Profit First* in a weekend, and realized quickly that his expenses were way out of control. "I couldn't immediately implement [cutting costs] without grossly damaging projects, or the business. I literally needed all of my employees and 90 percent of everything we had been paying for because were stuck and committed to it," Wesley said. "I was afraid of what could break or go wrong if I implemented Profit First too quickly. So I had to start thinking about how I could eliminate expenses carefully."

Little by little, Wesley started chipping away at his expenses. "Over the past year, unfortunately, I have had to release six employees, but have been able to replace their efforts by eliminating unprofitable products and services, re-creating and optimizing processes and streamlining other portions of the business," Wesley explained. "Now, I am able to determine what expense is allowed [for a project] before we take it on. Otherwise, we have to figure out another solution."

Figure out another solution. Music to my ears. Not, "We have to find more money to cover it." Nope. Time to crack the knuckles and find another way out of the corn maze, because the airlift ain't comin'.

In the first year of implementing Profit First, Wesley was able to double his profits, which allowed him to increase his annual income by approximately 46 percent, between salary and disbursements. "I have been able to set aside money for taxes and use profits to help toward a down payment to buy a house, which before would have been impossible."

There's that word again: impossible. At first, Wesley thought he couldn't possibly cut expenses and continue to serve his clients. And yet, after a year, he was able to do just that, which allowed him to do this other "impossible" thing, something he hadn't been able to do in more than ten years of kicking ass in business: save for a down payment on a house. In every year past, despite growth, he never had any money left over. And yet by cutting expenses and streamlining his systems, he *found* money in his business.

You don't have to slash and burn the moment you put down this book. You can take it slow. Just get started.

FIRE BAD CLIENTS

If you've read *The Pumpkin Plan*, you know that while the book is outwardly marketed as a system to help business leaders grow their companies into industry giants, it's secretly a book about efficiency. Letting go of clients who suck us dry and eat up our profit margins is a way of making space for clients we can serve exceptionally well by doing what we do best and with fewer resources. It is all about improving not only the top line but the bottom line, too.

A study facilitated by the Chicago-based growth-consulting firm Strategex analyzed the revenue, cost, and profit breakdown for a thousand companies. What they found was nothing short of a "duh" moment, as in the "Duh, I already knew this, but I still haven't done anything about it in my own business because I'm a glutton for punishment" type of duh.

Strategex sorted the clients for each company into four sections, in descending order based on revenue. For example, if a company had a hundred clients, the twenty-five clients who generated the most revenue were put in the top quartile, the next twenty-five highest revenue-generating clients in the second quartile, and so on. Strategex found that the top quartile generated 89 percent of the total revenue, while the lowest quartile only accounted for a meager 1 percent of total revenue.

It gets worse. The study found that each group of clients required pretty much the same amount of effort (cost and time). This means that it took the same amount of effort to serve a big-revenue client as it did a client who barely affected revenue at all.

Then came the awkward "gulp" moment. Strategex's profit analysis showed that the top quartile generated 150 percent of a company's profit. The two middle quartiles were effectively break-even, and the bottom quartile, the one that generated 1 percent of the total revenue, resulted in a profit loss of 50 percent! In the end, the profits generated from the top clients are used, in part, to pay for the losses accrued in serving the bottom clients.

I'm sure you know this scenario all too well. Those clients who barely pay you peanuts, yet constantly complain about how much you charge and how you do nothing right; the clients who demand you rework everything you've done for the third time and then never pay you for your work, or never pay you on time—those clients are costing you money. Get rid of them. Fast!

Dumping any client who makes you money (even if it is the worst client in the world) may seem counterintuitive at first. But never forget what I said earlier: All revenue is not the same. If you remove your worst unprofitable clients and the now-unnecessary costs associated with them, you will see a jump in profitability and a reduction in stress, often within a few weeks. Equally important, you will have more time to pursue and clone your best clients. I've lost count of how many readers have shared stories of how both their top line and bottom line improved after they implemented this and other growth strategies I revealed in *The Pumpkin Plan*. I know that sounds like bragging, but it's not. The system isn't some miracle I came up with; it is just simple math.

I know how scary it feels to dump any client when you are scrambling to cover this week's payroll, especially if you fought hard to get that client in the first place. But remember, profit is about the percentages, not a single number. So take it easy on yourself. Start by dumping one rotten little pumpkin in your patch, the one you occasionally fantasize about leaving on a deserted island or shipping off to Mars. The emotional distraction that client caused you and your staff will disappear immediately. The profits you earned from other clients and were spending to keep this bad client on board will now stay in your pocket. And since his special requirements no longer need to be serviced, you have time and headspace to find another, better client—an ideal client, a clone of your very best clients.

CLONE YOUR BEST CLIENTS

Just for a moment, I want you to think of your favorite client: the call you will always take, the person or company you say yes to without hesitation. This is the client who pays you what you're worth, on time, without question. This is the client who trusts you, respects you, and follows instructions. This is the client you love, and who loves you. Now imagine that this client had five identical twin companies that all wanted to work with you. Wouldn't that boost your business? Wouldn't it be easy to serve those clients? Wouldn't it help you keep your bottom line healthy? Now imagine ten clones, or a hundred clones.

For almost any B2B business in the world, landing a hundred clones of its best client would put it at the front of the pack. It would dominate. The same is true for B2C businesses. If just a mere 10 percent of their clients behaved like their number one client, those businesses would rule, too.

Having clients with similar needs and very similar behaviors offers a few magical profit-making benefits:

1. You will become superefficient, because you now serve very few but consistent needs, rather than an excessive array of varying needs.

2. You will love working with your clones, which means you will naturally and automatically provide better service. We cater to the people we care about.

3. Marketing will become automatic. Birds of a feather flock together (for real) and that means your best clients hang out with other business leaders who have the "best client" qualities you're looking for. Your best clients are awesome, remember? You love them and they love you, and that means they will talk you up every chance they get.

Clones of your best clients are the very definition of efficiency, which is why they are like gold. Find them. Nurture them. And then find out where even more best-client clones hang out and cultivate them, too.

THE PARETO OVERLAP

You may be familiar with the Pareto Principle, commonly known as the 80/20 rule. For the history buffs: Vilfredo Federico Damaso Pareto was an Italian economist who studied the distribution of wealth in Italy in the late 1800s. He discovered that 20 percent of the Italian population owned 80 percent of the land. Then he looked at his garden and observed that 20 percent of the peapods contained 80 percent of the peas. Then he looked down at his feet and exclaimed, "OMG, I own five pairs of clogs, yet I wear these superfly boots 80 percent of the time!"

Pareto's Principle also applies to your clients, in that 20 percent of them yield 80 percent of your revenue. It goes further—80 percent of your profit is derived from 20 percent of the products and/or services you offer.

The key to this advanced strategy is to connect the two—your clients and your offering. Some of your top clients buy most of your profitable offerings; some of your top clients go for the offering with the lowest profit margin. Likewise, some of your weakest clients consistently purchase your profitable stuff and some are just weak all the way around, buying the same no-profit stuff over and over again.

Once you see the overlap, the decisions become very easy. Get rid of the "bad" clients who only want your least profitable products and services. You are losing money here, catering to clients or customers who are not a good fit for your company.

Find a new way to manage the weak clients who do buy your most profitable offerings. Often, "bad" clients can become better clients if you meet with them to set new expectations and methods of communication. Meet with your top clients who don't buy profitable offerings, too. Find out how you can deliver profitable stuff to them.

When you focus on Profit First, even when choosing the clients and customers you are willing to work with, you increase your profit dramatically. Not only do you save money by cutting expenses related to serving weak clients, who don't buy profitable offerings; you also free up your time, energy and creativity to focus on the clients you love, who bring in the profit. Applied to your client base, the Pareto Principle is an advanced Profit First technique that does double duty—you save money and gain profit. Gotta love that!

SELL SMART

I've already mentioned Ernie, my lawn guy, briefly, but I want you to know a little more about his story. It speaks to how fast things can go down the "upselling" rabbit hole. In the fall I pay my lawn service to clean up all of the leaves in our yard. A few years ago, Ernie, the owner of the business, knocked on my door. He said, "I noticed that there are leaves in the gutters." He offered to remove them, for a fee. And I, my friends, was what they called an "easy upsell."

Ernie had just expanded his service offering. Easy money! To complete the job, Ernie bought some ladders for his truck. While Ernie was up on the roof, though, he realized he needed a tool to snake out the downspouts. He also spotted more opportunities—damaged shingles, a crack in the chimney, and a soft spot on the roof, a sign of rotting wood. Again he asked if I wanted them fixed; I said yes, and he ran out and picked up some roofing tools, a downspout snake tool, band saws, cement, and brick supplies, and he hired temporary labor. Ernie came back near the end of the day and pushed through to get it finished. He even bought floodlights to keep the work area lit as dusk approached.

At the end of the day, I paid $1,500 for all the work. Not bad for Ernie, considering he gets paid "only" $200 to clean the lawn. But the $1,500 he earned cost Ernie an investment of about $2,000 for tools and supplies that day, plus a lot of driving back and forth and the cost of hiring a laborer.

Ernie lost money on me, but he grew his sales by a lot. Tomorrow he intends to use his new equipment and tools to take care of other clients and will, in theory, earn his money back and then some. The problem is, that rarely happens. As the bills mount, the pressure grows to sell more and more; and you end up working on projects in which you have limited experience and sometimes little interest.

As the variety of things you do increases, you need to buy more tools and equipment and hire more specialized labor. And none of this gets used to its maximum potential because you do many different things, not one thing. Your stuff sits there unused. While you rake lawns, your ladders just lie there. As you fix roofs, the leaf blowers just sit in your truck.

You get stuck in the Survival Trap and end up not doing a very good job at any one thing. For example, when Ernie wrapped up for the day, he said, "I'll be back early tomorrow to clean the lawn again."

Why? Because he threw the leaves from the gutters onto the lawn he had just cleaned, as well as shingles and other things. His additional work required that he actually redo his original work, while all that new gear he bought just sat on his truck, not being used. What's efficient about that? Nada.

Across the street, my neighbors Bill and Liza hire a different guy, Shawn, to clean up their leaves in the fall. He also charges $200. On the same day Ernie worked on my house and earned $1,500, Shawn serviced four more properties and also knocked on the doors at two other properties that, by the look of their lawns, needed his help. I suspect that if Ernie and Shawn had had a beer together that night, Ernie would have boasted about doing one and a half times the sales Shawn pulled in, but Shawn would have ended up paying for the drinks. Shawn has achieved efficiency, and recognizes it as the secret sauce of profitability—getting more of the same things done with better and better results, using fewer and fewer resources.

Selling more is the most difficult way to increase profits, because in the best-case scenarios, the percentages stay the same; and in the worst-case more common scenarios, expenses generated to support sales increase faster, resulting in smaller percentages and a smaller profit margin.

Sales without first putting efficiency measures and systems in place is a dangerous game that only leads to bigger expenses and fewer ideal clients. Applying efficiency strategies to your top line—firing bad clients, cloning the good ones, refining your offering to get the most out of your resources and then selling smart—is a surefire way to increase profitability.

TAKE ACTION: LET GO OF DEAD WEIGHT

Step 1: Focusing on one aspect of your business (one that benefits your best customers), challenge yourself to figure out how to get two times the results for half the effort.

Step 2: Using the parameters outlined in this chapter, identify your weakest clients. Fire the weakest links. I'm not suggesting that you get into "Take This Job and Shove It" mode. Don't burn any bridges. Just politely end the relationships. You're not dating anymore, but you can still be friends.

Chapter 9

PROFIT FIRST— ADVANCED TECHNIQUES

You are invited to come to ProfitCON. It may well be the first conference in the world to be all about profitability. I started the conference in 2015, and to the best of my ability I couldn't find any other conference like it. At our first meet up we had just accountants, bookkeepers, and business coaches who were learning ways to help their clients, and themselves, increase profitability. It has subsequently grown to include all types of entrepreneurs, accounting professionals, and business experts who want to learn and share strategies on profitability.*

At the most recent conference, Erin Moger (we call her Mo), from our office, was delivering a Q&A presentation on Profit First when one of the attendees raised his hand and said the standard Profit First foundational five accounts did not work with his business due to its unique requirements.

Mo looked down from the stage and said, "When in doubt add an account."

There you have it. Maybe you have a seasonal business in which money spikes and sags. Another account, specifically a DRIP account, would help here. Maybe you need to outlay big cash for equipment every so often, then an EQUIPMENT account would help.

---

* Seriously, I would love to see you at ProfitCON and share the latest strategies in profit with you. To check out our upcoming events, visit (you guessed it) ProfitFirstProfession als.com or go directly to ProfitCON.us.

To take Profit First to the next level and customize it for your business, it is pretty simple. Follow Mo's rule: add another account.

When you start adding new accounts to suit your unique needs, consider yourself an advanced user of Profit First.

Here's the deal: You are about to learn the Profit First equivalent of running your first marathon. You need to be in shape and all stretched out before you do it. So please do proceed with reading, but don't implement this stuff until you have completed at least two full quarters (180 days, plus) with the core stuff you learned about Profit First. Are you making your biweekly allocations? Are you amassing some profit, no matter how small? Have you experienced a few profit distributions? Are you participating in some form of accountability? If you answered yes (a *real* yes) to all four, if you've mastered *not* breaking the rules, you're good to put on your running shoes and move forward.

You started out taking it easy with a walk around the block. Then you did that jog-walk-jog-walk thing. You started running faster and for longer distances. Now you're one of them: a runner. Time to train for a marathon.

ADVANCED SIMPLIFICATION

A few years after implementing Profit First for myself, I realized that I could really take my money management to the next level if I tweaked my system further. The stuff I taught you in the beginning of this book was working well, but there were certain times I still needed to do the accounting work to understand the financial health of my business. Sometimes my deposits weren't made as a result of sales; they were simply reimbursements for expenses. Other times, a client paid a wad of cash up front for work that I would do in dribs and drabs over the next year. Sometimes I needed to make big purchases, and I wanted to save for them. Mine wasn't the only business that needed tweaks; everyone I consulted with needed them. So do you. And the process is simple. You need just a few more accounts.

While it may not seem that opening additional accounts simplifies anything, it absolutely does. Whenever you can get a clear, accurate picture of how much you have to spend on a specific aspect of your business, you will make better decisions and be less likely to commit to projects, vendors, and expenditures that do not fall in line with the balances in those accounts. Likewise, if you know exactly how much cash is flowing into your business at any given time, you can make better decisions about where you need to focus your efforts.

You already have your five foundational Profit First accounts open—INCOME, PROFIT, TAX, OWNER'S COMP and OPEX—plus your two no-temptation accounts that don't get touched, the PROFIT HOLD and TAX HOLD accounts in a separate bank. Here are the additional accounts, contingent on your business needs, that I recommend you consider opening:

The Vault

Let's start with accumulating some cash, because that is my happy place (thanks, Suze Orman). The Vault is an ultra-low-risk, interest-bearing account that you can use for short-term emergencies. At a certain point, leaving 50 percent in your PROFIT account to act as a rainy-day fund is not prudent because the money flow is a little unpredictable. A bad quarter won't contribute much to the PROFIT account. Then you take 50 percent out for a profit share, and now that PROFIT account reserve might be too small to sustain a big business. Every business should have a three-month reserve, meaning that, if not a single sale came in, all costs could still be covered for three months (a quarter). The question isn't *whether* you will have a dark day (your supplier goes out of business, your biggest client goes bankrupt, your best employees leave to start a direct competitor, and your clients decide to go with them, etc.). The question is, *when?* The Vault is there for that.

When you set up the Vault, you *must* also establish certain rules for its use. What I mean is that when you have a situation so dire that you need to access this money, you also have instructions written in advance on how to proceed. For example, if the money is pulled due to a drop in sales, you will preplan that besides just trying to get more sales, you will also cut all the related costs in your business within two months if things haven't improved. Few people have the discipline to think clearly or act appropriately in times of panic, and that's why we document a simple set of instructions for ourselves in advance.

The idea behind the Vault and the entire Profit First system is that it puts your decisions well out in front of any money crisis. Your business dynamics may not, in fact, improve; but your decision making will be much further out in front of the actual financial impact. So the goal of the Vault is *not* to buy time; it may afford some time to address unexpected challenges, but it is really about forcing important decisions early, so your business doesn't go into a cash crisis (you know, back to the Survival Trap).

Stocking Account

This is an account for big purchases and to fund the stocking of your inventory. For example, my friend JB's roof decking company, RoofDeck Solutions, Ltd., sells the materials contractors need to complete their projects. JB includes some basic nuts and bolts with each order, usually fifty or a hundred of each; yet his supplier requires a minimum order of ten thousand at a time, which costs JB roughly $5,000. Each order will last JB ten months or longer, so he set up what he calls a large purchase account into which he allocates 1/20th (that's $250 each time) of the funds he will need for the next big nuts-and-bolts purchase. Why 1/20th? Because he knows he'll need the next order in ten months, and he is on the tenth/twenty-fifth rhythm. Ten months, two times a month, equals twenty allocations before the next big purchase. By doing this, JB is able to chip away at the big bill *before* it happens. Then when it's time to cough up the $5,000 for the next big nuts-and-bolts order, he's ready. In the past, this bill caught him off guard and he had to scramble to cover it. Now he barely feels the $250 he allocates to his STOCKING account twice a month.

Pass-Through Account

Some businesses receive income from customers that is not to be allocated for Profit or Owner's Comp. Sometimes you may provide a service or a product to your customer at cost (or near cost), and other times you may be reimbursed for costs outright. For example, I travel a lot for my work and in almost every case my clients reimburse my travel costs. That income is not allocated to cover payroll or added to my PROFIT account. It's a pass-through and goes directly into this account, and then off to the corresponding vendor to pay the bill. If I have paid the bill in advance, the money is deposited into the PASS-THROUGH account and then transferred (on the tenth or twenty-fifth) to the OPEX account, from which I paid the initial bill. By the way, with all these advanced accounts, the nickname you give each is entirely up to you. I call this one my REIMBURSEMENT account.

Because you don't want this money hitting your INCOME account, set this account up as a checking account and deposit the reimbursement (or pass-through) money right into it.

Materials Account

If most of your revenue (as indicated in the Instant Assessment) falls into top line revenue and does not flow through to Real Revenue, then most of your income is pass-through revenue and the core of your business is basically the management of that pass-through. If this is the case, set up a MATERIALS account for the money that is allocated specifically for purchase of materials. Do not allocate it for anything else. (Ever!) If for some reason there is money left over at the end of the quarter (in other words, you had a larger profit margin than you expected), move that balance to your INCOME account and make the allocations accordingly. The MATERIALS account functions in the same way the PASS-THROUGH account does, but it is broken out separately so that you know its exclusive purpose is for materials.

Subcontractor/Commission Accounts

If your business does not purchase materials, but uses contractors or people paid on commission instead, set up a CONTRACTORS or COMMISSIONS to allocate the funds to pay these fine folks. Treat it just like the MATERIALS account, but apply it to contractors and commission-based team members. In the case where you both purchase materials *and* use contractors, use both a MATERIALS and a CONTRACTORS account.

Employee Payroll Account

Employee pay is relatively predictable—full-timers are on salary and part-timers, for the most part, work an average number of hours per week. This means you can look at the cumulative gross pay for your employees plus the payroll taxes you'll incur and allocate funds from your INCOME account to the EMPLOYEE PAYROLL account every tenth and twenty-fifth. If you use a payroll service, set them up to pull the payroll from this account (not your OPERATING EXPENSES account).

Equipment Account

Similar to your STOCKING account, this account is for big purchases you may need to make further down the road, such as new computers or a high-end 3-D printer. Estimate how much you might have to spend on future equipment purchases, divide it by the number of months you have to save up for it, divide that number by two and allocate that amount every tenth and twenty-fifth to accumulate enough money for that big purchase.

Drip Account

This account is for retainers, advance payments, and prepayments on work your company will complete over a long period of time and for which you have yet to expend resources. Say you get a big project (congratulations, by the way), and you receive $120,000 from the client up front for work you will complete every month over the period of a year. That means that each month, you will really be earning $10,000. So when you get that check, put the $120,000 into the DRIP account and then automatically transfer $10,000 to the INCOME account every month (or better yet, $5,000 every tenth and twenty-fifth). You don't touch any of the balance in the DRIP account. You only make allocations when you drip a portion of the funds— in this case, the $10,000 each month—into the INCOME account.

The DRIP account will help you manage the true cash flow of earned money so that you can manage your expenses and costs. For example, the labor doing the work will be paid monthly. I helped implement a DRIP account with my friends at TravelQuest International in Prescott, Arizona. They provide their clientele with once-in-a-lifetime trips, from viewing solar eclipses from the best vantage points in the world, to visiting the South Pole to see the Aurora Australis, to experiencing zero gravity in outer space. People book these trips up to five years in advance, while the majority of the company's expenses occur during the year of the event. Enter the DRIP account.

Petty Cash Account

Set up a bank account and get a debit card for petty cash purchases, such as client lunches. Then allocate a regular dollar amount from your OPERATING EXPENSES account to petty cash. Me? I allocate $100 every two weeks for myself, and also for a few employees who need it. The funds cover gifts, lunches, and other small purchases. Sorry—if I'm buying, we likely aren't having an eight-course meal. If it's not in my PETTY CASH account, it ain't in my budget.

Prepayment Account

As I shared in Chapter 6, you can save a considerable amount of money by prepaying for services. Car insurance costs less when you pay for six months rather than monthly, and some services will give you deeper discounts if you pay for an entire year in advance. Set up an account specifically to set aside funds for prepayments so you can take advantage of those deals when they are available. If the discount is not offered to you, and you have enough money to cover several months or a year's worth of services, offer to pay it up front for a discount. Most businesses will be happy to comply.

Sales Tax Account

If your business collects sales tax, every single stinkin' penny of the sales tax you collect is immediately allocated to this account. For example, if you sell something for $100 and the sales tax is 5 percent, you will deposit $105 into your INCOME account. First, transfer that $5 into your SALES TAX account; then do your Profit First allocations with the remaining $100. Sales tax isn't even legally your money; you are just acting as a collection agent for the government, so never, *ever* treat that money as income. Just bang people over the head for the sales tax and turn it over to the king (the government).

Figure 6 is my own account setup. The account numbers are made up, of course, and the balances are not my real numbers. But they do show a

BANK 1 (FOR MY BUSINESS OPERATIONS)		
NAME	**ACCOUNT**	**BALANCE**
Income	**3942	$13,432.23
Profit 15% (TAP 18%)	**2868	$0.00
Owner's Comp 31% (TAP 32%)	**0407	$4,881.88
Tax - Gov't Money 15%	**4365	$0.00
Opex 39% (TAP 35%)	**5764	$3,676.18
Petty Cash $75	**4416	$142.66
Employee Pay $1,500	**8210	$1,845.46
Reimbursement 0%	**4247	$212.58
Drip 0%	**8264	$27,500.00

BANK 2 (TEMPTATION REMOVED)		
NAME	**ACCOUNT**	**BALANCE**
Profit Hold	**1111	$14,812.11
Tax Hold	**2222	$5,543.91
The Vault	**3333	$10,000.00

Fig. 6. Mike's Account Setup.

very typical breakout of the cash, and the names of the accounts are the real names I have assigned to my accounts. Next to each name I put either the dollar amount or percentage that goes into each account at the allocation times (the tenth and the twenty-fifth). In parenthis I have put the TAP I am targeting for that account. You should do the same.

Looking at the numbers, I can see instantly where my business stands. I can run an Instant Assessment at any time. For the purposes of this example, I set my required personal monthly income at $10,000 per month.

From there I can instantly calculate the total business income I need to make between every allocation period.

WRITE DOWN THE PROCESS

Create a single-page document that defines the function of each account. Explain what purpose each account serves, and the process you will follow. For example, document that on the tenth and twenty-fifth of the month, all the money in your INCOME account is distributed to the PROFIT, OWNER'S COMP, TAX, and OPEX accounts based on the respective percentages. Then the specific dollar amounts—$75 for PETTY CASH and $1,500 for EMPLOYEE PAYROLL—are transferred from the OPEX account into the respective accounts. Finally, the total money in Bank 1's PROFIT and TAX accounts are transferred to Bank 2.

This process is a system, so it needs to be documented. Your book-keeper might have to take this over for you; otherwise, you might drink too much one night and forget the rules you set up for your accounts. Heck, you could end up allocating all of your money to your Erik Estrada Fan Club fund, a fan club of which you are the only member (even Erik dropped out).

SHIFT YOUR FOCUS FROM THE "MONTHLY NUT"

The famed "monthly nut" is a horrible distraction. It's up there with reruns of *Jersey Shore*. The monthly nut is a remnant of the GAAP mentality that simply tells us the number we need every month to keep the doors open. And *that* is nonsense. The monthly nut is a focus on—you guessed it—expenses, not profit. The concept of the monthly nut makes you focus on expenses and do everything you can to earn your nut with enough sales. In other words, it has us put costs first and makes the goal to cover expenses, not to improve profitability. Can you say "Survival Trap?" Good. I knew you could.

You get what you focus on, so stop focusing on expenses. Focus on profit, and the expenses will be taken care of by default. Screw the monthly nut. Instead, focus on your Required Income for Allocation (RIFA). This is the money you need to deposit by the tenth and again on the twenty-fifth to have a healthy business, to pay the salary you want from your business, and to take the profits you deserve. Period.

My business partner, Obi-Ron Kenobi (I give everyone nicknames, if you haven't figured that out yet), teaches a simple method to achieve this. Take your monthly required personal income and divide it by two because you are getting paid twice a month. Then divide that number by the percentage being allocated in Owner's Comp. Using the (made-up) amounts on Figure 6, I would divide $5,000 by 0.31. The result is just over $16,000 in business income, which means that by the tenth and twenty-fifth of every month, I need to collect and deposit around $16,000 into the INCOME account to cover it. It's really that simple.

There are twenty-four allocations per year. So to annualize it, multiple that $16,000 by twenty-four and you will have your annual business income requirement, which in this case is $384,000. For you to take $5,000 every pay period, you need to generate $384,000 and, of course, live by the specified allocation percentages.

So when I look at my INCOME account (above), I know instantly that I am currently falling short by $3,000, and I need to keep the sales moving. Every two weeks the INCOME account drops to zero when it is allocated, and I need to rebuild it to $16,000 or more. Yes, there is a nice chunk of change in my DRIP account; but that money is for services I will render over another twelve months, so it will only account for about $1,000 every allocation period. Using this system, my sales revenue minimum becomes very, very clear.

WHEN YOU HAVE MORE THAN ONE BUSINESS OWNER

Just one more point about Owner's Comp: If you have a partner or multiple partners who are also getting paid, you need to add up the total income requirements for the owners. So if you need $10,000 a month and your partner also needs $10,000, the total owner pay is $20,000 per month. Divide that number by two; then divide again by 0.31, and you get a RIFA of more than $32,000.

WHY PROFIT AND TAX ARE $0.00 AT BANK 1

You may also notice that the PROFIT (15 percent) account with Bank 1 is at zero. That is because it is simply a holding tray for a day or two. Money gets allocated from the INCOME account and goes to the PROFIT (15 percent) account at Bank 1. Then on the same day, I initiate a transfer to Bank 2, to pull the entire amount of money out of the PROFIT (15 percent) account at Bank 1 and put it into the PROFIT HOLD account at Bank 2. That is where the profit accumulates. And I can see that it looks as though I will have a really nice $7,000-plus profit celebration at the end of this quarter. It's a simple calculation: $14,812.11 times 50 percent. Par-tay!

This same holding tray setup is in place for my TAX (15 percent) account. Allocate and then remove the temptation immediately.

Also, you may notice that no bank summary "grand total" is shown in the table. The accounts aren't all automatically added up to show a total combined balance. Many banks do this for your convenience, but I suggest that you disable the option (if you can). The grand total of all your accounts shows you all the money on one big plate again— exactly the thing we want to avoid. Looking at a grand total messes with your mind, so don't do it.

RAISING CAPITAL

Raising money is a risky endeavor. I generally discourage it, unless you have an extremely high confidence that an investment of money will bring in a lot more profit. How do you know if an investment will bring in more profit? You will know only if you are already profitable. Be profitable first and when you know what exact elements of your business are making that profit, you can consider using outside money to amplify what is working. There are many more considerations than just that, but profitability is a foundational requirement. Also, I hope you'll talk with an accounting professional or financial expert who understands raising money before seeking the money.

If you do raise money, you need to do a quick advanced technique with Profit First. You guessed it: set up another account. Call it OUTSIDE CAPITAL. All the money goes there, and it is used on the schedule and as specified with the use of funds you agreed to with the investor. If the dynamics of your business change, and there is a better use of funds, you agree to a new plan with the investor. And if you don't need the money just yet, it sits there until the right use and time presents itself. In fact, TSheets, a rapidly growing time-tracking software company did exactly that. Matt Ritter, the cofounder, raised $15 million for his company. He got the funds, and then smartly sat on the money until the right time and opportunity came together to use that money to amplify what was already working.

Note: Everything in this section also applies to getting and using loan funds. Wait until you're profitable, and then use the funds for amplification.

HOW TO DETERMINE WHETHER YOU CAN AFFORD A NEW EMPLOYEE

There is a really simple formula for determining whether you can afford a new hire—or if your business is currently understaffed or overstaffed. For each full-time employee, your company should generate Real Revenue of $150,000 to $250,000 (ideally more, but this is the minimum). So if you want a million-dollar company, you know that you can afford four to six employees (including yourself). This is just a ballpark number; every business is unique. But do not use your super distinctive status as an excuse to hire more people.

Efficiency is always the goal. Always. Not hiring your husband's cousin who is down on his luck and "could really use a job." Not finding space for the brilliant kid who has a ton of great ideas you could use . . . someday. You're a "bottom line" person now, remember? You're taking profit first. And that's why you're forced to be careful with your expenses.

And remember—we're talking about Real Revenue, not top line revenue. Subtract your material and subs cost *before* you divide by the magic number range to get to your ideal employee count.

Again, this is not an exact, perfect system, but it will give you a better and more realistic understanding of what it means to be over- or under-staffed. The reason these numbers aren't perfect is because labor costs vary tremendously. A guy cooking french fries at McDonald's will make much less than the lady who engineered the next generation smartphone. In this example, cheap labor is less costly but also has a smaller impact on revenue. The fry guy just facilitates the sale of fries, but the engineer creates an entirely new product and revenue stream.

According to Greg Crabtree, the author of *Simple Numbers, Straight Talk, Big Profits*, your Real Revenue must be two and a half times the total labor cost if you're running a tech business. This is because the tech industry traditionally requires expensive labor (highly trained people who have a big impact on revenue). If, on the other hand, you are in a cheap-labor field, such as the fast-food restaurant example I used above, your Real Revenue must be four times your total labor cost.

For example, let's say you're a manufacturer with $6,000,000 in Real Revenue. If you hire cheap labor, such as assembly line personnel, you will divide $6,000,000 by four to get $1,500,000. This means that your total labor cost (the people on the floor and the folks in the office) should not exceed $1,500,000. And if you are a manufacturer with $6,000,000 in Real Revenue but use expensive labor, such as scientists and engineers, divide the $6,000,000 in Real Revenue by two and a half to get a total labor cost of $2,400,000.

MINI POWER TACTICS

Some advanced Profit First strategies require very little time and are super effective. I am constantly tweaking and improving my system, so if you want to know about my latest discoveries, and share yours, visit my blog at Mike Michalowicz.com. Here are my favorites (so far):

The Government's Money

It's so easy to "borrow" from our TAX account. (It's really stealing, but you don't need me to tell you that. Oops, I just did.) The money is just sitting there, taunting us with all of those zeros we could put to good use. When we cave and pull from the TAX account, we don't feel the pain right away. But when tax time comes, we can get in *really* big trouble. Owing more taxes than we have money to pay means that at a minimum, we'll be paying interest and possibly penalties on the amount we owe.

A smart tactic is first to move this account to a third-party bank that you don't see, and then change the name of the TAX account to THE GOVERNMENT'S MONEY. Now, I suspect that like me, you would be *way* more reluctant to "steal money from the government" than you would be to "borrow money from the TAX account."

Hide Accounts

Following the "out of sight, out of mind" theory, you are less likely to justify transferring or withdrawing funds from your accounts if you can't see them. Some banks allow you to "hide" accounts so that you can't see them on first view when logging onto online banking. Try hiding all of your accounts except for the OPEX account. You can still do the disbursements and the entire Profit First system using this tactic; it just means that now you won't consider the other accounts when making spending decisions.

Outside Income Accounts

Chances are that as your business matures, you will add a variety of other accounts that collect income. You may have a PayPal account to collect funds, or a wire account for international business or local transfers. The challenge with these accounts is that you might start to view them as "extra," like your own additional petty cash fund. They're not extra. They are part of your revenue, and you need to make sure that you protect and allocate the funds just as you would any deposit into your main bank account.

For this tactic, set up all your outside income accounts so that any income is transferred to your main INCOME account on a daily basis. Some banks will let you set up an automatic transfer for the total balance in the outside account, which is ideal as long as you keep whatever minimum balance is required to avoid extraneous administration fees.

If you can't do this automatically, simply transfer the money to your INCOME account when you do your biweekly allocations. Just note that these transfers may take a few days, so you won't instantly have the money in the INCOME account and will have to wait until your next allocation period to move the money to all the individual accounts.

Account Snapshot

To keep track of your accounts, set up automatic notifications for your key accounts via email or text. Have the bank report the balances of your INCOME account and OPERATING EXPENSES account to you on the tenth (when all of your money has accumulated) and the fifteenth (when all of your money has been allocated and all checks have been mailed; and again on the twenty-fifth (accumulated) and the thirtieth (allocated). Set up a daily notification of the balance in your PETTY CASH account. Check the other accounts manually.

This quick report will ensure that you are acutely aware of how cash flows in (INCOME account) and what is available to go out of your business (OPEX account) and out of your own spending allotment (PETTY CASH account).

Bank Checks

Until we see that a payment has cleared, we still think of the money as ours. And sometimes we forget we wrote the check. Hello, insufficient funds charges and a ticket straight to the ninth circle of hell. This technique changes that dynamic immediately. Rather than pay with checks you write by hand and mail (if you don't lose the envelope on the floor of your car), pay with bank checks.

Also called bank pay or bank payment processing, bank checks are processed by your bank quickly. More important, the bank will pull the money for the checks you "write" immediately. This way, you know the money is gone forever as soon as you process a payment.

Yes, the bank makes money on the float, and you lose any interest you may have earned in the few days it would take your payment to be received and processed by vendors. But I say, "Who cares?" Here's the deal: If you manage hundreds of millions or billions by processing checks and transfers manually, it's a good strategy to cling to your money for a few days because the interest earned on your operating capital in even just a few days is significant. But for most entrepreneurs, the interest earned in the float is embarrassingly negligible—usually around five dollars per year, and you'll spend more than that on postage to mail your payments! So let the bank do the dirty work, why don't ya?

TAKE ACTION: PLAN TO ADVANCE

Choose one of the advanced tactics or strategies detailed in the chapter and add it to your to-do list for six months from now. It may seem silly to add a to-do item so far out, but if you don't put it on your radar, you may end up forgetting that there are advanced strategies that could help you take Profit First—and your company—to the next level.

Chapter 10

THE PROFIT FIRST LIFE

When you make enough money, you don't have to budget."

In Chapter 6 I shared some of my update from Jorge, cofounder and owner of Specialized ECU Repair. Toward the end of our conversation, he dropped that little bomb on me. I have to admit, the frugal monster in me initially rejected Jorge's comment as being totally out of hand. But Jorge is my kitesurfing badass Profit First poster child, so I kept my mouth shut while he explained what he meant.

"My mom had a good job as a pharmaceutical executive," Jorge began. "A long time ago, when I was in college, we were shopping in Bed Bath & Beyond. She was buying stuff like crazy. Since I had about sixty dollars in my bank account at the time and couldn't imagine buying so much stuff, I asked her, 'Do you ever budget for the things you buy?' That's when she said, 'When you make enough money, you don't have to budget.'"

"It might seem incorrect, but because I use Profit First, I don't have to budget that much," Jorge continued. "When we go on vacation, we do whatever we want. We're not crazy; we don't stay in the Four Seasons. But we go where we want, do whatever adventure we want to do. We never think, *can we afford it?* I'm not a millionaire, but because I follow Profit First, I don't have to restrict myself when I travel, or spend my disbursement."

Ah, I get it. A budget, in this case, is a restriction. And when it comes to Profit First, we implement a lot of (good) restrictions to make the business profitable. But when the money comes out and it's reward time, the restrictions, within reason, come off.

Like me, Jorge doesn't like to use credit cards. Because he follows Profit First, he doesn't have to. He and José simply watch the sales, and when they cross their minimum each month, they know all will be fine. They created a lifestyle they love, and they can fund it because they know the profit disbursement is not only coming, but their business can also continue to grow without it.

Profit First helps you create the lifestyle you want, even if you're just starting the system. Laurie Dutcher, CEO, accountant, and owner of Secretly Spoiled, a company that started using Profit First three years back, shared with me that she took her family on their first Disney vacation using her first-ever quarterly profit disbursement (which was two years and nine months ago). A type-A numbers person, Laurie had been investing everything she had in her business—most of her time and all of her revenue.

"I was living check to check," Laurie told me. "I wasn't taking a salary."

All of that changed as soon as Laurie started plugging Profit First into her well-organized system. Within months, her personal finances stabilized; and by the time her first quarterly disbursement came around, she had enough to take her family on their first trip to Disneyland.

"The trip was amazing, and we've already taken quite a few more," Laurie said. "But what really surprised me was, after funneling all of my money into my business thinking that it was the only way to make it grow, my business actually started to grow *faster* when I started paying myself and focusing on the profit first!"

Like so many of us used to "doing anything" to build our businesses (including going without pay and delaying profit indefinitely), Laurie had to learn how to give herself permission to use her hard-earned money not only to pay herself, but also to *enjoy* herself—to provide experiences for her family that would enhance their quality of life and create a lifetime of treasured memories. The business was no longer a cash-eating monster. Not even close. It said, "Bon Voyage!" to Laurie and her family as they cruised off to Disneyland for the seventh time. No one gets tired of that place.

This won't come as a shock to you: everything you just learned about creating a Profit First business also applies to your personal life. I mean, if you think about it, running your life is like running a business. You generate income and spend money. Your income likely varies at times. You never know when a crisis might hit and make a huge dent in your bank account. And you have a vision for your life, just as you have a vision for your business—one that, before reading this book, you may have thought hinged on a lucky lottery ticket or some other sudden windfall.

Now you know better. You know that in order to save enough money for a rainy day and the celebratory pleasures of life, you need to pull that money out before you spend a dime on other things. You know that a smaller plate will help you trim the fat from your lifestyle and zero in on what's most important to you and find fun, creative solutions to get what you want. And you know that the big vision you have for your life does not have to hinge on luck or fate—it can be earned, not with two dollars for the Powerball, but with a simple change in habit, practiced consistently.

You know what? That's a big, big deal. You created the miracle that is your business and now, by implementing the Profit First system, you have ensured its greatness—not just in terms of profitability, but also in terms of the positive impact your business will have on the world.

THE PROFIT FIRST LIFESTYLE

The ultimate goal of the Profit First lifestyle is financial freedom, which I define as doing what you choose to do whenever you choose to do it. That will change over time. Jorge and José used their Profit First distributions to fund a lot of vacations in Central America, Canada, Europe, and Australia. Today their choices are different. Jorge still loves to go on adventures, but he's more focused on helping his wife complete her law degree and pass the bar. His business partner, José, focused on buying and renovating an incredibly beautiful house for his family, which, because it's HGTV awesome, has now been featured in commercials. Financial freedom means that you have reached a point where the money you've saved yields enough interest to support your lifestyle and continues to grow. The path to financial freedom is paved with simple, small habit changes that become systematized and apply to both your business and personal finances.

Now, I did not write this book to teach you about your family budget or your 401(k), but I do know this: If you own a business, your personal financial health is in lockstep with the financial health of your business. In fact, the analogy of your business being your child is only partially accurate. A better analogy is that your business is your conjoined twin. Separating yourself from it must be done with absolute surgical precision, and even if the operation is successful, you will always share a soul.

So, soul mate, you need to apply everything you're doing right now (and planning to do) to fix your business with Profit First to your life, too.

1. Face the music. This step should be easier now that you've faced the truth about your company's finances. Add up all of your monthly bills, plus your annual bills and the debt you owe.

2. If you have any debt at all, stop accruing more. Put a freeze on all purchases you cannot pay for with cash.

3. Establish a personal Profit First habit. Set up an automatic withdrawal so that every time you get paid, which should now be twice a month on the tenth and the twenty-fifth, a percentage immediately transfers into a retirement savings account. If you are carrying any amount of debt, keep the retirement percentage at 1 percent until the debt is paid off. Use every penny you have after necessary expenses to eradicate your debt.

4. Set up your "small plates." Create five foundational accounts, multiple Day-to-Day accounts and Big Event accounts.

    A. INCOME Account. This is the account into which you make deposits. From this account, allocate money to the other accounts. Don't use it for any other purpose.

    B. The VAULT Account. Initially, this is the "oh shit" account, the amount of savings you must have on hand to get through the month if—scratch that—*when* something dire happens. Now, Suze Orman recommends saving eight months' worth of living expenses, but that's not doable right off the bat for the average human being on this planet. However, you will work toward it slowly and methodically—you know, Profit First style. A good starting balance for the Vault is one month's rent or mortgage payment. If you can spare that right now, transfer it to the Vault immediately. Remember, this account must be difficult to access (e.g., different bank, no online banking, no checkbook, etc.). Once you eradicate debt, the Vault will grow and grow, with the intention of having the cash you save here eventually become a source of income. This is where money makes you even more money.

C. RECURRING PAYMENTS Account. This account is for payment of your recurring bills, including fixed (e.g., your mortgage or car loan), varying (e.g., utility bills) and short-term (e.g., an installment plan for your kid's braces). Determine the monthly average for your varying recurring bills, plus 10 percent. Then total your fixed recurring bills. Add the two totals plus the cost of your short-term recurring bills: this is the amount you will transfer from your INCOME account into your RECURRING PAYMENTS account every month. If you have it, transfer that amount now.

D. DAY-TO-DAY Account (multiple, if needed). There are many day-to-day costs in keeping a family running—groceries, clothes, school supplies, Girl Scout cookies, date night, running shoes, Girl Scout cookies, babysitting, toiletries, snow tires, Girl Scout cookies . . . okay, maybe I've had enough of those . . . just one more Samoa? No? Okay, I'll stop.

Set up a DAY-TO-DAY account for anyone in the house who's responsible for paying for these types of expenses, and transfer the amount that each person needs every tenth and twenty-fifth from the INCOME account, based on spending requirements. For example, my wife and I both buy stuff for the house—I'm the Costco king; she handles the grocery stores. And we both gas up cars and pay for kid expenses. Get a debit card for each person so that purchases are deducted from the account immediately.

E. DEBT DESTROYER Account. This account receives all remaining funds and goes toward eradicating debt. Following Dave Ramsey's advice, make the minimum payment on each debt. Then, regardless of interest rates (unless they are extreme), pay off your smallest debt first. Wipe that sucker out and then move on to the next one. Ramsey wisely says that paying off a debt, however small, creates a mental momentum that will motivate you to pay off the rest of your debt faster. Remember, we are emotional beasts, not logical ones.

F. You will have big events in your life, such as buying a house, buying cars, paying for weddings (likely your kids' weddings . . . maybe yours), college, college and yet another kid going to college. Here's the deal: there are good financial programs out there for this stuff, such as 529 plans. These are just ideas for accounts that you may benefit from and are not mandatory.

If you are carrying debt, I want you to cut up your credit cards. Remember, it's much easier to go with human behavior than it is to fight it, so removing temptation is the best solution.

However, I do have one exception. An entrepreneur's income can be highly unpredictable. You could have an amazing month followed by a zero-dollar month, followed by a not-bad month, followed by a why-do-I-bother month. If you follow Profit First, your OWNER'S COMP account should address this and your income should become consistent. But in the beginning, it probably won't be. And if you're a start-up, you may not get any cash at first. For these reasons, I believe in keeping one credit card line to buffer you in dark months. Put the credit card in a sealed envelope labeled "Emergency Only" and give it to a trusted friend to hold on to. I am serious. You must remove temptation.

Here's how you manage your emergency credit card the Profit First way:

Every quarter, as you make progress paying down debt, reduce your credit limit by 50 percent of the amount you paid down. Say you have a maxed-out card with a $10,000 limit. By the end of the quarter, you've managed to pay down $3,000 of that debt (nicely done, my friend). Now you have $7,000 in debt and a $10,000 limit. What I want you to do is call the credit card company and ask them to reduce your limit by $1,500, which is 50 percent of the amount you paid down in the first quarter. Now your debt is $7,000 and your credit limit is $8,500. In doing this, you put up a guardrail of sorts, a mechanism to protect yourself and keep your debt total down (should you convince yourself it's okay to max out your credit card again), while keeping a credit line buffer in place should you need the card for emergency funds during slow months.

Keep following this method every quarter until your credit card balance is zero and your credit limit is $5,000. Put that credit card in a sealed envelope and store it in a safe place (your wallet, it goes without saying, is *not* safe). Better yet, have that reliable friend hold on to it for you. This is your emergency line.

Now, for those of you who say, "But Mike, if I drop my credit line, my debt-to-credit-limit ratios will fall out of favor with lenders and my interest rates will go up!"

To that I say, "Who cares?"

The goal here is to remove financial stress from your life by eradicating debt, not to get better rates on *more* debt. We can worry about improving your credit score once you are debt free. Remember Jesse Cole, owner of the Savannah Bananas? If he can wipe out a $1.3 million debt in less than two years, you can commit to burning through your debt. That's right, burn it. Burn it in effigy—get a mini keg and some kale smoothies and start your own damn Burning Man. Burn that debt *to the ground*.

RIP OFF THE BAND-AID

The day my daughter handed over her piggy bank in an effort to help solve my self-made financial crisis, I still had all three of my luxury cars parked in the driveway. I was still a member of the country club I never went to and had a ton of recurring expenses that, quite frankly and even more embarrassing, I could not name.

In the weeks and months leading up to that moment, I knew I was running out of time, but I still held on to the trappings of the lifestyle I had earned (but not "learned"), the lifestyle I thought I deserved and did not want to give up. But my daughter's amazing act of selflessness woke me up to the reality that none of that stuff mattered.

It's common for us emotional humans to give up the stuff we can no longer afford (or couldn't afford in the first place) by small degrees. We cling. We keep hoping that something will "turn up" and "save the day," and so we dole out the pain in small increments, biding our time. We do this because we hate loss. More specifically, we have a far greater desire to avoid losing something than we have to acquire something. This behavioral response is called loss aversion.

Loss aversion is everywhere, and it is mighty powerful. Combine it with the Endowment effect—the theory that states that we place a much higher significance on something we possess than on an identical thing that we *don't* possess—and you are dealing with a stubbornness resembling that of a three-year-old in a tug-of-war for a beloved blankie. ("Mine!")

For example, the beautiful red Porsche you've been eyeing—it would be nice to have, for sure. But once you have it, it's way past "nice." Now, it's badass (and so are you). You polish the car. You take friends for rides in it. You take selfies with that red beauty in the background of each photo (just by chance, of course). You love it because now that you own it, your relationship to it has changed, even though it's the same car you once idly admired from the showroom floor.

Then you get the notice: you missed yet another payment. If you miss one more, they will repossess your baby. *Your* baby. So what do you do? Return the car? No, you cancel your daughter's ballet class (she kinda sucked anyway), and your gym membership (you kinda sucked anyway), and that trip to the Cape (because everyone knows that anyone who goes to the Cape sucks . . . a lot). You eat ramen noodles every night. Shoot, you even cancel the insurance on the damn car and keep it parked safely in your garage until "better days" come along. So what if you can't drive it? At least you didn't lose it. At least it's still *yours*.

I behaved the same way. I cut back everywhere I could, but nowhere I should. Then, when I couldn't pay a bill and the credit cards were maxed, I cut just enough things to get by. The next month it happened all over again, only worse. Juggling bills and drumming up money were a source of constant stress.

The night after my "piggy bank moment," I remembered what I used to do in the past, when money was tightest in the early days of starting up a new business: I wouldn't cut expenses in ineffective dribs and drabs. I would cut them all.

It was time for me to return to what worked. It was time to rip off the Band-Aid.

I cut everything. The luxury cars? Gone. (I replaced the three cars with two used basic models.) The swanky club membership? Gone. The little extravagances like the Netflix account? Gone. And here is what made it easier—I realized that no one gives a crap. I mean truly, no one cares. I'm guessing you had no idea I was slashing and burning when I was in the throes, never thought for one second, "Hey, I wonder how good ol' Mikey is making out with his financials?" And I'll bet you aren't crying about me right now either. And that's cool because that's reality.

When you realize that 99.99 percent of the people who know you or know of you won't care what you own or where you hang out or what your circumstances are, and that the 0.01 percent who, for whatever reason, can't stand you will simply point a finger at you, laugh evilly, and then direct their self-loathing misery at someone else, it's easier to ditch the pimped-out ride.

And when you realize that 99.99 percent of the people who *do* know you and truly love you will rally around your courage, as my family did for me, that, *that* is when you will stand up, brush yourself off, and say, "Let's do it."

DEATH TO DEBT

Now, your business will be sending you a quarterly profit disbursement check. Yippee! Celebration time! And do you know the best way to celebrate when you have mongo personal debt? Have a death-to-debt party. It's super fun and goes something like this: As soon as you get your disbursement check, turn on some tuneage that gets you fired up—my choice would be Metallica's "Seek and Destroy," but if you don't have a mullet, do your thing. For God's sake, though, don't crank up the Barry Manilow or "Escape (The Piña Colada Song)" by Rupert Holmes . . . we want to destroy debt, here, not make love to it.

Then, make sure you have a glass of libation, or whatever floats your boat. Finally, take 99 percent of your profit disbursement and use it to pay down debt (smallest first). Call it in using your debit card, or go online and get it done immediately. Then, and only then, raise your glass and say, "Cheers to me!" Then we dance (or swing our sweaty, stringy mullet hair around while listening to Metallica). The party is over in about ten minutes, but that debt? It's gone forever. Hey, wasn't that a total blast?

You may think I'm being sarcastic here, but I'm not. To me, paying down debt is *winning*, and winning is fun.

Use the remaining 1 percent of your profit disbursement however you please, but it needs to feel like a reward. Go out to dinner. If you don't have enough for dinner, go out for ice cream. No matter what your disbursement is, cherish it. Celebrate with it. Your business is still serving you and killing debt at the same time.

Rewards are an important feature of Profit First. We must celebrate. Many experts will tell you to eradicate debt only. The problem is, while debt reduction alleviates pain, it doesn't provide much pleasure. Experiencing both is ideal—it packs more punch. Destroying debt feels good, and reminiscing about tearing up credit card statements while enjoying a nice bottle of wine feels better.

After you've eradicated your core debt—credit cards, bank loans, and student loans—start using 45 percent of your quarterly profit disbursement to kill remaining long-term debt and keep 55 percent for your splurge item or experience. This is another psychological move. It's more gratifying to get the bigger chunk of the fruits of your labor and spend it on whatever the hell you want than to take the smaller chunk. So use 45 percent to expedite the payoff of long-term debt beyond your normal monthly payments (mortgage, car payments) and keep the rest for whatever crazy antics you are up to. (What? I don't judge. And I totally didn't see *anything*.)

After you own your cars and home outright and have wiped out debt from every nook and cranny of your life, 100 percent of the profit disbursement goes to you. And this time the party had better be legit. I'm talking a band and some good booze, maybe stuffed pizza instead of plain. And my wife and I had better get an invite. We'll kiteboard over.

LOCK IN YOUR LIFESTYLE

According to Parkinson's Law, if you have ten dollars in your pocket, you will spend ten dollars. As our income increases, Parkinson's Law takes over and we spend every extra penny we earn.

Now that you know your salary and actually take it, you need to live within your means. Then you're going to lock in your lifestyle. What that means is, no matter how good things get (and this is going to be a challenge for you, because now that you follow Profit First, things will get *amazing*), you will not expand your lifestyle in response. You need to accumulate cash—lots of it—and that means no new cars, no brand-new furniture or crazy vacations. For the next five years, you will lock it in and live the life-style you are designing now so that all of your extra profit goes toward giving you that ultimate reward: financial freedom.

Don't freak out on me now. I'm not telling you that you shouldn't go out to dinner with your sweetie or go away for the weekend. (Were you thinking a B & B? I like B & Bs.) You need to enjoy life. I get it and support it. What I am telling you is, in order for Profit First to have a permanent im-pact on your life, you need to build as big a gap as possible between what you earn and what you spend. The more cash you can collect, the better, because at a certain point money starts *earning* you substantial money, all by itself. Money yields interest and returns from investments. And remem-ber, once the money you have collected yields more new money every year than you spend in a year, you have achieved financial freedom.

Here are five rules to help you stay locked in to your lifestyle for the next five years:

1. Always start by looking for a free option.
2. Never buy new when you can get the same benefit you would if you bought used. (It's used as soon as you buy it anyway.)
3. Never pay full price if you can avoid it.
4. Negotiate and seek alternatives first.
5. Delay major purchases until you have written down ten alternatives to making the purchase and have thought through each one. Save your splurging for Profit First quarterly disbursements! Yay!

The Profit First lifestyle is a frugal lifestyle, for sure. But the frugal lifestyle is not the same as a cheap lifestyle. You can and will live very well (actually better) when you are frugal than you would when you are posing as a big spender. Why? Because frugality removes financial stress, enabling you to better appreciate and enjoy the things and experiences you pur-chase. Big spenders buy the same things, but their purchases are served with a big ol' heaping serving of massive stress. Who's got time for that? Remember, well-dressed poverty is still poverty.

If staring down the next five years is too much for you, that's cool. I have a plan B for you. (And if you do rock the five years, this is your next step after your locked-in lifestyle term is up). It's called the *Wedge*, a term that has been floating around entrepreneurial circles for a while, which as far as I can tell was originally coined by Brian Tracy. The idea of the Wedge is to only gradually (and mindfully) upgrade your lifestyle as your income increases. Every time your income increases, you set aside half of the increase as savings so that you don't expand your lifestyle to, as Parkinson's Law suggests, "use all available resources."

So, for example, if you're taking home $100,000 (post-tax, paid by your business) and your Profit First lifestyle means you're setting aside $20,000 every year and living on $80,000; this is where you will start your Wedge. Half of every income bump over and above $100,000 will go directly into the Vault. The Vault starts piling up cash, and changes from a "Holy crap, I have no money" fund to a "Holy cow, that's a lot of money" fund.

Let's say your take-home income goes up to $135,000, an increase of $35,000 over the previous year. You would take 50 percent of the $35,000 ($17,500) and drop it into the Vault. This leaves just over $117,000. Because you live the Profit First lifestyle, you now take 20 percent and set it aside for savings. With the increase in income, that number is now $23,400. That brings your annual savings up to around $50,000. And you are now living on more as well—$93,600, to be exact, an increase of more than $13,000. Your life moves forward, but the Wedge system, combined with Profit First, allows your savings to climb super fast, getting you that much closer to financial freedom.

PROFIT FIRST KIDS

Regardless of how you get your money, the universe seems to find a way to make us earn it. This is why I don't gift my kids an allowance. Instead, I set up a job list (a variant on chores) with corresponding pay rates and post it on the refrigerator. (You can download one from the Resources section at MikeMichalowicz.com.) The kids decide how much they earn by how much they work for it. As I write this, my daughter is on a six-week vacation in Hawaii that she paid for herself. Three years back she went to Spain on her own dime. This is surely a little bit of Daddy's bragging, but also I want to drive home the point that the goal of Profit First for kids is to make them appreciate the value of money, learn to manage it, and strip away any sense of entitlement. Here's the basics of how to do it:

Give your kids some mailing envelopes (you know, the snail-mail type) and have them label each one:

1. One for the big dream, like my daughter's horse. Have them stash up to 25 percent of their chore money in this envelope.

2. One to help support the family. This number should be a recurring number, such as five dollars a week to contribute to groceries or entertainment. The key is to have a recurring fee so they get used to having to pay out something on a regular basis. Make sure the number is age appropriate.

3. One for impact. Have them put 5 to 10 percent into this envelope to give to a charity of their choice, or to use in a meaningful way . . . like starting their own business, one that both serves the community and makes money!

4. One for the Vault. This is where they will sock away 10 percent of their funds for a critical emergency (hopefully your kids will never have one, but you want them prepared from day one), which will also become an investing source as the money accumulates.

5. One envelope for mad money, to buy whatever they need or want—toys, music, books, etc. Let them earn money and have fun!

It goes without saying that the kids must follow the Profit First golden rule: always allocate the money to the different accounts (envelopes) before doing anything else. This system will teach your kids so much about the value of money—how to manage it, how to earn it, how to finance their dreams. It may feel strange at first (I'm talking to you, helicopter parents), and you'll surely get some pushback, but this is a massive gift to them. Imagine how your financial life might have turned out differently had someone taught you these important lessons and strategies. Or if you are lucky enough that your parents did teach you, just think about how well it served you and can do the same for your kids.

It's funny—the "piggy bank" story is one that readers mention the most. It stays with them; I know it sure stayed with me. It is forever implanted on my brain and I know it will be my final thought before I die.

My daughter, Adayla, is all grown up now, and was accepted to attend Virginia Tech, my alma mater. (Go Hokies!) When I drove her down to the orientation, we stopped at a Cracker Barrel. Over lunch, I brought up the piggy bank story; I hadn't asked her about it since she was nine.

"What are you talking about?" she said.

I recounted the story and she shook her head. She didn't remember it at all. For a second, I was saddened that such a pivotal moment was simply a fleeting memory for her. Then I realized, *of course she won't remember.* For her, offering me her hard-earned pennies, nickels, and dimes was an automatic thing to do, like holding the door open for an elderly person. Good money management and caring for others is just automatic for her. It requires no extra skills or thought; it's just who she is.

When I dropped Adayla off at campus, I gave her the usual spiel about getting the most out of college, yadda yadda, dad stuff, yadda yadda. Krista and I require all of our children to participate in paying for their college education. What Adayla doesn't know yet is that the last few profit distributions have already paid for her college. The money she put in toward her college is actually going toward paying for her wedding—and a big ol' wedding cake in the shape of a piggy bank.

TAKE ACTION: LIVE PROFIT FIRST

Step 1: Set up corresponding Profit First allocation accounts for your personal expenses.

Step 2: Based on your most recent pay and the "lifestyle lock" explained in this chapter, figure out how much you should truly be living on.

Step 3: Have a sit-down with your entire family and talk numbers. Tell them what you're doing with Profit First and the positive impact it will have on your family's long-term financial health. And if it helps, you can tell the kids that this method was something suggested by "Uncle Mikey."

Chapter 11

HOW TO KEEP IT FROM FALLING APART

The worst enemy of Profit First is not the economy, your staff, your customers, or your mother-in-law. (Well, it *could* be your mother-in-law.) The worst enemy of Profit First is *you*. The system is simple, but you have to have the discipline to implement it consistently, and that's where most of us fall short. We won't do the Debt Freeze all the way, or at all. We won't cut back on our staffing expenses or move into a grade-D office space. We surely won't challenge the industry norms and try to innovate. But we *will* steal from ourselves, taking money we originally allocated for profit to pay bills. We will steal from our TAX account to pay our own salaries. We'll borrow. We'll beg. We'll steal (from ourselves). And when we let Profit First fall apart, what is the single biggest reason why? We go it alone.

When I wrote the original version of this chapter, we were having a mother of a bad winter here on the East Coast. I hear other parts of the country also had it rough, but I had been snowbound in my house for what seemed like eighty-four years. I remember being afraid to turn on the Weather Channel for fear that I might finally, permanently lose my mind. I'm not sure which state had had the worst of it, but while my heart feels it was my beloved Jersey, I'm pretty sure it was Minnesota. Actually, I know for sure it was Minnesota.

Anjanette Harper, one of my best pals (as in, we have shared deodorant on road trips type of best pal) and the best damn writer on this planet, lives across the border in New York. We were trading war stories over the phone about how the latest storm had affected each of our towns when she said,

"Mike, I survived a mile-long hike in the Minnesota Northwoods . . . in January. We were sent out in waist-deep snow with nothing but a compass, some matches, and a bag of granola. This winter has nothing on me."

Anjanette went on to tell me a hilarious story about Camp Widjiwagan (yes, that's its real name), a winter camp she attended with her classmates near Ely, Minnesota, when she was thirteen.

"It was ridiculous—we were this group of city kids sent to an environmental camp way up north during the coldest month of the year. We weren't allowed to use the one indoor bathroom except to brush our teeth—seriously, the toilet seat had duct tape over it—instead, we had to put on three layers of clothes plus outerwear to trek out to the biffies [outhouses] in the woods to pee. Just try going to the bathroom in the middle of a pitch-black night on a frozen toilet seat in a tiny wooden shack, with two active wolf packs howling at each other nearby."

I laughed so hard as Anjanette went on to tell me about more of her adventures at Camp Widjiwagan, but it wasn't until she explained how the counselors managed to get the campers to change their wasteful habits that I realized I *had* to share her story with you.

"The first night, after we had dinner, we were asked to scrape the leftover food on our plates into a bucket. One of the counselors weighed our combined leftovers and announced that we had managed to waste several pounds of food. Being a bunch of privileged brats, we responded with, 'Yeah, so?'

"We were then lectured about how a few pounds of waste, repeated daily, adds up to a few tons of waste, and soon enough that adds up to a few landfills full of waste. Next, we got the ultimatum: We had to get the waste-per-meal down to a few ounces by the end of the week. I can't remember what the exact consequence was if we didn't pull it off, but it was something outrageous, like forcing us to square-dance . . . with each other."

Anjanette went on to explain how, in the days that followed, she and her classmates held each other accountable for the amount of food they left on their plates at the end of each meal. They strategized and came up with solutions—the most important of these was to take smaller portions to begin with.

"We helped each other out," Anjanette explained. "If, after I was done eating, I still had vegan mashed potatoes on my plate and Ted and Brian wanted second helpings, I would pass them my leftovers. We nudged each other (or shouted at each other, take your pick) when our plates were piled too high with food. Toward the end, when it looked like we might not reach our goal, we really put the pressure on each other. Because, let's face it—we'd just hit 'puberty. We would have done *anything* to avoid having to touch each other, much less partner up for a square dance."

By the last dinner, Anjanette and her fellow campers surprised even themselves—they got that bucket down to zero waste. Zero. Zilch. Squat. As in, no one needs to do anything with the two words that should never be said together . . . square and dance.

In essence, what Anjanette and her friends did was to buddy up to ensure that they met their goal. The benefits of using an accountability buddy or group are numerous. Chief among them:

1. Your sticktoitiveness skyrockets because someone else depends on you, and good old friendly competition doesn't hurt either.

2. When you go through a painful process with others, the pain is diminished.

3. The action of enforcing a plan or system with someone else ensures that you are more likely to do your part.

4. When you meet regularly with your buddy and/or group, you get into a rhythm that makes it easier to stay the course and achieve your goal. Big aspirational goals get broken down into smaller achievable milestones.

Profit First works, and getting an accountability buddy will make sure you let it.

Going it alone is the biggest mistake **(Mistake #1)** entrepreneurs make when implementing Profit First, but there are others. In this chapter, I'll share a few more pitfalls and how to avoid them as you work the Profit First system. Don't worry—none of my solutions require you to square-dance. (No offense to my square-dancin' readers.)

MISTAKE #2: TOO MUCH TOO SOON

It is extremely common for entrepreneurs new to Profit First to start putting 20 percent or even 30 percent into their PROFIT account right out of the gate. The next month they realize they can't afford it and pull the money back out to pay bills, which defeats the entire process. You must allocate profit and not touch it, so you've got to be sure that your business can handle the reduction in operating income.

To increase your profit, you need to become more efficient, to deliver the same or better results at a lower cost. Profit First works from the end goal backward. Once upon a time, you used to try to get more efficient in order to turn a profit. Now, by taking profit first, you must become efficient to support it. Same result, reverse engineered.

This is why I suggest you start with a small percentage. Don't fall into the trap of hogging all of the grub, taking too much profit up front and then shuffling most of it back into your OPERATING EXPENSES account when payroll comes due. Start with a small percentage to build the habit. Every quarter, move your Profit First allocation percentages closer to your goal by increasing them by an additional 1 or 2 percent. Starting slowly and moving slowly and deliberately will still force you to look for ways to get better and more efficient at what you do, but you won't be tempted to throw in the towel on the entire system because the pressure is too great or the task impossible.

Jorge and José, once pumped by the results they had achieved with lower percentages, allocated 20 percent to their Profit Account and quickly realized their business could not support both that much profit *and* the way they were growing. So they adjusted the percentage until they achieved a balance with their PROFIT account allocation. They discovered that 9 percent in profit is high enough to make a real difference in their rainy-day and celebration funds, but low enough that it did not hinder their current strategy for market domination.

Their strategy is constant in-front-of-the-industry innovation. To achieve that, they established a powerful retention plan of paying their employees 30 percent more than the industry norm. Yes, they pay their employees *more* than the competition, allowing them to retain the best engineers in the market and—wait for it—are still wildly profitable for their industry. That's the power of reverse engineering your profit. You identify the elements that support the profit—in this case, great employees who stay with you for the long haul—commit to it, and jettison the things that don't.

Jorge and José adjust the PROFIT account percentages on a regular basis, factoring in short- and long-term needs. They've done everything right—and have a successful, thriving business to show for it.

"Too much of a good thing" is possible, even when it comes to watching your PROFIT account grow rapidly. Whether you make this mistake at the outset of implementing the Profit First system or down the road when the future looks especially rosy, be sure to correct it as soon as possible, or you'll find yourself slipping back into the Survival Trap.

MISTAKE #3: GROW FIRST (AND PROFIT LATER)

"I like the idea of Profit First, but I want to grow my company."

This is probably the most common objection I get when I share Profit First with others. Too many entrepreneurs believe that you can have only one or the other: profit or growth. It sickens me that so many entrepreneurs think it is a trade-off. Pick growth or pick profit, but you can't have both. Bullshit! Profit and growth go hand in hand. The healthiest companies figure out how to consistently be profitable first and then do everything to grow that.

Maybe the lure of the four or five magical success stories we hear over and over again has caused this myth about profit and growth to take hold among entrepreneurs. You know, the stories about companies that skyrocket in growth, and after enough investors throw money at them, they turn a profit big-time. I mean, don't you want to be the next Google or Facebook? If so, the path is clear: copy them. The problem with this strategy is the companies behind these same magical success stories are the lottery winners of the entrepreneurial game. They are not the rule, not even close. They are the one-in-a-million oddball successes, where the right approach was to grow, grow, grow, and that sparked the turn to profit. Yet the "grow at all costs" approach rarely results in profit. In fact, it is hard even to find stories you would recognize because the "grow at all costs" mentality has produced a landscape of trashed, dumped, and destroyed businesses that you never heard of because no one ever talks about the failures (and that's another quirk of our behavior, called selection bias). But perhaps you are familiar with Twitter.

After ten years in business, Twitter still isn't profitable. It has *lost* $2 billion since 2011, and has yet to figure out a way to make a penny in profit. It keeps hiring new management teams, new leadership, new anything to figure out a way to become profitable, but it can't. Isn't that crazy? To grow first and then try to figure out profit later? Twitter is trying to do just that, and unless it pulls a miracle out of thin air, its well of investor capital is going to run dry. At the time of this printing, rumors have been circulating for years that the company is for sale, but it seems no one is interested. Maybe buyers are getting savvy and have decided that if a company can't figure out how to be profitable, they can't do it either.

The irony is that Twitter is just a massive example of what goes wrong when the focus is growth, leaving profit to be addressed in the future. This mentality is everywhere,* and the scenario plays out in every size business. Grow at all costs. Until there is no money left and the end is a miserable lonely death. Fun times.

When profit comes first, your business will automatically show you the path to growth. I wonder how different Twitter would be had its founders committed to be profitable from day one? It would likely be a very different, and a much healthier company indeed.

Maybe the decree by Mark Cuban, the wildly successful entrepreneur and shark on *Shark Tank*, will set the record straight. In his February 2009 blog post titled "The Mark Cuban Stimulus Plan," he outlines what it takes for businesses to thrive and for him to invest money in their growth; my favorite bullets are 1. and 4.:

"1. It can be an existing business or a start-up.

"4. It must be profitable within ninety days."

---

* A February 18, 2016, article titled "Uber Says It Is Now Profitable in the US" by Dan Primack states that Uber states it is now profitable overall in the US, but that it is unclear how expenses are being allocated throughout Uber's global presence and therefore it is unclear when and/or how profitable Uber is. I suspect that if they used Profit First, it would be very clear . . . look at the profit account. http://money.cnn.com/2016/03/21 /technology/twitter-10th-anniversary/.

I believe you need to be profitable starting today. One of the world's most famous investors gives leniency. He gives you the quarter.*

MISTAKE #4: CUTTING THE WRONG COSTS

By now you know I'm a frugality junkie. I get a high from saving money, and I get the biggest rush when I find a way to eliminate an expense altogether. Still, not all expenses should be cut. We need to invest in assets, and I define assets as things that bring more efficiency to your business by allowing you to get more results at a lower cost per result. So if an expense makes it easier to get better results, keep it or purchase it.

I once toured the factory of a company that makes knives. When I noticed they were using old tools, one of the owners said, "Yup. We even have systems from the 1960s! We save so much money by keeping our old equipment."

During my tour, I also noticed that the knives they produced were inconsistent in terms of quality. Some of the knives were sharp; some were not. The handles rarely had a snug fit. Coincidentally, I had toured a different knife company earlier that week and noted that in one cumulative hour of manufacturing time they were able to turn out one perfect knife after another at a volume four times that of the company stuck in the decade of screaming Beatles fans and free love.

Money is made by efficiency—invest in it. If a purchase will bring up your bottom line and create significant efficiency, find ways to cut costs elsewhere, and consider different or discounted equipment (or resources, or services) rather than sacrifice efficiency for what you think are savings.

MISTAKE #5: "PLOWING BACK" AND "REINVESTING"

We use fancy terms to justify taking money out of our different allocation accounts to cover expenses. Two that are used most often are *plowback* and *reinvest*, which are really just other ways to say borrow. I have done this. I "plowed back" money from my PROFIT account to cover operating expenses, and boy, do I regret it.

---

* Check out Cuban's entire investing strategy, as posted on his Web site at http://blog maverick.com/2009/02/09/the-mark-cuban-stimulus-plan-open-source-funding/.

When you don't have enough money in your OPEX account to cover expenses, it is a big red flag that your expenses are too high and you need to find a way to fix them fast. Once in a blue moon, it could also mean that you are allocating too much to Owner's Comp or Profit. This only happens when you start with a high Profit or Owner's Comp percentage. And when it happens, it is because you are taking a percentage of profit or pay that you are not yet able to sustain; the efficiencies are not yet in place to support your profitability. But again, this is rarely the reason your OPEX account is in the red.

Likewise, some entrepreneurs continue to use their credit cards for day-to-day operations and call them lines of credit. This is not accurate. It's money you don't have. Your credit card spending limit is almost never a bridge loan to carry the business for short cash flow gaps (e.g., a big profitable job isn't paying the bill on time, as it was committed to). Nope. Credit cards are used simply to pay expenses, resulting in debt, plain and simple. Using a credit card to cover what you can't afford is also a red flag that your expenses are too high. Stop using the credit card and reserve it for legitimate emergencies or unique circumstances (like for a purchase you must make to yield income).

When you find yourself in a situation where you feel the need to "plow back" your profits, *stop* to reassess. There is always a better, more sustainable way to maintain the health of your business. You need to invest thought, not reinvest money.

MISTAKE #6: RAIDING THE TAX ACCOUNT

In the first year or two of doing Profit First, you may get caught in a tax bind because you only pay your estimates. For example, your accountant may prepare estimates based on your business's prior year's income and profitability that say you should make payments of $5,000 every quarter.

As your PROFIT account and TAX account grow, you may be surprised to see that you're reserving about $8,000 in taxes each quarter. Seeing this, you might think, "Hey, my accountant said I should pay $5,000 per quarter. I'm reserving too much for taxes." A little voice inside your head may even say, "Don't touch that money; you'll probably need it for taxes." And then a louder voice will say, "Nah, don't worry about it; you probably won't owe it and even if you do, you have time." Cue the $3,000 withdrawal to pay your-self or pay bills. (A still louder voice—one I may have heard myself—might say: "Why not start leasing a brand-new sports car with that money? Not only is it a business expense, you will instantly become the sexiest beast on this planet." Do not listen! Danger, Will Robinson! Danger!)

Big mistake.

As your profitability grows, your taxes will, too. In fact, paying more taxes is an indicator that your business health is improving. Now, I am not saying you should ever pay more taxes than you need to (tax is just an ex-pense like any other), but do realize that your taxes will grow as your busi-ness health does. So don't steal from your TAX account, thinking you won't need that money for taxes. You will.

At times, you may even need more than you think. One year I messed up when I paid my estimated taxes every quarter and then used the extra money to increase my Owner's Comp when I discovered there was money left over. Dummy! Tax estimates are based on your prior year's income. If you make more profit this year (which you will), you will pay more taxes, but your tax *estimates* will not change. If you spend "leftover" money from your TAX account simply because you allocate more than the estimate, you will be in shock come tax time.

Talk to an accountant who specializes in *both* profit maximization and tax minimization (if you are unsure whether they do, ask them to share their method*) every quarter to gauge how you are doing on taxes. And don't take money out of that TAX account! Your business is growing by leaps and bounds, and higher taxes are definitely in your future.

Another tax issue has to do with paying down debt. I call this paying for your sins, because if you have debt you need to wipe out, implementing Profit First is going to hurt in the beginning. I should know—it happened to me.

Here's the problem: the government gives you a tax break on expenses but does not consider the money you reserve to pay down debt an expense. The actual charges on your credit card and the interest and credit card fees can be expensed, but not your payments to pay down your cards.

---

* I have created a list of Profit First Professionals who specialize in not just maximizing your profit, but also reducing your taxes. Choose the FIND option at http://ProfitFirst Professionals.com and we'll recommend an expert for you to consider.

I can't believe I'm saying this, but in this case, the government is right. You get the tax benefit in the year that you make the purchase—no matter if you paid for the expense in cash, by credit card, or with funds from a bank loan or line of credit. As you become profitable and pay off debt, you will pay taxes on that income. Eliminating debt and paying taxes will feel like a double whammy. It isn't—you just need to pay for your "sins."

MISTAKE #7: ADDING COMPLEXITY

As Profit First grew in popularity, I found a completely unexpected failure point: people think it needs to be more complex. It is a weird phenomenon, but many entrepreneurs are so used to struggling with accounting details that they feel they need to struggle with Profit First. And if they are not struggling, they think something must be wrong. So they just make up rules to add confusion. I know this sounds odd, but I have seen it happen time and time again.

I have seen entrepreneurs modify their bank balances by introducing depreciation or amortization of stuff. Don't do this. Cash is cash. Either you have it or don't.

I have seen entrepreneurs take a profit distribution, put it in their savings, then pay for a purchase or make a hire with the money and say it is not an expense because it came out of their pocket. Ahhh! That is a shell game. And it is an expense. Profit is a reward (in the form of a cash distribution) for the equity owners of the business, and is above and beyond their pay from working in the business (Owner's Comp).

The system is super easy. It has been designed to work with how you naturally work; hence it is fluid. Don't overthink it. Don't add complexity. Don't try to "outsmart" the system. Just get comfortable with the fact that sometimes getting the results you want is way easier to achieve than all the hard work you have put in to get the results you don't want.

MISTAKE #8: SKIPPING THE BANK ACCOUNTS

Some folks try to "simplify" Profit First by not setting up the bank accounts. They just have their bookkeeper manage it. They are entrepreneurs, after all, and don't have the time for "unnecessary" nuances. So they use a spreadsheet or modify the chart of accounts in their accounting system to emulate the Profit First "small plate" bank accounts. Then, immediately, Profit First fails to work. When this happens, they blame the system, but the problem is, they didn't *use* the system.

Profit First must be set up to be directly in the path of the natural behavior of you, the entrepreneur. Because you log on to your bank account to look at your balance and make decisions, you must have Profit First there. Spreadsheets and your accounting system's general ledger reports are also great, but they are also too late. You don't look at them when making in-the-moment money decisions; you look at them after the fact. Coming up with a battle plan after the battle is over is useless.

Profit First at the bank will be in your face every time you look at the accounts, enabling you to manage profitability and cash flow decisions in real time. Setting up your accounts means you can't avoid it, and that is exactly how it needs to be.

PROFIT FIRST PROFESSIONALS (PFPS)

While you can absolutely stick with Profit First and avoid the biggest mistakes on your own, working with a Profit First Professional (PFP)—bookkeepers, accountants, business coaches, and other experts trained and certified to help you drive profitability to your business—will make it easier. You want to work with someone who has seen problems with other companies before you (sadly) discover them for yourself. It's like working with a trainer at the gym rather than going it alone. Trainers help you reach your fitness goals faster; PFPs get you to profit faster, and with fewer problems. When you have a trainer waiting for you at the gym, you have built-in accountability, and your workouts will be safer and more effective as well.

If you are having trouble getting your bookkeeper or accountant on board with Profit First, I humbly ask you to consider working with a PFP. You can find one at ProfitFirstProfessionals.com.

My own business—and life—has turned around for the better because of Profit First. I am eternally grateful for the financial stability and freedom it has given me. But I also know how easy it is to fall off of the Profit First wagon. Before my ninja bookkeeper Debra started holding my feet to the fire, it happened to me, and I've seen it happen to many businesses. Not only do people fall off the wagon, it rolls all over them.

It's easy to fall back into the old ways because they seem to make sense (they don't), or because our accountant says we shouldn't bother (we should), or because we think we were happier doing things the old way (we weren't).

I'll leave you with a quote from the great athlete Sir Roger Bannister, who busted through the myth that the four-minute mile could not be beaten: "The man who can drive himself further once the effort gets painful is the man who will win."

Right-o, Sir Roger.

TAKE ACTION: GET REAL WITH YOUR ACCOUNTANT

Sit down with your accountant, bookkeeper, or coach (ideally, all three), preferably a PFP trained in this system, and come up with a game plan to ensure that you don't end up allocating too much revenue to your PROFIT account and you *do* allocate enough to your TAX account. Schedule quarterly check-ins to make sure you are consistently building up your profit and other allocations while reducing your operating expenses.

And if for any reason whatsoever, you have not yet set up Profit First at the bank, for the sake of all that is holy, do it now. Follow the lead of Claudio Santos, who emailed me from South Africa just as I was typing the final words in this chapter and said, "Just started with your book. Can't seem to put it down. Anyway, just following your instructions and doing what you said." Claudio opened his account and sent me an email to tell me about it, just as I asked you to do in Chapter 1. I strongly suspect he is about to see a positive turn in his profits.

That's it. Just do it.

EPILOGUE

Rick Barry is one of the greatest foul shooters of all time. He is a twelve-time NBA All-Star and member of the Naismith Memorial Basketball Hall of Fame. His free-throw record is 89.3 percent. In the NBA, the average is 75 percent, and many players miss half the time. Two of the greatest basketball players of all time, Shaquille O'Neal and Wilt Chamberlain, had a free-throw percentage of less than 53 percent, and both missed more than five thousand free-throw attempts over the course of their careers.

How did Barry sink so many free throws? He shot "granny style"—underhanded.

The underhand shot, ironically, is not with the hands under the basketball. The shooter's hands grip the sides of the ball, with the ball held down about waist high. Then the shot is made by swinging the arms up and throwing the ball forward. Two interesting things happen. First, the arm movement is greatly simplified. As opposed to the overhand shot that requires the coordination of a lot more joints (read that as more variables), the underhand shot keeps the arms locked and the wrists cocked (read that as fewer variables). The result is a much more consistent shot. The other part is that it puts much more backspin on the ball, allowing it to land with a better placement. If it hits the rim, it bounces vertically more often, which allows the ball to stay near the rim and means it is more likely to fall in.

If you try (and stick with) a Rick Barry granny-style shot, your free-throw shot percentage will increase dramatically. And yet you probably wouldn't do it in front of your buddies. College and pro basketball players adopting granny style? Hell, no. Even though the most elite players are being paid millions to score points, and using the granny-style shot will even help them *score more points*, pro players don't take advantage of it. The fear of looking stupid or inexperienced wins out over logic, which tells players that the underhand shot will give them a higher success rate. It might also help them get into the record books. You see, Wilt Chamberlain, the guy with the meager free-throw percentage, became a legend, in part when he scored a record-breaking one hundred points for the Philadelphia Warriors over the New York Knicks in 1962, and he did it by scoring more free-throw points. In fact, he broke a free-throw record in that game. How did he do it? In that game, Chamberlain shot his free throws granny style.

Who knew that Granny was such a badass? I wish I could shoot like good old Granny. Scratch that; I wish I'd kept shooting like her (because I did when I was a little kid) and never became "too cool" to compromise points. Lesson learned, Grandma. I will never be too cool to score more points. And never, ever too cool to compromise profit (even if no one else gets putting profit first).

I couldn't be more thrilled that Profit First is catching on, big-time. But chances are you're still the first of your friends to implement Profit First. And just as good friends would behave when you are the first to try something new, they might mock you. Welcome to the granny shot of accounting and money management: Profit First. By implementing it, the odds for success and fulfillment in business are now in your favor. But to those unfamiliar with the system, it might appear to be an awkward or overly simplistic approach to accounting and bookkeeping.

As you walk up to your own free-throw line—the bank—and open up a bunch of accounts that you now know will change your life, you may hear snickers and taunts. That's okay. Just like Barry, you know it works. And you're in good company. Daily—literally, every single day—I receive at least five or six emails from people who have read *Profit First* telling me how applying it helped them turn their businesses around. That's just email. I also consistently get Facebook posts, Tweets, snail mail (believe it or not) and calls, and some people have even written articles about their Profit First success stories. Some stories I shared with you in this book. Others I share in my keynote addresses. Some folks I interview on my Profit First

Podcast. And all of them are saved or photographed and stored on my hard drive for all of eternity. Eradicating entrepreneurial poverty is my life's mission, and my readers are part of that. *You* are part of that.

I struggle to remember all of the names, but I remember the stories. Like the organic farmer, who, after fourteen years of losses, decided to give up and close the farm. Before she acted on her decision, she decided to try Profit First. Within six months, she had turned her first profit. She was reinvigorated, and her business was growing and profitable. A couple who raises horses in the middle of Australia, in a town with a population of ten, wrote to me not too long ago. Their marriage was on the rocks because their business was slowly sucking away at their souls. Then they read *Profit First* and applied what they learned. It saved their business, and their marriage. I've heard from countless CEOs and entrepreneurs who got their confidence back, their joy back, their sanity back, their weekends back, and from people who are no longer plagued with anxiety, insomnia, and other ailments caused by the challenge of running an unprofitable business.

As for me, running a Profit First business and lifestyle has given me complete confidence over my own finances and freed me from the endless search for a big payout. I'm no longer looking for the Holy Grail—I don't need it. I'm not hoping that one day someone will swoop in and save me from a check-by-check business by buying me out. My businesses are profitable today, and they will continue to be profitable tomorrow, next month, and in the years to come. I am debt-free and stringing together one small financial win after another—every tenth and twenty-fifth of the month.

The normal response to fixing problems is to try to change our habits. In *The Power of Habit* Charles Duhigg says habits are "click, whirr." Triggered by something (like an empty bank account)—click—we go into our reactionary routine, like making panicky collection calls, for example—whirr. As Duhigg points out in his book, changing habits is possible but is also really, really hard. Instead, simple systems that capture the good parts of our habits and guard us from the bad parts will bring about positive and permanent change, fast.

That's all Profit First is—a simple system that works with us *as we are*. All you have to do is follow it. You don't have to get an MBA, or take an accounting course, or start devouring articles in the *Wall Street Journal*. You don't even need to know how to read your own income statement, cash flow statement or balance sheet. You don't have to change or "fix" who you are for this to work. It just does.

Why would I ask you to change who you are? You have been able to grow your own amazing business doing what you do, and that's remarkable by any measure. Now all we need to do is capture your good money habits and put guardrails up to protect you from your "humanness."

It really is that simple. We are going to put profit first. Period.

Step up to the line. Ignore the naysayers. Grip the ball and throw that granny shot. Don't pay any mind to what others think; they just don't get it yet. Just as Barry—and Chamberlain, for one legendary game—racked up the points, you'll watch your profit *and* your business grow while you do what comes naturally to you. And trust me, you surely won't look like a granny—you'll look more like an entrepreneurial genius.

You don't need a miracle, or a lucky night in Vegas. You don't need a windfall, a colossal client, or a worldwide phenomenon to realize the vision you've held for your business since you opened your first box of business cards. You simply need to put your profit first and everything else will fall into line. It's not rocket science, and you don't have to have a truckload of karma to get it. Financial freedom really is just a few small plates away.

ACKNOWLEDGMENTS

If I had to do this project alone it would have taken me ten times longer and this book would be one tenth of what it is today. As I flip through the pages one final time before it goes to the printer, I have chills. I truly believe this book will change the world. And the reason it will is because of the relentless effort of an army of amazing colleagues and friends, all driven to serve entrepreneurs and help them become permanently profitable.

First and foremost, I want to thank Anjanette Harper, my writing partner. When we created the first version of *Profit First*, the goal was simple: "Write a book that *can* change the world." Rebuilding *Profit First* into this second book has made the good stuff even better, and I can proudly put a stamp of "this *will* change the world" upon it. Anjanette, you are the yin to my yang. Five books down, twenty to go!

When a man orders a beet sandwich and four coffees for lunch, you know you are working with someone who plays at the next level. Kaushik Viswanath, my editor at Portfolio, went page by page, sentence by sentence, dozens of times to make Profit First even easier to master, while never compromising the system, the tone, or my style. Thank you, Kaushik, for further empowering the Profit First concept, and further empowering me to be me.

Thank you to Liz Dobrinska, my graphic designer, who said, "Oh! I have an idea," and brought powerful visuals to vague concepts. A big shout-out to Go Leeward (goleeward.com), the best speaking agency on the planet, hands down, which has helped me travel the globe to speak about Profit First to anyone and everyone who will listen.

There are a few behind-the-scenes people who spend every day educating accountants, bookkeepers, coaches, and entrepreneurs on Profit First. They are true profit warriors. Ron Saharyan (better known as Obi-Ron Kenobi), who is the biggest supporter of Profit First I have ever known. If you run into Obie-Ron on the street, chances are he will give you a Profit First sticker, book, or T-shirt. Big thanks to Kristina Bolduc (better known as Kebby), who keeps the Profit First Professionals team humming; and Erin Moger (better known as Mo) and Mike Scalice (better known as the Hawaiian Lumberjack), who, together, help business after business master Profit First.

My thank-yous would not be complete without acknowledging you, the courageous entrepreneur. You are the definition of a superhero. You are fighting for profitability for yourself, your family, your employees, your community, and our world. Keep fighting, superhero. Keep fighting.

And last, but certainly first in my soul, to Krista, I live you. (That is not a typo.)

Appendix 1
THE PROFIT FIRST QUICK SETUP GUIDE

ONE TIME SETUP:

1. Set up the five foundational bank accounts with your current bank as checking accounts. We'll call this bank **Bank 1**. 1. INCOME; 2. PROFIT; 3. OWNER'S COMP; 4. TAX; 5. OPEX.
2. Set up two new savings accounts at a different bank: We'll call this bank **Bank 2**. The purpose here is to remove the temptation of "borrowing" from these accounts.1. PROFIT HOLD; 2. TAX HOLD.
3. Determine the TAPs (Target Allocation Percentages) for your business using the Instant Assessment (see Appendix 2 or MikeMichalowicz.com/Resources). But start by implementing CAPs (Current Allocation Percentages) that your business can reasonably manage for the rest of the current quarter.

EVERY DAY:

1. All receipts from sales or other business generated revenue go into the INCOME account.
2. If you are using Advanced Profit First accounts, deposit receipts for reimbursements, retainers, etc., into the respective accounts.
3. Spend a minute daily to review your account balances at **Bank 1** to see cash flow trends for the key aspects of your business. That's all the time you need to see where things stand!

EVERY TENTH AND TWENTY-FIFTH:

1. Transfer all funds that have accumulated in the INCOME account to the other accounts at **Bank 1** based on the CAPs you are using.
2. Transfer all the money in your PROFIT account at **Bank 1** to the PROFIT HOLD account at **Bank 2**. Transfer all money in your TAX account at **Bank 1** to the TAX HOLD account at **Bank 2**. This will leave a $0.00 balance for PROFIT and TAX at **Bank 1**.
3. If you are using Advanced Profit First techniques, transfer Employee Payroll or other fixed dollar amounts from OPEX to the respective accounts.
4. Disburse the salaries for the business owner(s) from the OWNER'S COMP account. Leave any remaining money, above and beyond the salary distribution, in the OWNER'S COMP account.
5. Pay your bills from the OPEX account.

EVERY QUARTER:

1. Take 50 percent of the money that has accumulated in the PROFIT HOLD account as a profit distribution. Remember, this money is for the business owners and not to be used to "reinvest" in or "plowback" to the business.
2. Pay your tax liabilities from the TAX HOLD account.
3. Meet with your accounting practitioner or Profit First Professional and adjust your CAPs for your Profit, Tax, Owner's Pay, and Operating Expenses to maximize your financial health.

EVERY YEAR:

1. Review your financials with your Profit First Professional or accountant and financial experts.
2. Make year-end contributions to the VAULT, retirement accounts, or make appropriate capital purchases as determined by you and your financial expert.

Appendix 2
THE INSTANT ASSESSMENT FORM

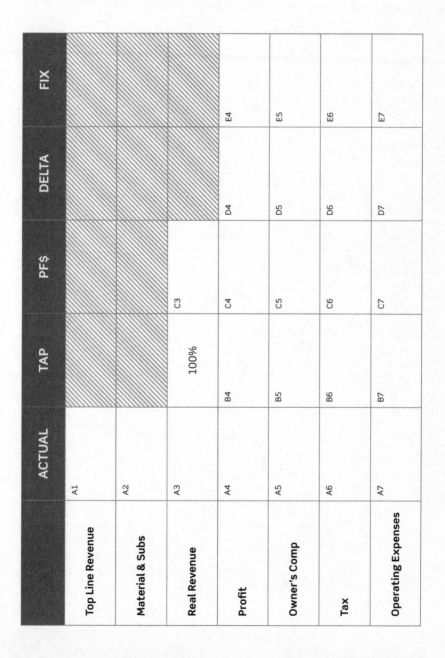

	ACTUAL	TAP	PF$	DELTA	FIX
Top Line Revenue	A1				
Material & Subs	A2				
Real Revenue	A3	100%	C3		
Profit	A4	B4	C4	D4	E4
Owner's Comp	A5	B5	C5	D5	E5
Tax	A6	B6	C6	D6	E6
Operating Expenses	A7	B7	C7	D7	E7

Appendix 3
GLOSSARY OF KEY TERMS

CAPs (Current Allocation Percentages): These are the current percentages you use to allocate money to your various accounts. A profit CAP of 5 percent means that twice a month, you will transfer 5 percent of the balance in your INCOME account to your PROFIT account.

Day Zero / Day One: Day Zero is the day before you implement Profit First. Day One is the day you implement Profit First.

Debt Freeze: The Debt Freeze means more than just "no more new debt." It's a rigorous, step-by-step process to cut your unnecessary expenditures, to stop incurring new expenses, and find ways to become more profitable.

Debt Snowball: Coined by Dave Ramsey, the Debt Snowball is an approach to tackling debt that pays off your smallest debts first. This helps you build momentum toward tackling your larger debts and achieving financial freedom.

Endowment effect: Studies in behavioral economics have shown that we tend to value what we own more highly than what we don't own.

GAAP (Generally Accepted Accounting Principles): Generally Accepted Accounting Principles are a set of accounting standards and procedures used by most businesses. GAAP assumes Sales – Expenses = Profit, thereby treating profit as an afterthought.

Instant Assessment: Income statements and balance sheets can be tedious and confusing. The Instant Assessment is a tool that gives you a quick, clear view of the current financial health of your business.

Loss aversion: Related to the Endowment effect, loss aversion is the psychological phenomenon that makes us resistant to giving up what we already have, even if it is for an equal or greater gain.

Margarita: A delicious cocktail made with tequila, triple sec, and lime. It should always be served with salt on the rim. You are encouraged to enjoy one as a reward for making it to the end of this book.

OPEX (OPERATING EXPENSES): Short for Operating Expenses. In the Profit First system, you should be paying all your bills out of your OPEX account.

Pareto Principle: Otherwise known as the 80/20 rule, the Pareto Principle states that 80 percent of effects come from 20 percent of causes. In other words, 80 percent of your revenue tends to come from 20 percent of your clients. To further boost your revenue, try to replicate and do more business with this top 20 percent.

Parkinson's Law: C. Northcote Parkinson's adage that work expands to fill the available time is the same tendency your business has to use up all available resources. This is also known as induced demand. That's the main reason why you need to stow away your profits before you find ways to spend it.

Primacy Effect: Our tendency to place greater emphasis on what we encounter first. So, if profits are important to you, you'll put profit first.

ProfitCON: My annual Profit conference. More details are at www.ProfitCON.us.

Profit First Professional (PFP): Certified accounting professionals who are well-versed in the Profit First system. To find one, go to www.ProfitFirstProfessionals.com.

The Pumpkin Plan: My book about how to optimize your business for maximum growth.

Real Revenue: When performing the Instant Assessment, we use Real Revenue as an alternative to gross profit. In the cases where there is a significant use of subcontractors and/or materials, those costs are subtracted from Income to derive the "true revenue" (i.e., Real Revenue) that the company generates. Calculations to gross profit in traditional accounting can vary based on different interpretations. The objective of Real Revenue is to simplify the calculations variable.

Sales – Expenses = Profit: The traditional accounting formula that we are going to flip to achieve profitability: Sales – Profit = Expenses.

Surge: My book about timing and catching the wave of consumer demand.

Survival Trap: When you operate your business check to check, you'll find yourself in the survival trap, doing anything to generate revenue, even when it goes against your company's vision and is outside the bounds of your top clients' needs.

TAPs (Target Allocation Percentages): The ideal percentage of revenue you should eventually aim to allocate to Profit, Tax, Owner's Comp, and Operating Expenses. You will gradually increase your CAPs toward your TAPs for Profit, Tax, and Owner's Comp. You will gradually decrease your CAPs for OPEX.

The Toilet Paper Entrepreneur: My first book about how to create a business with limited or no money, education, or experience.

Wedge: A system to gradually upgrade your lifestyle as your income grows.

INDEX

accountability buddy or group, 178–79
accountants, selecting and using, 91–93
accounting, traditional. *See* GAAP
   accounting
accounts, 45, 52–54, 93–94
   adding accounts to customize for your
     business, 148–56
   assigning CAPS to, 94–99
   COMMISSIONS account, 152
   CONTRACTORS account, 152
   distributions to, 99–101
   documenting function of, 156
   DRIP account, 153–54
   EMPLOYEE PAYROLL account,
     152–53
   EQUIPMENT account, 153
   GOVERNMENT'S MONEY
     account, 160
   hiding accounts from view, 160–61
   INCOME account, 45, 52–53
   keeping track of, 161–62
   MATERIALS account, 152
   mistake of not setting up, 186–87
   Operating expenses (OPEX) account,
     45, 52–53
   OUTSIDE CAPITAL account, 158
   outside income accounts, transfers to
     INCOME account from, 161
   OWNER'S COMP account, 45, 52–53
   PASS-THROUGH account, 151–52
   for personal life, 166–68
   PETTY CASH account, 154
   PREPAYMENT account, 154
   PROFIT account, 45, 52–53, 80, 108, 112
   PROFIT HOLD account, 53–54
   SALES TAX account, 154–55
   sample account setup, 154–56, 157–58
   STOCKING account, 151
   TAX account, 45, 52–53
   TAX HOLD account, 53–54
   VAULT account, 150–51
action steps
   for advanced techniques, 162
   for building efficient companies, 147
   commitment, emailing, 33
   for debt reduction, 131–32
   for implementing Profit First, 113
   Instant Assessment, completing, 74
   for living Profit First lifestyle, 176
   opening PROFIT account and placing
     1% of current money in it, 48
   for setting up Profit First, 57–58
   Target Allocation Percentages (TAPs),
     determining, 88
advanced techniques for Profit First,
   148–62
   action step for, 162
   capital, raising, 158–59
   employee, determining whether you
     can afford new, 159–60

advanced techniques for Profit First (*cont.*)
mini power tactics, 160–62
monthly nut, avoid focusing on, 156–57
multiple owners, accounting for, 157
Required Income for Allocation (RIFA),
156–57
Amazon, 85
assessment, of health of business. *See*
Instant Assessment
automatic withdrawals, 125

bank balance accounting, 21–23, 25–26,
50–52
bank checks, making payments with, 162
banks, selection of, 55–57
Bannister, Roger, 188
Barry, Rick, 189, 192
behavioral science, 39
best clients, cloning, 143–45
Bezos, Jeff, 85
Bieber, Justin, 3
bookkeepers, selecting and using, 91–93
Bridezillas (tv show), 27

capital, raising, 158–59
cash consumption of businesses, 6, 11–33
author's experience with, 11–16
bank balance accounting and, 21–23,
25–26
emailing commitment action step, 33
growth and, 18–21
money as foundation of business,
16–17
power of business, directing and
controlling, 31–33
profit, maximizing, 19–21
revenue-focused check-to-check
methodology, problems with, 17–18
Survival Trap and, 23–26
traditional accounting and, 26–29
cash flow management, tenth/twenty-fifth
rhythm for, 103–7
Chamberlain, Wilt, 189, 190, 192
children, using Profit First for, 174–76
clients
best clients, cloning, 143–45
unprofitable clients, letting go of, 141–43

Cole, Jesse, 46, 128–30, 169
COMMISSIONS account, 152
CONTRACTORS account, 152
costs and expenses, reduction of, 72–73,
101–2
Debt Freeze and (*See* Debt Freeze)
efficiency and, 140–41
wrong costs, cutting, 183
Courtright, Debra, 103
Crabtree, Greg, 135–36, 159–60
credit cards
mistake of using for day-to-day
operations or as bridge loan, 184
personal, for emergencies, 168–69
reissuance of, 125
crisis, 24
Cuban, Mark, 182–83
Current Allocation Percentages (CAPs),
77–78, 94–99
Day One CAPs, determining, 94–95, 99
Day Zero percentages, determining,
96–98
starting with small percentages,
purpose of, 95–96

DAC Management, 103
debt, 22, 114–32
action steps for reducing, 131–32
building momentum through small,
repetitive acts for reduction of, 130–31
choosing profitability even when in,
128–30
crisis-mode response to, 115–16
enjoying saving more than spending,
117–18
freeze of, 120–28
importance of percentages in allocating
money to accounts, 119–20
pain-pleasure motivation and reduction
of, 117–18
personal, 166, 168–72
purpose of implementing Profit First
while reducing, 116–17
worst month, preparing for, 118–20
Debt Freeze, 120–28
amount of expenses that need to be cut,
calculating, 122

automatic withdrawals, ending, 125
credit cards, reissuance of, 125
goal of, 120–21
"just one more day" technique and, 126
labor costs, cutting, 122–24
negotiation of expenses, 126–27
pay cuts, avoiding, 124
print and mark up documents relating
   to debt, 121
recurring expenses, ending, 125–26
Debt Snowball, 131
distributions
   of income to accounts, 99–101
   quarterly profit distribution, 107–9
Dobrinska, Liz, 104
DRIP account, 153–54
Duhigg, Charles, 31, 191
Dutcher, Laurie, 164

Eckler, Greg, 85–86
efficient companies, building
   action steps for, 147
   asking big questions to achieve
      substantial results, 139
   best clients, cloning, 143–45
   cost cutting and, 140–41
   doubling results with half the effort,
      136–40
   increased profit margins from, 137
   innovation and, 138–40
   interplay between efficiency and
      sales, 137
   Pareto Principle and, 144–45
   profit squeezes and, 135–37
   Survival Trap and, 25
   top line sales focus versus building,
      134–35, 137
   unprofitable clients, letting go of, 141–43
   upselling, pitfalls of, 145–47
employee count, determining, 159–60
EMPLOYEE PAYROLL account, 152–53
E-Myth Revisited (Gerber), 83–84
Endowment effect, 169–70
Enron, 28
envelope system, 49–50
EQUIPMENT account, 153
estimated taxes, quarterly payment of, 110

Exorcist, The (movie), 92
expenses, reduction of. *See* costs and
   expenses, reduction of
"Eye of the Tiger" (song), 34

Fear, Keith, 7–8
financial professionals, selecting and
   using, 91–93
finding money within company. *See*
   efficient companies, building
Fisher, Roger, 127n
Ford, Henry, 77
Frankenstein (Shelley), 11
Fried, Jason, 19
frugality, 40, 71–72, 173

GAAP accounting, 26–29
   complexity of, 28
   profits formula under, 6, 26
   profits/salary as afterthought in, 28
   reports, 29
   sales and expenses as primary metrics
      of, 27–28
Gerber, Michael, 83–84
Getting to Yes (Fisher, Ury & Patton), 127n
glossary of terms, 199–200
Google Finance, 78–79
GOVERNMENT'S MONEY account, 160
growth
   chasing profit for sake of, effect of,
      18–21
   mistake of growth at all costs approach,
      181–83
   prioritizing profit and, 43–44

Harper, Anjanette, 177–79
health of business, assessing. *See*
   Instant Assessment
Heath, Chip, 47
Heath, Dan, 47
Hedgehog Leatherworks, 46, 126, 139
Hill, Andrew, 119
Horovitch, Debbie, 1–2, 9

implementing Profit First, 89–113
   accounts, setting up, 93–94
   action steps for, 113

implementing Profit First (*cont.*)
  assigning CAPS to each account,
    94–99
  distribution of income to accounts,
    99–101
  estimated taxes, payment of, 110
  evaluation of current percentages and
    making adjustments towards TAPs,
    110–11
  expense reduction, 101–2
  financial professional, selecting and
    using, 91–93
  profits to be used for personal benefit
    only in, 109–10
  quarterly profit distribution, 107–9
  rainy day fund, 110–11
  tenth/twenty-fifth cash flow rhythm
    and, 103–7
  yearly tax finalization, 111–12
INCOME account, 45, 52–53
induced demand, 39
innovation, 40, 138–40
Instant Assessment, 1–2, 59–88
  action step for, 74
  completing Instant Assessment Form,
    62–71
  cost cutting and, 72–73
  Current Allocation Percentages (CAPs),
    77–78
  frugality, 71–72
  Materials & Subs cell, 63
  for new businesses, 73
  Operating Expenses cell, 66
  Owner's Comp cell, 65
  Real Revenue cell, 64–65
  sample form, 197
  Target Allocation Percentages (TAPs),
    66–67, 68–70, 75–88, 94
  Tax cell, 65
  Top Line Revenue cell, 62

"just one more day" technique, 126

labor costs, 122–24
Laughter, Peter, 56
layoffs, 123–24
Li, James, 136

lifestyle of Profit First, 163–76
  accounts, setting up, 166–68
  action steps for, 176
  applying Profit First to personal life,
    165–69
  celebrating debt eradication, 171–72
  children, using Profit First for, 174–76
  debt and, 166, 168–72
  facing debt head on, 169–71
  financial freedom as goal of, 165
  locking in, 172–74
  Wedge system and, 174
LinkUSystems, 140
longevity of business, 80
loss aversion, 169
lowering the bar, 47–48

McDonald's, 138
margins, 80–81
"Mark Cuban Stimulus Plan" (Cuban),
  182–83
Marketwatch.com, 78–79
MATERIALS account, 152
Materials & Subs cell, for Instant
  Assessment Form, 63
Michalowicz, Adayla, 176
mini power tactics, 160–62
  bank checks, making payments with,
    162
  GOVERNMENT'S MONEY account,
    creating, 160–61
  hiding accounts from view, 160–61
  keeping track of accounts, 161–62
  outside income accounts, transfers to
    INCOME account from, 161
mistakes entrepreneurs make when
  implementing Profit First, 179–87
  accounts, skipping, 186–87
  allocating to much to PROFIT account
    to soon, 180–81
  complexity, adding, 186
  going it alone, 179
  grow at all costs approach, 181–83
  plowbacks or reinvesting to cover
    expenses, 183–84
  raiding TAX account, 184–86
  wrong costs, cutting, 183

Moger, Erin, 148
monthly nut, 156–57
Morales, Jorge, 89–91, 96, 102, 109,
    112–13, 163–64, 165, 180–81

negotiation of expenses, 126–27
new employees, determining whether you
    can afford, 159–60
Nudge (Thaler and Sunstein), 37
Nunn, Gary, 119

Olmec Systems, 98
O'Neal, Shaquille, 189
Operating Expenses cell, for Instant
    Assessment Form, 66
Operating expenses (OPEX) account, 45,
    52–53
Orman, Suze, 117, 118, 131, 166
OUTSIDE CAPITAL account, 158
OWNER'S COMP account, 45, 52–53
Owner's Comp cell, for Instant
    Assessment Form, 65
Owner's Comp Target Allocation
    Percentages (TAPs), 81–85
  business entity status and, 82–83
  selection of, considerations for, 81–82
  separate Owner's Comp account,
    purpose for having, 82
  underpaying most important employee,
    avoiding, 83–85
  working "on versus in" business
    philosophy and, 83–85

Pain, José, 89–91, 96, 102, 109, 112, 164,
    165, 180–81
pain-pleasure motivation, and debt
    reduction, 117–18
Pareto, Vilfredo Frederico Damasco, 144
Pareto Principle, 144–45
Parkinson, C. Northcote, 39
Parkinson's Law, 39–40, 172, 174
PASS-THROUGH account, 151–52
Patton, Bruce, 127n
pay cuts, 124
PETTY CASH account, 154
Power of Habit, The (Duhigg), 31, 191
PREPAYMENT account, 154

Primack, Dan, 182n
Primacy Effect, 27–28, 41
principles of Profit First, 34–48
  accounting formula for Profit First,
    44–46
  action steps for, 48
  income versus cost and, 36–37
  lowering the bar and, 47–48
  Parkinson's Law and, 39–40
  physical health principles, applicability
    of, 38–39
  Primacy Effect and, 41
  rhythm, enforcing, 42–43, 45–46
  serving sequentially, 45
  small plate philosophy and, 45
  temptation, removing, 42, 45
PROFIT account, 45, 52–53, 80, 108, 112
ProfitCON, 148
Profit First, 6–10
  accountability buddy or group, using,
    178–79
  adding accounts to customize for your
    business, 148–56
  advanced techniques for, 148–62
  as cash-management system, 61
  common problems entrepreneurs face
    when implementing, 76–77
  debt and, 114–32
  as designed for existing habits and
    tendencies, 30–31
  efficient companies, building, 25,
    133–47
  growing to profitability, problems with,
    18–21
  implementing, 89–113
  Instant Assessment, 1–2, 59–88, 197
  living Profit First life, 163–76
  mistakes entrepreneurs make when
    implementing, 179–87
  principles of, 34–48
  quick setup guide, 195
  setting up, 49–58
Profit First (first edition) (Michalowicz),
    3, 7, 10
Profit First Podcast, 9
Profit First Professionals (PFPs), 8–9, 187
PROFIT HOLD account, 53–54

profit margins
   competition and, 80–81, 136–37
   efficiency and, 137
profit/profitability
   cash consumption of business and, 6,
     11–33
   committing to, 33
   defined, 29
   formula for, 6
   on Instant Assessment Form, 65
   lack of, as reason for business
     discontinuation, 4–5
   maximizing, 19–21
   Profit First system and (*See* Profit
     First)
   traditional systems for attaining,
     problems with, 5–6, 26–29
profit squeezes, 135–37
Profit Target Allocation Percentages
   (TAPs), 78–81
   business longevity and, 80
   purpose of PROFIT account and, 80
   researching public companies to set
     industry-specific, 78–79
Pumpkin Plan, The (Michalowicz), 1, 3,
   141, 143

quarterly profit distribution, 107–9

rainy-day fund. *See* reserves for
   emergencies
Ramsey, Dave, 131
Real Revenue cell, for Instant Assessment
   Form, 64–65
Required Income for Allocation (RIFA),
   156–57
reserves for emergencies
   PROFIT account and, 80, 108, 112
   VAULT account and, 150–51
revolving line of credit, 115
rhythm, enforcing, 39, 42–43, 45–46
Ritter, Matt, 158
Robbin, Lisa, 59–61
Robbins, Anthony, 117
Rocha, Wesley, 140–41
RoofDeck Solutions, Ltd., 151

Sales - Expenses = Profits, 6, 26
Sales - Profit = Expenses, 44
SALES TAX account, 154–55
Santos, Claudio, 188
Savannah Business, 129
Scheiter, Paul, 126
Secretly Spoiled, 164
serving sequentially, 45
setting up Profit First
   action steps for, 57–58
   bank balance accounting, use of, 50–52
   banks, choosing, 55–57
   envelope system and, 49–50
   foundational accounts, setting up, 52–53
   no-temptation accounts, setting up,
     53–54
   reasons for using Profit First accounts,
     54–55
Shark Tank (tv show), 182
Shelley, Mary, 11
Simple Numbers, Straight Talk, Big Profits!
   (Crabtree), 135, 159
size of business, 19
Small Business Administration (SBA), 3
small businesses, 3–4
small plate philosophy, 45
Solutions Tax & Bookkeeping, 119
Specialized ECU Repair, 89–90, 163
Star Trek (tv series), 30
STOCKING account, 151
Stratagex study on clients, 142
Sunstein, Cass, 37
Survival Trap, 23–26
   actions taken in response to crisis as,
     24–25
   crisis and, 24
   efficiency, importance of in reaching
     sustained profitability, 25
   profitable income versus debt-generating
     income, 24
   vision and, 24
Switch (Heath), 47

Target Allocation Percentages (TAPs),
   66–67, 68–70, 75–88, 94
   action steps for, 88

Current Allocation Percentages (CAPs)
as starting point for, 77–78
Owner's Comp Target Allocation
Percentages (TAPs), 81–85
Profit Target Allocation Percentages
(TAPs), 78–81
quarterly evaluations and adjustments
to move closer to, 110–11
Tax Target Allocation Percentages
(TAPs), 85–88
TAX account, 45, 52–53
Tax cell, for Instant Assessment Form, 65
taxes
estimated, 110
raiding TAX account mistake, 184–86
yearly tax finalization, 111–12
TAX HOLD account, 53–54
Tax Target Allocation Percentages
(TAPs), 85–88
approaches for determining, 87
income tax rate, determining, 86
math for, 87–88
purpose of, 86
temptation, removing, 38, 42, 45
tenth/twenty-fifth cash flow rhythm,
103–7
Thaler, Richard, 37
Tirone, Phil, 46
Toilet Paper Entrepreneur, The
(Michalowicz), 3, 12, 28, 46, 71, 89, 90

Top Line Revenue cell, for Instant
Assessment Form, 62
Total Money Makeover, The (Ramsey), 131
Tracy, Brian, 174
TravelQuest International, 153
TSheets, 158
Twitter, 182

"Uber Says It Is Now Profitable in the
US" (Primack), 182n
United Parcel Service (UPS), 139–40
unprofitable clients, letting go of,
141–43
upselling, pitfalls of, 145–47
Ury, William, 127n

Van Ittersum, Koert, 38
VAULT account, 150–51
Villalobos, Michelle, 20
vision, 24
Vistage, 133

Wall Street Journal, 3
Wansink, Brian, 38
Wedge system, 174
working "on versus in" business
philosophy, 83–85

Yahoo! Finance, 78–79
Young Frankenstein (movie), 56

Also by MIKE MICHALOWICZ

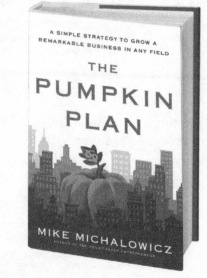

www.MikeMichalowicz.com

PORTFOLIO
PENGUIN

Want Mike to keynote your next event?

CONNECT WITH MIKE

Li Hayes • Speaking Coordinator for Mike Michalowicz
888-244-2843 x7008 • Li@MikeMichalowicz.com
MikeMichalowicz.com/Speaking